How To Turn Down A Billion Dollars

How To Turn Down A Billion Dollars

The Snapchat story

BILLY GALLAGHER

1 3 5 7 9 10 8 6 4 2

Virgin Books, an imprint of Ebury Publishing,
20 Vauxhall Bridge Road,
London SW1V 2SA

Virgin Books is part of the Penguin Random House group of companies
whose addresses can be found at global.penguinrandomhouse.com

Penguin
Random House
UK

First published in the United Kingdom by Virgin Books in 2018
This edition published by Virgin Books in 2019

www.penguin.co.uk

A CIP catalogue record for this book is available
from the British Library

ISBN 9780753557594

Printed and bound in Great Britain by Clays Ltd, Elcograf S.p.A.

Penguin Random House is committed to a sustainable future for
our business, our readers and our planet. This book is made from
Forest Stewardship Council® certified paper.

MIX
Paper from
responsible sources
FSC® C018179

To my mom, Eileen. Thank you.

CONTENTS

PART I: AN EVAN SPIEGEL PRODUCTION

PART II: TOYS ARE PRELUDES TO SERIOUS IDEAS

AUTHOR'S NOTE

I first interviewed Snapchat cofounder and CEO Evan Spiegel over six years ago, as Snapchat was just gaining traction and Evan and I were both still undergraduates at Stanford University. I have been following the story ever since. Because no one reads book dust jackets, and I occasionally use the first person in this book, let me tell you a bit about myself: I was two years behind Evan Spiegel and Reggie Brown at Stanford University. They were the class of 2012; I was the class of 2014. Bobby Murphy, Snapchat's other cofounder, was the class of 2010. Most of the principals in this book, especially the early Snapchat team, went to Stanford between 2010 and 2013.

While at Stanford, I joined the same fraternity that Evan, Reggie, and Bobby were members of, although they had all left the fraternity by the time I joined (more on this later). I was the editor in chief of the school newspaper and a writer for one of the major tech blogs, *TechCrunch*. I interviewed Evan several times for *TechCrunch* during Snapchat's early days in 2012; however, he stopped granting me interviews in 2013 when I covered ousted cofounder Reggie Brown's lawsuit against Snapchat. After I graduated from Stanford, I worked on the investing team at Khosla Ventures, a prominent Silicon Valley venture capital firm (though not a Snapchat investor).

This book is based on nearly two hundred interviews, thousands of pages of court documents, and hundreds of articles. I personally visited (and in some instances lived at) many of the locations in this book; I reviewed primary characters' emails, text messages, internal Snapchat documents, calendar appointments, and more. Evan, Bobby, and Snapchat, alas, declined many requests for interviews for this book, which is of course their prerogative. Why didn't they want a book written about them? You'd obviously have to ask them, but I suspect the answer is a mix of a company culture that is very protective of its secrets and the fact that they were working long days during most of the period of writing this book, fending off significant challenges from competitors and driving the innovations necessary to keep Snapchat relevant in advance of taking the company public. You will find more on both in the pages that follow.

As often as possible, I have let the principals share this story through their own words, in speeches, emails, interviews, or other forms. In a few instances, I have made minor edits to these texts to correct misspellings or grammatical errors. Most quotes in this book are from recorded interviews, lawsuit documents, emails, text messages, and other permanent records; others are based on what multiple sources said another person said at the time. Beyond the permanent records, this book is necessarily based on anonymous sourcing. It simply wasn't possible to do it any other way. I needed to get the unbiased truth from sources, and since the principal characters chose not to participate and asked employees and friends not to participate, those who spoke to me risked their livelihoods, significant amounts of money, and relationships, both professional and personal. Many of these sources only agreed to speak under the condition of anonymity. I have not shared the names of anyone who spoke on the record for fear that doing so might help expose, by process of elimination, those who chose to remain anonymous.

I would caution readers not to assume that just because I have written about a person's thoughts or actions that that person is the direct source. People typically share their thoughts and feelings with friends and colleagues, especially during times of high stress and notability, which many of the events in this book were. There are often discrepancies between sources' memories, as they have different recollections and versions of the truth. I have done my best to triangulate on the truth from witnesses' memories and other documents. In some cases, I have had to use my best judgment as to what happened based on the information available. I have changed some minor characters' names and personal details to both protect sources and private citizens who have nothing to do with our main story.

Other excellent reporters have worked hard to crack Snapchat's tough shell. I have included a works cited list detailing the articles I have referenced. I am particularly indebted to the excellent work of Josh Constine, Jordan Crook, Alyson Shontell, Mike Isaac, Austin Carr, and Kurt Wagner.

I do not claim that this is an impartial account. This is one version of the Snapchat story, undeniably colored by my experiences and those of my many sources. If Evan has his way, there will be many books written about Snapchat and Evan Spiegel.

It has been a significant challenge to write about a medium as visual as Snapchat, especially knowing that many readers have never used the app. I urge you to download Snapchat if you haven't and try it out as you read this book. At the very least, you'll understand what those damn teenagers are doing.

PROLOGUE

Initial Public Offering

MARCH 2, 2017

NEW YORK
STOCK EXCHANGE

NEW YORK, NY

Smiling in their navy blue suits, Evan Spiegel and Bobby Murphy stood next to New York Stock Exchange president Thomas Farley on a balcony at the exchange. A large yellow screen with the black letters SNAP INC., the parent company of the hit app Snapchat, hung behind them. The company's logo shined on seemingly every screen in the building. In a few short moments, Snap would go public on the New York Stock Exchange.

Farley turned and took a selfie using Snapchat as Evan and Bobby smiled and looked out at the crowd. Evan's fiancée, supermodel Miranda Kerr, stood on the floor of the stock exchange, as did early Snapchat employees Dena Gallucci and Nick Bell and Snap chief strategy officer Imran Khan. Bobby and Evan pressed a button together and a bell rang out loudly, signaling the opening of the day's trading. The assembled throng of Snap employees, friends, and reporters cheered. Farley encouraged the crowd to cheer louder. Evan, in a white shirt and gold tie, and Bobby, with a blue shirt and darker blue tie, smiled at the crowd, then turned and shared a moment. Bobby patted Evan on the back in celebration as Farley turned and shook hands with them each in turn. This was actually happening.

$SNAP was priced at $17 a share, but it opened at a much loftier $24. Snapchat CFO Drew Vollero watched the stock jump and exclaimed, "That's crazy!"

After Snap began trading, Evan, Bobby, Kerr, and Khan headed over to the fourth-floor equities trading desk at Goldman Sachs on 200 West Street. When Snap's stock jumped up to $24 right out of the gate, the Goldman trading floor broke out in jubilant cheers. The stock closed at $24.48, up 44 percent, with a closing market cap of $34 billion, on par with Marriott and Target. By the end of the day, Evan and Bobby were worth more than $6 and $5 billion, respectively.

Never before had so much economic value been created by a consumer product, used by millions of people daily, that was still so misunderstood.

As Snapchat rose from a silly photo-sharing app with a bad reputation for sexting to one of the hottest startups in the world, it became an increasingly common topic of conversation, particularly in the media. But it was little understood. A 2016 *New Yorker* cartoon depicted a man whose head had exploded, leaving behind his corpse holding his phone with Snapchat on it; in the caption a coroner explained to a cop, "Looks like another case of someone over forty trying to understand Snapchat." In a 2015 *New York Times* article, "Campaign Coverage via Snapchat Could Shake Up the 2016 Elections," the writer, commenting on Snapchat's seriousness as a platform, still referred to Snapchat as "a company known for enabling teenagers in various states of undress to send disappearing selfies to each other." Another *New York Times* writer said, "The user interface and design looks like the cross between a weird Japanese animation and a 1980s sitcom."

Evan occasionally tried to control the narrative surrounding Snapchat. In June 2015, he posted a video on YouTube titled "What is Snapchat?" In the video, Evan is wearing his usual white v-neck t-shirt, sitting in what looks like a windowless room. He spends four minutes awkwardly using slides written on a pad of paper to discuss the history of social media and how to use Snapchat. The video did not do much to clear up the perplexity surrounding the app.

But Evan has also embraced opaqueness at Snapchat. The app is designed for existing users rather than new ones; this helped early growth at Snapchat as users showed friends how to use all of the app's features in person. Confusion also lets Snapchat work in private, building hardware, computer-vision software capable of analyzing Snapchat pictures, and other moonshot projects that are key to the company's future. This attitude, combined with Snapchat's youth-focused design, has led outsiders to question how serious the company is.

As Snapchat set out on its IPO roadshow, Evan, Bobby, and the team found themselves pitching the company to potential investors far outside Snapchat's core demographic. There is a generational divide that Snapchat illuminates. As with many new social apps, Snapchat's user base skews very young. Some of this is inherently age based—young people tend to experiment more and have wider social circles. But a lot has to do with what age you were when you initially joined Facebook or Myspace. Older people who arrived to Facebook in its more constant state don't understand the appeal of Snapchat. Indeed, it was easier for me to write this book than teach my mom how to use Snapchat.

So what is Snapchat? To fully understand the company, you have to understand Evan Spiegel and how the thinks. Evan and Snapchat are inseparable. So we must go back to the beginning and examine how Evan approached his previous ventures, how Snapchat was created, and the environment it was born into. We will look at how the Snapchat team approached problems when they were a scrappy underdog with few resources and how that approach changed over time as their assets grew exponentially. By understanding the company's challenges and decisions, we can explore how the tech world's most creative product minds are approaching the future of communication.

As eventful as Snapchat's story has been to date, the company still has far to go to carry out Evan's grand ambitions. The night before the IPO, Evan emailed Snap's two thousand employees, noting that the IPO was merely a milestone and that the company had much left to accomplish. The next day, three thousand miles from the New York Stock Exchange, employees at Snapchat's headquarters in Venice, California, celebrated with doughnuts and champagne before returning to work.

One notable figure was missing from the celebrations: the guy who came up with the idea behind Snapchat.

Part I

AN EVAN
SPIEGEL
PRODUCTION

CHAPTER ONE

RUSH

APRIL 2010
STANFORD, CA

Sam leaned against the shopping cart, forearms bulging as he pushed with all his strength, picking up his pace from a trot to an all-out sprint. On most days, he used his athleticism to play wide receiver for Stanford's football team. Tonight, he was using that same athleticism to push his friend Stuart in a shopping cart because they were freshman boys trying to get the older guys' attention at fraternity rush.

Pushing Stuart off a makeshift ramp designed for frat bros to tricycle over seemed like a good way to make an impression. It was working. As they rounded the corner of Kappa Sigma's parking lot, several fraternity brothers standing on the concrete steps and sidewalk realized that these freshmen weren't using the normal Target-bought tricycles.

Where the hell did they get a shopping cart? one of the guys thought as he joined his brothers and started cheering as Sam steered the cart around the turn of the parking lot.

Stuart, a thin, goofy kid with his dark brown hair in a bowl cut, sat in the cart, looking diminutive next to his friend Sam and wondering why he'd thought this was a good idea. The Jack Daniels had initially calmed his nerves, but Sam was pushing him pretty damn fast. He didn't have time to rethink things.

Sam whipped the cart around the corner of the parking lot, its wheels rattling over bits of broken beer bottles. The parking lot's lone light cast a faint orange glow over the scene. The cart went up on two wheels as it turned; Stuart almost fell out, but Sam grabbed it and slammed it back down.

Steadying the cart, Sam sprinted toward the hastily constructed ramp and threw the cart forward into the warm California night.

The plywood ramp sagged atop its cinder block supports. Rather than soaring gloriously into the air as the boys had intended, the cart slid right off the end, its old wheels digging straight into the asphalt with a harsh screech. The cart violently ejected its cargo—Stuart flew through the air and tumbled end over end against the hard asphalt.

The onlookers paused.

Rolling over, Stuart rose gingerly. He turned and looked back at the group watching him and triumphantly raised his fists in the air over his head, like a snowboarder who had just won Olympic gold.

The older brothers exploded into hollering and cheering. This kid was getting a bid.*

Evan Spiegel smiled and sipped his beer from a red Solo cup, watching the chaos from the crowd. Tall and lanky, Evan had brown hair that he kept short and styled up across his sharp, angular face. He was often seen partying on campus in a tank top and shorts. As a sophomore rush chairman, Evan held the keys to the kingdom for these potential newcomers. All around him, nervous freshman engaged in the same small talk with active brothers: Where are you from? What freshman dorm are you in? Did you play any sports in high school? How's freshman year going?

All told, there must have been more than a hundred people there, milling about between the makeshift tricycle track in the parking lot and the fraternity house. The freshmen had come sporting a variety of

---

* A bid, or bid card, is an invitation to join a fraternity.

attire, from the East Coasters in polos to Southern Californians in tank tops, most trying too hard to look cool and casual at the same time. All the brothers were wearing yellow t-shirts for rush; the front depicted Curious George passed out next to a tipped-over bottle of ether. The lower right side of the back showed a small anchor with the fraternity's letters, KΣ, on each side—it was Evan's signature. The anchor was his way of saying, "This is an Evan Spiegel production."

Evan was born on June 4, 1990, to a pair of highly successful lawyers. His mother, Melissa Thomas, graduated from Harvard Law School and practiced tax law as a partner at a prominent Los Angeles firm before resigning to become a stay-at-home mother when Evan was young. His father, John Spiegel, graduated from Stanford and Yale Law School and became a partner at Munger, Tolles & Olson, an elite firm started by Berkshire Hathaway's Charlie Munger. His clients included Warner Bros. and Sergey Brin.

Evan and his two younger sisters, Lauren and Caroline, grew up in Pacific Palisades, an upper-class neighborhood bordering Santa Monica in western Los Angeles. John had the kids volunteer and help build homes in poor areas of Mexico. When Evan was in high school, Melissa and John divorced after nearly twenty years of marriage. Evan chose to live with his father in a four-million-dollar house in Pacific Palisades, just blocks from his childhood home where his mother still lives. John let young Evan decorate the new home with the help of Greg Grande, the set designer from *Friends*. Evan decked out his room with a custom white leather king-size bed, Venetian plaster, floating bookshelves, two designer desk chairs, custom closets, and, of course, a brand new computer.

From kindergarten through senior year of high school, Evan attended Crossroads, an elite, coed private school in Santa Monica known for its progressive attitudes. Tuition at Crossroads runs north of $22,000 a year, and seemingly rises annually. Students address teachers by their first names, and classrooms are named after important historical figures, like Albert Einstein and George Mead, rather than numbered. The school devotes as significant a chunk of time to math and history as to Human Development, a curriculum meant to teach students maturity, tolerance, and confidence. Crossroads emphasizes creativity, personal communication, well-being, mental health, and the liberal arts. The school focuses on the arts much more than athletics; some of the school's varsity games have fewer than a dozen spectators.*

In 2005, when Evan was a high school freshman, *Vanity Fair* ran an exhaustive feature about the school titled "School for Cool."† The school, named for Robert Frost's poem "The Road Not Taken," unsurprisingly attracts a large contingent of Hollywood types, counting among its alumni Emily and Zooey Deschanel, Gwyneth Paltrow, Jack Black, Kate Hudson, Jonah Hill, Michael Bay, Maya Rudolph, and Spencer Pratt. And that's just the alumni—the parents of students fill out another page or two of who's who A-listers. Actor Denzel Washington once served as the assistant eighth grade basketball coach, screenwriter Robert Towne spoke in a film class, and cellist Yo-Yo Ma talked shop with the school's chamber orchestra.

Evan was attracted to technology early on, building his first computer in sixth grade and experimenting with Photoshop in the Crossroads computer lab. He would later describe the computer teacher, Dan, as his best friend.

Evan dove into journalism as well, writing for the school newspaper, *Crossfire*. One journalism class required students to sell a certain amount of advertising for *Crossfire* as part of their grade. Evan walked around the neighborhood asking local businesses to buy ads; once he had exceeded his sales goals, he helped coach his peers on how to pitch businesses and ask adults for money.

By high school, the group of 20 students Evan had started with in kindergarten had grown to around 120. Charming, charismatic, and smart, Evan threw parties at his dad's house that were "notorious" in his words. Evan's outsized personality could rub people the wrong way

---

* The basketball team did have its moments—the 1996–97 Crossroads Roadrunners were led to the state championship by Baron Davis, who went on to be an NBA All-Star.

† Funnily enough, the founder or Crossroads, Paul Cummins, had an epiphany as a freshman at Stanford that drastically impacted his life's work. He shared this story every year with Crossroads students at assembly, recounting, "While standing in line to register at Stanford, I met this guy who asked me what I was reading. I said, 'What am I reading? Classes haven't started.' And he kind of rolled his eyes, like, 'What kind of an idiot is this?'" The new classmate then bought him a copy of George Orwell's *Animal Farm*. "And I just thought it was fantastic; There hasn't been a day since that I haven't been interested in learning something."

at times, but his energy, organizing skills, and enthusiasm made him an exceptional party thrower. He possessed a bravado that could be frustrating and off-putting but was great for convincing everyone that the night's party was going to be the greatest of all time.

Obsessed with the energy drink Red Bull and the lifestyle the brand cultivated, Evan talked his way into an internship at the company as a senior in high school. The job involved throwing parties and other events sponsored by Red Bull. Clarence Carter, the head of the company's security team, would give Evan advice that would stand him well in the years to come: pay attention to who helps you clean up after the party. Later recalling the story, Evan said, "When everyone is tired and the night is over, who stays and helps out? Because those are your true friends. Those are the hard workers, the people that believe that working hard is the right thing to do."

In the fall of 2008, Evan burst onto the campus scene at Stanford. Known as "The Farm" because Leland and Jane Stanford founded the school on their old Palo Alto farm, Stanford has an idyllic 8,000-acre campus in northern California, just south of San Francisco. He lived on the top floor of Donner, a three-story all-freshman dorm. Evan quickly became friends with the guy who lived right across the hall from him, Reggie Brown. Evan could not possibly have imagined it at the time, but meeting Reggie would become one of the most important things he did at Stanford.

Reggie was born on January 17, 1990, in Isle of Palms, an affluent coastal town just outside of Charleston, South Carolina. Reggie had a masterful way of making people feel welcome and comfortable around him, like he was genuinely interested in getting to know you. He could come across as a goofball at first, as he smoked and drank and made lowbrow jokes, but he was deeply intelligent and creative. Reggie knew from the day he got to Stanford that he wanted to be an English major and focus on writing. Reggie was a beefy, good-looking kid with shaggy blonde hair that was typically tucked under a backward cap. A wide, silly smile usually brightened his face. His Southern manners set him apart in Northern California, as he would frequently address professors and friends' parents more formally.

Evan and Reggie spent a lot of time partying together. The group in Donner was unusually social that year, not least because the two fast friends frequently threw parties in their dorm. This was not common for freshmen because it was frowned upon. These gatherings were typically lubricated by handles of vodka and Red Bull Evan had shipped to him, as he was still working for the company as a brand manager, giving out free samples.

Most freshmen did not have a car and were adjusting to life without their parents. Evan drove a Cadillac Escalade and thrived in his new environment. In addition to his ever-growing group of friends he met through his and Reggie's parties, he started dating a pre-med student named Lily, and they were soon attached at the hip.

Lily was a steady, positive influence on him. She was a very patient, understanding girlfriend and put up with some of his absurdity because the good times—from fraternity parties to adventures for just the two of them to a spring break trip to Cabo San Lucas in Mexico—were so much fun.

Throughout the year, Evan designed and printed tank tops for his Donner crew. He had befriended the owner of a printing shop and was able to negotiate discounted prices and short turnarounds on orders. Evan created a tank top mimicking the Stanford athletes' Nike gear. The shirts said STANFORD across the chest, but instead of a team sport underneath "Stanford," it read HUSTLING. In the spring, a friend tossed out the idea for a "Sun's Out, Guns Out" tank top; later that day, Evan emailed the dorm a Google doc to collect people's orders and sizes, and by Friday everyone who paid him could rock their shirt.

By the time spring quarter arrived, Evan's reputation had grown—he was the kid from LA who liked to throw parties. Most of his Donner crew joined a fraternity or sorority that spring. Reggie, Evan, and their friend Will rushed the Kappa Sigma fraternity.

The Kappa Sigma brothers had a work-hard/play-hard ethos; they prided themselves on being able to excel on campus while drinking and throwing ridiculous theme parties. The leaders of the house typically did very well academically and balanced sports teams and other extracurricular commitments with heavy drinking binges. *The Stanford Flipside*, the school's beloved *Onion* wannabe, summed up the culture best with an article titled, "Kid Vomiting in Stall Next to You to Run Fortune 500 Company Someday."

In April 2009, Evan, Reggie, and Will were awoken in Donner by Kappa Sigma brothers, offering them Natty Lights and little manila bid cards—invitations to join the fraternity. They were in.

Evan and Reggie took widely divergent routes through the fraternity pledging process. Most of the new members went with the flow during pledging and did what the older brothers told them to do. Evan constantly questioned: Why do we do it this way? Why are we letting other people tell us what to do? Why can't we go do this? Reggie, on the other hand, simply couldn't be bothered to show up or take pledging seriously. During the process, the older brothers frequently wrote out the pledges' names on a big whiteboard and gave them points for tasks well done, events they showed up to, and generally how much they were liked by the active members. Reggie was always at or near the bottom of the list.

While he didn't put any effort into the setting up, cleaning up, or planning of parties, Reggie excelled at one part of the process: the parties themselves. All pledges were given tasks: one had to carry a lunchbox around to classes, another had to roller blade around campus, and a third had to wear a bike helmet to every party. All received nicknames as well: Reggie earned the nickname Blue Suit, given every year to the pledge who parties the hardest. He was handed down a baby blue men's suit that was rarely, if ever, washed. He had to wear it to every party, adding more layers of liquor stains to its illustrious history.

Evan moved into the Kappa Sig house his sophomore year and was assigned a room in the Mid, so named because it was located right in the middle of the house, where the bedrooms met the kitchen, lounge, and chapter room to form a T. Five pledges lived in two small bedrooms, with a larger common room connecting them in the middle.

Choosing to live in the Mid meant committing to a quarter* where keg stands would take precedence over classes. Mid residents who wanted to get homework done had to escape the fraternity for the library. And it was difficult to get to bed before two o'clock in the morning most nights, as fraternity brothers would drink and party or smoke

---

* Stanford is on the quarter system, so each year is divided into fall, winter, and spring classes rather than two semesters (fall and spring).

and play *Super Smash Bros.* on a beat-up N64 in the middle room. In the larger common room of the Mid, Evan and his friends would throw regular weeknight parties, inviting everyone they knew.

Evan had a private text group with a bunch of the girls in his year to which he'd regularly send mass texts like, "Raging tonight at Kappa Sig, be there." Almost inevitably, Evan's Thursday-night parties would explode into all-campus events. Sorority girls, overeager freshmen, and jaded-but-drunk seniors alike would wander over and cram into the Mid to slam back Natty Lights, take pulls from plastic handles of bottom-shelf vodka, and forget that they had class the next morning. During these parties, Evan was in his element. He could often be found sitting on top of a speaker DJing in a tank top, gauging the mood of the crowd, and making sure everyone was having a blast. He even came close to getting LMFAO, a hip-hop duo best known for their "Party Rock Anthem" hit, to come play at one of the fraternity's parties.

Fraternity life posed a continual challenge for Evan—he always wanted to take things to the next level. Instead of planning mere parties, he constantly increased their vision and scale until they became planned events with specially built props and specifically designed tank tops. "Spiegel, we can't do that" became the most common phrase uttered at house meetings. Evan would type up ridiculous event descriptions for emails and Facebook invites, describing parties in the most absurd, dramatic ways.

Evan was elected a social chair and quickly went way over budget. As Stanford's football team embarked on their first winning campaign in nine years and the busy student body started to pay attention to the games, Evan pushed to make tailgates into bigger spectacles. For every home game, he would cart his own enormous speakers down to the dirt parking lot next to Stanford Stadium. The Kappa Sig brothers invited every girl they knew and threw a full-on frat party in the parking lot. Evan worked the crowd with ease, greeting people left and right with a thin, wide smile on his face. When his head wasn't thrown back laughing, he was typically drinking from his red Solo cup or gesticulating with his long, gangly arms to make a point. The tailgates kept growing, week after week, riding the unstoppable waves of the football team's success and Evan's party-throwing acumen.

In addition to obsessing over his parties looking a certain way, Evan had already begun to think about his future. Evan decided to study product design, to learn how to look at the things he used in his daily life and see how he could make them better and cooler. David Kelley, the head of Stanford's famed design school, took Evan on as his advisee. One thing was clear; as he frequently put it, "I'm not going to work for someone else." And this gave him freedom from the heavy grind of Stanford. Nobody would ever see his résumé or grades, so he took classes for what he actually wanted to learn.

Evan was actually unique on a campus where most of the bright sheep were only unique in their own minds.

During his sophomore year, a family friend introduced Evan to Peter Wendell, the founder of venture capital firm Sierra Ventures. Wendell had been teaching a class for second-year MBA students, Entrepreneurship and Venture Capital, at Stanford's business school for over twenty years. Stanford MBA students take the class hoping to learn how to start their own businesses. Wendell let Evan sit in on the class and put his visitor's chair right next to the guest speakers. A thrilled Evan sat on the edge of his seat next to prominent venture capitalists and entrepreneurs like Google's Eric Schmidt and YouTube's Chad Hurley. The class poured fuel on the fire of Evan's desire to found his own company. He learned directly from Silicon Valley superstars who had accomplished exactly what he aimed to do.

From Red Bull to his dorm-room tank-top business to frat parties to Wendell's class, Evan threw himself into the endeavors that managed to hold his interest. And, typically, these projects were different from what most Stanford students found captivating.

After class one day, Intuit cofounder Scott Cook told Wendell he was impressed by the intelligence and reasoning of Evan's response. Wendell replied, "Well, you will be surprised to know he isn't an MBA student. He is an undergraduate who is auditing this class." Wendell introduced Cook to Spiegel, who promptly begged to work with Cook. Cook let Spiegel join him on a small Intuit project called txtWeb, which aimed to make available online information accessible via SMS messages in India. The txtWeb team consisted of Cook, Spiegel, and an engineer. Evan didn't work there very long, but he learned how much he could accomplish with a small team—and how much he wanted to work for himself, where he could call the strategic shots.

One day, Evan had coffee with Peter Wendell and talked to him about his experiences working for Cook and his desire to get involved with startups. "Being your own boss is great," Peter told him. "There's no boss more kind, more generous than yourself."

◉

If you made a country out of all the companies founded by Stanford alumni, it would have a GDP of roughly $2.7 trillion, putting it in the neighborhood of the tenth largest economy in the world. Companies started by Stanford alumni include Google, Yahoo, Cisco Systems, Sun Microsystems, eBay, Netflix, Electronic Arts, Intuit, Fairchild Semiconductor, LinkedIn, and E*Trade. Many were started by undergraduates and graduate students while still on campus. Like the cast of *Saturday Night Live*, the greats who have gone on to massive career success are remembered, but everyone still keeps a watchful eye on the newcomers to see who might be the next big thing.

With a $17 billion endowment, Stanford has the resources to provide students an incredible education inside the classroom, with accomplished scholars ranging from Nobel Prize winners to former secretaries of state teaching undergraduates. The Silicon Valley ecosystem ensures that students have ample opportunity outside the classroom as well. Mark Zuckerberg gives a guest lecture in the introductory computer science class. Twitter and Square founder Jack Dorsey spoke on campus to convince students to join his companies. The guest speaker lineups at the myriad entrepreneurship and technology-related classes each quarter rival those of multithousand-dollar business conferences. Even geographically, Stanford is smack in the middle of Silicon Valley. Facebook sits just north of the school. Apple is a little farther south. Google is to the east. And just west, right next to campus, is Sand Hill Road, the Wall Street of venture capital.

Silicon Valley has always had an influence on Stanford, and vice versa. But starting in the late 2000s, tech started to dominate the university. In the fall of 2010, as Evan began his junior year, I arrived on campus as a freshman. Coming from the East Coast, I knew that Stanford and Silicon Valley were closely linked and that tech companies were a big deal out there on the West Coast. I just didn't realize how big. One of the guys in my freshman dorm made a new social networking app that he was trying to get this tech blog called *TechCrunch* to write about. My friends and I went to see *The Social Network* in Mountain View, right next to Google's campus. You never expect one of your friends to start a billion-dollar company. But watching *The Social Network*, we all had a strong feeling: *This could happen again. Here.*

It wasn't just the nerds starting companies, either. Even fraternity guys and sorority girls had ideas for apps and companies. Perhaps especially them—the Greek system naturally drew out the more social students, who mixed that outgoing nature with the brains and work ethic that got them into Stanford into a potent recipe for creating popular consumer companies. Instagram cofounder Kevin Systrom was a member of Sigma Nu a couple of years before Evan, Reggie, and Bobby arrived on campus. Other high-profile companies like Chubbies, a men's shorts and lifestyle brand, and Robinhood, a stock-trading app that would eventually be valued north of $1 billion, would be founded from the fraternities' members in the years to come. The founder of Hewlett-Packard was a brother in Kappa Sig at Stanford as well, but that was many years ago.

Most of the ideas people pitched sounded idiotic. And there was a definite fatigue that set in among students who were sick of hearing so many classmates pitching so many apps. But there was nevertheless an energy on campus. People were creating and building.

CHAPTER TWO

FUTURE FRESHMAN

OCTOBER 2010
STANFORD, CA

When we last saw him, Stuart was a freshman getting thrown from a shopping cart while trying to join the Kappa Sig fraternity. Six months later, having achieved his goal, he was a sophomore living in the fraternity house. It was a typical Wednesday night, and Stuart was anxious. He was supposed to meet up with some classmates to work on a group project. Instead, he was sitting with two dozen of his fellow pledges in the End, one of the three rooms where new members lived, like a more laid-back version of the Mid. As with the Mid, it was quite cleverly named because it sat at the east *end* of the house, overlooking a large parking lot.

The main room, a large, fat rectangle with a vaulted ceiling, was furnished with couches and low tables; the sophomores had set up a big projector and would watch movies on the room's largest wall. They'd managed to jam one desk into a corner for when someone had to work but didn't want to make the trek to the library. Other guys in the house would come through the room to smoke weed and cigarettes off the balcony. Two smaller rooms, which connected to the main room on either side, were filled with two bunk beds and dressers in one room and three bunk beds and dressers in the other. Sometimes the guy sleeping in the top bunk would drunkenly roll off and crash onto the floor, causing the other inhabitants to run in and check on him.

The pledges were awaiting the arrival of Evan Spiegel. Stuart wasn't the only one who was anxious about what fate awaited them. Evan had spearheaded a number of rollouts that fall—these involved active members rolling pledges out of bed in the middle of the night to perform various drinking stunts. Evan's rollouts were feared because they featured complicated tasks and lots of booze. The practice had become an increasingly vital part of the house shenanigans, as the fraternity had been placed on a year-long probation, banning them from throwing any of Evan's precious parties.

But Evan wasn't focused on rollouts tonight. As he entered the End, he excitedly addressed the group, telling them about a new startup he was working on.

"It's going to be this platform where kids in high school can go on and learn about all these different universities," he told them, his face lighting up with enthusiasm. "They can put in their credentials, then the system will give suggestions on what schools they should apply to."

The iPhone had only reached its third generation, the iPhone 3GS, and mobile app development was not ubiquitous, so students and entrepreneurs at the time would still think to build a website first and foremost. Evan explained that he and Bobby Murphy, one of the brothers who had graduated the previous spring, had been working on the website throughout the summer. The problem, Evan said, was that the way high school students searched for college information was tedious, slow, and inefficient. They had to look at every school's website individually. He and Bobby had designed a site that would solve that problem. Future Freshman would aggregate information on most of the country's colleges and universities; the site offered ancillary material like videos of college counselors talking about life on campus. Parents and guidance counselors would pay a monthly subscription fee to access the database. It was a potential goldmine.

Unfortunately, someone had to do the work of aggregating all of that data, which involved manually pulling it from college websites and inputting it into Future Freshman. That's where the pledges came in. They'd each have to dig up a whole host of information on the colleges like population, location, Greek Life: Yes/No, and much more and add it to a shared Google spreadsheet.

Wrapping up his short pitch, Evan handed each pledge a slip of paper with 25 colleges on it, and told them get to work. Then he turned and exited the room.

"Fuck this," Stuart blurted out.

Some of them argued that they should just get up and leave immediately. Evan was totally abusing the pledging process—it wasn't the sophomores' job to get his startup off the ground by doing mind-numbing data entry. They had their own homework and student groups to deal with. Cole had soccer practice early the next morning. Chris had rehearsal for his a cappella group. Sam was trying to get into Harvard Law School. Jeremy was struggling with the pre-med core classes. Others argued that alternative pledging events would suck more.

The room was split—some of the guys were good friends with Evan and looked up to him. His ease with girls, ability to throw great parties, and flair for the absurd bought him significant social capital. Others thought he was an obnoxious clown who spent too much time and energy on impassioned speeches at house meetings about inconsequential things like party themes.

They huddled around a leftover keg, half of them drinking and bitching about Evan and pledging, the other half drinking while doing the work, all inhaling a scent equal parts stale weed and beer. A few of the guys had come right from the gym, and it really would have been great if they'd found some time to shower. Some of them sat around texting their girlfriends on BlackBerrys or checking to see if anyone had sent anything funny to the fraternity email list. Others typed away diligently, some even buying into Evan's dream, wondering if Future Freshman would change the way their younger siblings looked at colleges.

The sophomores sat in the crowded End for hours. Evan anxiously checked in on them periodically. In the end, only about a quarter of the work got done. Evan was pissed, but one of the other older brothers pulled him aside and told him to let the pledges go.

A few days after the pledging event, Evan gave a few of the sophomores who had contributed a full tour of the site. They had to admit it looked very professional with its striking background and intertwined "FF" logo. In Evan's hands, it could be something huge. A few were sufficiently convinced of its promise to keep helping Evan get all the college information into the database. They sat together in the fraternity's single small study room and entered the data for two or three hours at a time. In a few weeks, Future Freshman was packed with information about colleges across the country.

Evan and Bobby Murphy got ready to launch the site. Bobby was two years older than Evan and had grown up in El Cerrito, California, near Berkeley. His parents were California state employees, one of whom had emigrated from the Philippines. Like Evan and Reggie, he had also been placed on the third floor of Donner* when he was a freshman in 2006–7. He rushed and joined Kappa Sig with his Donner buddies as well, living in the Mid like Evan. He was almost exactly the same height as Evan, but Bobby's face was rounder than Evan's angular facial structure, and he had black hair that he typically styled up and to the side.

When Evan was first learning computer science, he would frequently bound into Bobby's room at two in the morning, interrupting Bobby's *Starcraft* sessions to ask for coding help. While Evan and Bobby were just two years apart in school, Evan's class had already started to shift from favoring more traditional career paths toward studying computer science and working at startups after graduation; this drift would accelerate in the coming years. Before Future Freshman, Bobby recruited Evan to work with him on a new social network that was a different spin on Google Circles. It went nowhere.

Bobby was quiet, introverted, and unassuming to the point that most of his fraternity brothers didn't know he was a part of Future Freshman until Evan told them. Bobby was more than happy to let Evan run the show and take meetings with Teach for America, tell customers about the service, and make pledges input data, while Bobby quietly worked on the company's technical backbone. Evan could sometimes get on his nerves, but they worked well together, and Evan respected Bobby's opinion.

---

* While joining Kappa Sigma was a choice, Evan, Reggie, and Bobby all being placed on the third floor of Donner was complete coincidence. Maybe there's something in the water there . . .

At the end of the fall quarter, Evan left to spend the winter studying abroad in Cape Town, while Reggie headed off to study for a quarter at Oxford. Evan was pulled toward new ideas and projects in South Africa as Future Freshman found itself battling for mindshare and dollars with well-established companies that had deep pockets and large sales teams.

And there were signs all too close to home that the product wasn't connecting with its intended users. "Both of [Bobby's and my] siblings were applying to college at the time and neither of them used it," Evan later said. "So that was a sign that that was probably not the right way to go." Eventually, they pulled the plug on Future Freshman. While the outcome was disappointing, Evan learned a valuable lesson: in order to avoid getting destroyed by better-funded competition, his next idea had to be more original.

As if the startup's failure wasn't enough, in the middle of the winter quarter of their junior year, while Evan and Reggie were still abroad, the University completed its review of Kappa Sigma's probation. University administrators said the fraternity had a toxic drinking culture causing incidents that went "beyond shenanigans," an admonishment that became something of a catch phrase for the group. In order to be reinstated, the members would have to prove that the organization had changed. The fraternity would be kicked out of their house for the 2011–12 school year, Evan and Reggie's senior year. They would be allowed to stay in the fraternity house through June 2011, but they could not throw any parties.

With rent in Palo Alto exorbitant, 96 percent of undergraduates lived on campus, making it a heavy blow to the fraternity Evan had worked so hard to build up. Several guys questioned whether the fraternity should even go on. A number of the fraternity's members, focused on their own startup dreams, job prospects, and academic careers, seemed ready to give up on the house. The fraternity's leadership did a membership review, interviewing every member and weeding out any brothers who were deemed unfit to be a part of the house. Evan and Reggie were picked as two bad apples and kicked out of the fraternity.

Reggie's expulsion came as no surprise to anyone who'd been paying attention.

He was known principally for getting wasted, breaking things, and leaving a mess in the kitchen. His room, which reeked of weed and to-bacco, was filled with cups and plates from the house's kitchen that he hadn't bothered to return. He never showed up for house meetings or lent a hand on house cleans or party setups. Although he was very book smart and super friendly to everyone, he was a downright nuisance to live with.

Evan's case was not so clear-cut—ask ten people why he got kicked out and you'll get ten different answers. Some say he was a willing scape-goat, volunteering to be kicked out because he knew he wouldn't have the house for his senior year anyway. Others say he was scapegoated because he had angered younger guys by pushing for parties while the house was on probation. Others say Evan deserved to be kicked out because he didn't want to fight hard enough get the house back, and he had been taking too cavalier an attitude toward the trouble the frater-nity faced.

No matter the reason, Evan was out. Guys in the fraternity blamed him for their house being taken away. Friends who he thought would have his back didn't.

Bad news came in threes for Evan. He had already lost Future Fresh-man. He lost the fraternity. Then, his girlfriend Lily told him she'd had enough and dumped him after two-plus years of dating.

CHAPTER THREE

MILLION-DOLLAR IDEA

SPRING QUARTER
APRIL 2011

STANFORD, CA

Reggie carefully ran his fingers over the blunt, admiring its tightly rolled perfection. It was almost a shame to smoke such a work of art. He leaned back on the couch in his Kimball Hall dorm room as he discussed the weekend's social events with two of his former fraternity brothers, David and Zach.

Reggie, now in the spring of his junior year, had plateaued—academically and socially.

What's more, he didn't seem bothered by it—he didn't really have any sort of a plan beyond enjoying himself and going to classes. Most students at Stanford throw themselves into academics, student organizations, athletics, and part-time jobs and generally continue their over-achieving habits that got them into the school in the first place. Reggie didn't do much of that. He seemed to many of his friends like a more subdued Van Wilder, just a regular guy who wanted to hang out and have a good time without worrying about the future.

The subject of the conversation moved on to the girls. A dreamy expression appeared on Reggie's face.

"I wish I could send disappearing photos," he mused, almost absentmindedly.

David and Zach laughed and agreed that it would be useful if photos disappeared, then turned to who was coming to their party that weekend. Reggie withdrew. He was thinking.

Through the haze of smoke, David and Zach's chatter faded. Reggie focused on the usefulness of this new idea. A way to send disappearing pictures. He wouldn't have to worry about sending a hookup a picture of his junk! And girls would be way more likely to send him racy photos if they disappeared.

Suddenly, he jumped up, and rushed down the hall to see if Evan was around. Having both recently returned from studying abroad, and with their Kappa Sig lives now over, Evan and Reggie had moved into Kimball Hall, a dorm not far from Donner, where they had lived freshman year. Mulling his disappearing photos idea—how would he best explain it to Evan—Reggie's topsiders barely touched the worn dark blue carpet as he surged down the hall in a half run/half walk.

Bursting into Evan's room, Reggie exclaimed, "Dude, I have an awesome idea!" Even before Reggie finished explaining his idea, Evan lit up. He was immediately energized—almost intoxicated. It was just like all those nights of partying together, except they were drinking in Reggie's idea.

"That's a million-dollar idea!" Evan finally exclaimed.

Reggie felt relief and validation; more importantly, he felt hope. Even though Future Freshman had failed, Evan hadn't given up his dream of starting the next transcendent tech company. He was the best operator Reggie knew, capable of taking this stroke of inspiration and making it a reality. And now they had an idea that actually seemed fresh and new. Unique.

The two friends excitedly discussed all of the celebrities whose nude photos had been leaked to the press. Their app would solve this problem! Evan gesticulated quickly and animatedly as he explained to Reggie how he could see people sending disappearing pictures back and forth. Most of us had barely moved past flip phones and BlackBerrys to iPhones at this point. And just as we moved from talking to texting to apps for everything else, people were starting to make the app transition for sex. Tinder would come out a year later, followed by a whole host of copycats. With this early photo-sharing idea, Reggie and Evan imagined a walled garden for couples to share intimate photos.

They would divide the company, vote on everything, and share any losses or gains they might see. Since Evan had more experience from running Future Freshman and other projects, he would be the CEO. Reggie would be the chief marketing officer.

But neither knew how to code well enough to make the app. They would need to recruit one of their friends to join them. They started a list of their fraternity brothers who had taken computer science courses. Most of the seniors that year were still economics majors heading off to Wall Street and the major consulting shops after graduation—it would be a few more years until most sought to make their fortunes in the Valley. But they came up with a couple names and headed off to the fraternity to recruit them.

Evan was a particularly persuasive salesman but he struggled to convince people with the initial pitches.

Evan and Reggie walked up the concrete steps of Kappa Sigma and opened the door to the foyer. The smell of stale beer wafted through the lounge as they greeted a few of the older brothers, turned left, passed the Mid, and headed down the hallway. Entering the End, Evan and Reggie found Jack Dubie using the room's lone desk to work on one of his assignments.

Jack was a tall, athletic, vivacious programmer from Vermont who let his dirty blonde hair flow in a somewhat shaggy mane; sometimes he would grow a beard to accompany it. A brilliant coder, Jack would go on to complete three degrees from Stanford in mathematics and computer science over the next two years. He was one of the fraternity's friendliest members, and when he wasn't cracking jokes, he could often be found helping friends with their CS assignments. He eventually became the computer science department's main student advisor. Jack frequently sported basketball shorts and t-shirts bearing the logo of his high school sports teams or his family's Maple Syrup company.

The three of them sat in the End, on the same couches Jack and his pledge brothers had sat on when they were inputting Future Freshman data for Evan a few months earlier. Evan dove right in. They had an idea, possibly a big one. More than one member of the frat lived in fear that photographs of their debauchery would come back to haunt them once it came time to get serious and have a career.

What if people could send each other wild pictures of themselves partying without worrying about future consequences? Jack listened intently, nodding along as Evan spoke in fast, clipped sentences. Evan talked about how weird it was that whoever started the internet and Facebook just decided that everything should stick around forever. Reggie jumped in now and then with anecdotes about drunken pictures he had sent and how he wished he had an app like this. Evan told Jack they were going to work on it as much as they could this spring, then full time during the summer when classes, which now seemed less important than ever, were out of the way.

Sinking back into the couch, Jack thought about the idea for a few moments. Evan was right, it did seem odd that everything was permanent, but this seemed like it was primarily a sexting app. Jack had already signed his offer letter to work at another startup that summer, at an email app called Mailbox that would later be acquired by Dropbox for $100 million. He explained that while it was an interesting project, it wasn't right for him. But he could introduce them to classmates who could code the app for them.

Reggie and Evan turned to Julian Okuyiga, a sophomore from Houston. Okuyiga had a flair for the ridiculous that almost rivaled Evan. Wearing pastel pants and polos, Julian frequently looked like he had just stepped out of a J.Crew catalog. He was black, had close-cropped hair, and was a bit on the short side. Okuyiga was known for writing prodigious code, and he would later go on to work for Goldman Sachs before founding his own startup.

A few days after speaking to Jack, during the midafternoon lull between classes and dinner, Evan pulled Julian aside in the fraternity and brought him into the Mid to pitch him on the idea, this time without Reggie. Evan's pitch was almost identical to the one he gave Jack. Julian seemed interested but was not yet ready to commit. Evan exited the Mid trying to contain his excitement and keep his big idea under wraps until it was ready for the world to see. He walked through the hallway looking like he was doing the world's worst job of hiding the world's best surprise party.

But his excitement was ultimately short-lived. The next day, Julian told Evan that he, too, had too much going on with school to devote time to something else at the moment. In reality, Julian didn't want to work with Evan, whom he found overbearing and overly intense. He also just didn't think much of the idea and couldn't see how it would take off socially. Couldn't people just text each other photos? Plus, everyone was already uploading pictures to Facebook and Instagram every day. Did they really need another way to share pictures?

Upon hearing the news, Reggie was momentarily discouraged. He still thought the idea was sound, but if Jack and Julian thought so little of it, then maybe he was wrong. Anyway, without a coder, they'd never know.

Fortunately, Evan was not so easily deterred. And he had the perfect person in mind—his old Future Freshman cofounder, Bobby. Evan was sure he could convince Bobby to work on the app. He called Bobby and explained Reggie's idea. But Bobby wasn't convinced. Would people really want to use this? Evan nervously urged him that this idea was different from anything other people were working on. It wasn't like Future Freshman where they would run into an army of competitors. They had learned a lot from their past two projects, and this was the most unique idea yet. Bobby, at last convinced, agreed to write the code, hoping the third time would be the charm for him and Evan.

Evan, Reggie, and Bobby's first crack at the idea was dreadful: they created a clunky website where users uploaded a photo then set a timer for when the picture would disappear. They quickly realized it would be much easier and more private for users, and thus more widely used, if they built a mobile app instead of a website; to this day, Snapchat still does not offer a web product.

They sat around in their dorm room, debating how users should interact with their friends and what features would make people tell their friends to download it. Evan ran the group, making sure things were coming together on time and keeping everyone focused, while boisterous Reggie offered up ideas on all the different ways people would use the app. Bobby, much quieter and more reserved than the other two, kept the group grounded and generally agreed with Evan on the app's direction.

Bobby put in eighteen-hour coding days for the next week to get them to a working prototype. Reggie came up with a name for the app: Picaboo, a riff on the childhood game Peek-a-boo. Evan designed the app's interface, digitally mocking up what it would look like and how users would interact with it, so that Bobby could turn his visions into reality.

When users opened the app, which was only available for iPhones, it showed a camera screen so they could immediately take a picture.* Once they took a picture, they could set a timer from one to ten seconds, tap to the right, and select which of their Picaboo friends they wanted to send it to. Then when their friend opened their picture, it would display for the set number of seconds before disappearing. If users tapped left they could see what photos their friends had sent them. The interface was simple but had the ugly clumsiness of a rough draft, with big square buttons and a jumble of icons crowding the screen.

They finished a working prototype of Picaboo just days before final exams. They needed people to download the app, test it out, and hopefully tell their friends about it. Evan decided to approach his former fraternity brothers; despite having been kicked out, he was still friendly with most of the guys from his year, and they were still some of the most social people on campus. Evan needed the popular crowd to use this if it was going to catch on.

Evan quickly typed out a few lines about the app. He had told a lot of the guys about the idea before but not in such a broad, public way. He imagined people forwarding the email, downloading the app, and being instantly addicted. Facebook had launched a mere seven years earlier and ripped through Harvard like wildfire before spreading to other campuses, and then the world. *The Stanford Daily* wrote at the time about how many students were skipping classes because they were consumed with Facebook. Instagram had been downloaded over forty thousand times on the day of its initial release. Evan used an analytics platform

---

* There's an inherent strangeness to writing about such a visual medium. If you haven't downloaded Snapchat yet, I would suggest you download it and explore the app while reading this book.

called Flurry to track how many people downloaded the app, how often they used it, and how often they sent pictures to each other. It was time for the world to see Picaboo. Putting the finishing touches on the email, Evan hit send.

And then . . . nothing. It was a dud.

The fraternity brothers who downloaded the app that first week had fun with it, sending each other silly photos of themselves bored in class or pics of themselves partying. Even more so, it was cool because it was one of the first times they could hold something in their palms, on their phones, that one of their friends had built. But it wasn't serious; it was just Evan's little toy. A few dozen people had downloaded it and were toying around with it because their friends had created it. But they weren't totally sure what it was and how they were supposed to use it. It was too early to call Picaboo a failure—the thing had just launched and barely worked. But it was far from the fairy-tale launch Evan had dreamed of.

Evan was enrolled in a mechanical engineering class called "Design and Business Factors" that encouraged upperclassmen product design majors to create a prototype and business plan for an app or other product. The final project, presenting this prototype and business plan, was a third of the grade for the course. Reggie's idea was much more intriguing than the ones Evan had been considering, so he adopted it for his class. While most of the other students worked in groups of three to five, Evan worked on his idea alone.

At the end of the class, everyone presented their prototypes to a panel of venture capitalists. There are dozens of entrepreneurship classes like this at Stanford, and while there is the allure of a team making it big, the vast majority of the students are just playing startup. If most startups fail, most of these class projects don't even reach a stage where they can accurately be called a startup.

Like a school science fair, everyone put together a visual presentation to display on tables in the back. Each group sent a presenter to sell the judges on their project and receive feedback. Evan sat in the back of the classroom and watched his peers pitch their ideas. They ran the usual gamut from overpolished presentations by excited students seeking approval to underprepared undergrads just running out the clock until their turn was over. For the first time, Evan worried what other people would think about his app. The fraternity brothers enjoyed playing with it—surely Evan's peers and these venture capitalists would understand the value of what he had been working so hard to build. They had to, right?

Finally, it was Evan's turn. Showtime. He approached the front of the room like the entrance to a party, strutting confidently to show the crowd what he, Reggie, and Bobby had been working on tirelessly for the past six weeks. Confident and comfortable, Evan enthusiastically explained to the other thirty students, two professors, and half a dozen venture capitalists that not every photograph is meant to last forever. He passionately argued that people would have fun messaging via pictures.

The response? Less than enthusiastic.

Why would anyone use this app? "This is the dumbest thing ever," seemed to be the sentiment underlying everyone's tones. One of the venture capitalists suggested that Evan make the photos permanent and work with Best Buy for photos of inventory. The course's teaching assistant, horrified, pulled Evan aside and asked him if he'd built a sexting app.

The scene was reminiscent of another Stanford student's class presentation half a century earlier. In 1962, a student in Stanford's Graduate School of Business named Phil Knight presented a final paper to his class titled "Can Japanese Sports Shoes Do to German Sports Shoes What Japanese Cameras Did to German Cameras?" Knight's classmates were so bored by the thesis that they didn't even ask him a single question. That paper was the driving idea behind a company Knight founded called Nike.

The VCs sitting in Evan's classroom that day likely passed up at least a billion-dollar investment return. But it's very easy to look at brilliant ideas with the benefit of hindsight and see that they were destined to succeed. Think about it from their perspective—Picaboo's pitch was basically, "Send self-destructing photos to your significant other." Impermanence had a creepy vibe to it, belonging only to government spies and perverts. With the benefit of hindsight, we can see that Facebook developed the conditions that allowed Snapchat to flourish. But it wasn't at all obvious watching Evan's pitch in 2011 that this was a natural rebellion against Facebook or that it would grow beyond our small Stanford social circle.

If anyone was searching for the next Facebook killer, they were hopefully looking at a little photo-sharing app called Instagram that had just raised Series A funding valuing the company at $25 million; it's much more likely that they were looking at any number of apps or websites that have since died without your ever hearing of them.

In spite of this third failure to successfully pitch people on the idea, Evan remained undaunted. And as he hoped to keep Reggie and Bobby engaged and driving on the project, he told them that everyone really liked their idea.

Most of their peers were pursuing internships—or, in Bobby's case, full-time jobs—at prestigious banks and big tech companies. But Evan and Bobby were used to ignoring the norms to chase their startup ideas. And Reggie was committed to it. Most importantly, they really liked the app. While primitive, it was fun to use. And they really believed that people would want to send pictures that deleted themselves, whether for sexting or otherwise.

The trio agreed to move south for the summer, to Evan's dad's house in Pacific Palisades. There, they would develop the app, gain users, and take their shot at becoming the next big Stanford startup. As they agreed on the logistics of the summer, Reggie felt his excitement grow. As long as he had Evan, nothing could go wrong.

CHAPTER FOUR

THE OTHER STARTUP

JUNE 2011
STANFORD, CA

Around the same time that Reggie had his idea for a disappearing-photos app, another Stanford student, a sophomore named Lucas Duplan, had an even bigger idea.

Duplan was a member of the Sigma Nu fraternity and a year younger than Evan and Reggie. He grew up in Orinda, California, which borders Berkeley. After his freshman year at Stanford in 2010, Lucas was studying abroad in London and became frustrated that he could use his phone to do any number of things, from messaging friends to playing music, but not to pay for a sandwich. Money could be transported and sent back and forth as little electronic bits of information just like anything else. So, Lucas wondered, why was it so much harder to buy something than it was to do anything else on his phone?

Lucas recruited two Stanford engineers, Frank Li and Jason Riggs, to cofound a new company with him. Li and Riggs agreed to work with Lucas despite the fact that Lucas was a year younger than Li and two years younger than Riggs. Their new company, Clinkle, would completely replace your wallet. Anything you used to pay friends or businesses, from credit cards to debit cards to checks to cash, would become obsolete thanks to this magical new app.

Lucas asked his professors to connect him with the very best designers and engineers. Some professors pushed back, saying there was no objective list, but they eventually relented and gave Lucas some names of talented students. Lucas, merely a sophomore, recruited two seniors: Rob Ryan to head up design and John Rothfels to run engineering.

The 2008 financial crisis was fresh on the undergraduates' minds as they set out to change the financial world. The system was unfair. The process of exchanging money was clunky and outdated. They intended to build a proper financial system for the twenty-first century, eventually maybe even expanding into areas like microlending. It would certainly be a more meaningful project than the silly photo-sharing apps their classmates were building.

They felt like the next generation of the PayPal Mafia, a group of roughly two dozen entrepreneurs who left PayPal after selling the company to eBay in 2002. Members of the group went on to found Tesla, SpaceX, LinkedIn, YouTube, Yelp, and Palantir, among many other successful companies and venture capital firms. Not coincidentally, many of the members of the PayPal Mafia had studied at Stanford, often as classmates.

Duplan received some money from his parents and a $15,000 grant from a summer program at the venture capital firm Highland Capital. It had become quite easy for students to raise initial funding for their startup ideas. Venture capitalists were frequently on campus, often as professors or guest lecturers. Sand Hill Road, which runs from the 280 highway right past the edge of Stanford University in Menlo Park bordering Palo Alto, is home to the world's major venture capital firms; think of it as Wall Street for venture capital. In the summer of 2011—the same summer that Evan, Reggie, and Bobby moved in to the Spiegels' house to start Picaboo—Lucas and ten members of team Clinkle rented a house in Palo Alto to build the company's first product.

I first heard of Clinkle soon after I heard of Snapchat, in 2012, during my sophomore year at Stanford. Clinkle worked wonderfully. It looked like a beautiful wallet on your phone, and you could pull dollars out of it and swipe them to send them to friends. Instead of trying to split bills over credit cards or remember how much cash you owed a friend, you could just send them money phone to phone, instantly. This may sound dull to current readers, but this was before Venmo, Apple Pay, and a number of other payment services launched. It felt like the future.

It was an amazing time to be on campus. We knew some people would become wildly successful; we just weren't sure who yet. There was this amazing feeling of possibility, of untapped potential. This would be the time we'd look back upon, the days we first knew each other before everyone became who they were going to become.

Lucas believed users would only use Clinkle en masse if it were able to replace their entire wallet from day one. So the team held off on launching the peer-to-peer payment app and worked on its solution for paying businesses, which involved transmitting high-frequency sounds between smartphones and payment terminals. Lucas also didn't want users to get Clinkle only to find that it didn't work at their favorite restaurant or bar. So he planned to start at college campuses, insular communities in which the Clinkle team could get every business signed up before launch. So, like Facebook before it, Clinkle would launch college by college and dominate these campus networks before opening up to the broader world.

In the spring of 2012, Clinkle design chief Rob Ryan was a teaching assistant for a class on campus called CS 183: Startup. Peter Thiel, perhaps *the* crucial member of the PayPal Mafia as the company's cofounder, taught students "how to build the future." The course was so popular that Thiel and one of his students, Blake Masters, eventually published a book, *Zero to One*, based on the class and Masters' notes.*

Thiel told the teaching assistants that they each had one golden ticket: an opportunity to pitch him their startup idea for venture capital funding. Rob signed Lucas and himself up for a half-hour slot to pitch Clinkle to Thiel at the office of Founders Fund, Thiel's venture capital firm.

---

* *Zero to One* is really quite a good read, and I would recommend it to any readers interested in startups and the future.

As Lucas talked about Clinkle and their dreams for a new wallet-less future, Thiel canceled other appointments and sat there, captivated, for ninety minutes. When Lucas finished, Thiel paused for almost a minute, just sitting there. The room was filled with a deafening silence. Thiel asked Lucas, "What is the maximum I can invest right now?"

Lucas replied that Thiel could invest between $250,000 and $2,000,000 in Clinkle. They agreed to the principles of a deal right there in the room. It was like a scene out of *The Social Network*—Thiel had actually put the first $500,000 into Facebook back in 2004.* Now, he was putting money into Clinkle. After that, money, investors, advisors, employees—everything flowed into Clinkle easily.

Let's take a minute to look at how most startups raise funding. A genius hero founder is walking along one day when a brilliant idea pops into her head, or so the creation myth goes. She then goes out and raises some money. This can be anything from raising several thousand dollars from "angels," rich people who help startups get going, to raising millions of dollars from professional investors. While startup funding is a bit hard to generalize across sectors and companies, seed funding usually gives a company six months to two years to get going.

If the company survives on this seed money, the founders next raise a round called a Series A from professional venture capitalists. Subsequent rounds continue in alphabetical order until the company dies, gets acquired, goes public, or starts making enough money that it turns down investors.

If you take a hundred startups that manage to raise seed funding, only thirty-one of them on average will raise Series A funding. Only seventeen will raise a Series B; seven will raise a Series C; and two will raise a Series D. It isn't, or at least shouldn't be, surprising that the success rate hits single digits by a Series C, as these are large funding rounds in the tens of millions of dollars set aside for highly successful companies. But the descent from seed-funded startups to Series A and B is often much steeper than people expect. Raising some money for an idea is not that difficult. Staying in the game round after round, as the world changes and targets are met or not met, is extraordinarily difficult.

At each stage, the company gets a valuation. This is often confused

* This $500,000 investment literally appears as a scene in *The Social Network*.

with what the company is actually "worth," and it is this number that usually has talking heads up in arms about how a no-revenue app is "worth" hundreds of millions of dollars. But these are not publicly traded companies; this valuation is merely what one private investor is willing to pay. The company is almost certainly worth far less than this number if you break down its assets. Odds are, it will be worth zero or close to zero in the years to come. But a minuscule number of these companies will break out and be worth billions, if not hundreds of billions, of dollars.

It's important to reiterate again that the valuations are not the same as public companies' market caps. Venture capitalists invest in startups to hold their equity for years until the company goes public or gets acquired. The current valuation doesn't matter in the long run to investors. What matters is how the company grows and what percentage of the company the venture capitalists own. So while a startup might haggle over whether it should be valued at $80 or $90 million, a VC cares much more about whether his equity stake is 18 percent or 19 percent.

For example, take Sequoia Capital, Silicon Valley's premier venture capital firm, founded in 1972 far before VC became sexy, with investments in Apple, Google, Oracle, PayPal, and a litany of others. In 2011, Sequoia invested $8 million in the messaging app WhatsApp. Over the next three years, Sequoia led two more rounds of funding in WhatsApp, investing $60 million in the company. When WhatsApp sold to Facebook in February 2014 for $19 billion, Sequoia earned roughly $3 billion.

With Peter Thiel on board, Lucas Duplan set out to lure other investors. He succeeded wildly; his investors would include Accel Partners, Andreessen Horowitz, Intel, Intuit, Qualcomm cofounder Andrew Viterbi, and Salesforce founder and CEO Mark Benioff.

VMWare cofounder Diane Green and her husband and fellow VMWare cofounder Mendel Rosenblum invested in Clinkle after teaching Lucas at Stanford.

Stanford University president John Hennessy, a successful entrepreneur himself and a member of Google's and Cisco's boards of directors, was Lucas's computer science advisor and became an advisor to Clinkle. Mehran Sahami, a Stanford professor who teaches the popular introductory computer science class, invested in Clinkle after teaching

Lucas and several members of the early Clinkle team. The former dean of Stanford's business school, Bob Joss, invested as well.

All told, close to sixty people and institutions invested a sum of $30 million in Clinkle before the company even told the world what they were doing. The company had at this point been in "stealth mode," a sexy term meaning they weren't telling anyone what they were working on.

Stanford has been intertwined with Silicon Valley for more than a century. In 1909, a Stanford graduate founded one of the earliest big Silicon Valley startups, Federal Telegraph. David Starr Jordan, Stanford's first president, was an angel investor. But Clinkle made students, faculty, and alumni uneasy. Should the university president be advising a company that is recruiting students to drop out of school? Should professors be investing in their students' companies? The questions around Clinkle had no easy answers, but certainly it would look better for everyone involved if Clinkle turned out to be a massive success—the kind of endeavor obviously worth leaving school for.

Lucas raised convertible debt, which is common for early stage startup funding. Early stage funding is typically either equity—stock in the company—or convertible debt. This debt then converts into equity in the startup's next round of funding, usually a Series A. Had any venture capital firm or person invested $30 million on their own, they would have gone through a rigorous due diligence process, vetting Clinkle's team and technology inside and out. But none of the sixty-odd investors had a significant amount of money on the line. And so, there was no one with sole responsibility, let alone a board seat, when things started to go to hell for Clinkle.

And it didn't take long for things to head south. In October 2012, half of the company walked out feeling Lucas had misled them about the stock options they would be receiving. As with many startups, employees took salaries well below their market rate to join Lucas and Clinkle, expecting to be rewarded with equity in the hot new startup. But for many, the equity never came.

Nonetheless, Clinkle pushed forward. Every startup hits bumps in the road to glory, and while the October 2012 exodus was tough, it would be a footnote once Clinkle hit it big, many still thought.

In April 2013, *The Wall Street Journal* ran a breathless story about

Clinkle, complete with a quote from President Hennessy suggesting that Clinkle might well be different from the many startups started by undergraduates that "won't make it past the summer." The story, which featured a picture of Lucas crowdsurfing on top of nearly two dozen employees, was light on details about how Clinkle's product actually worked.

"This isn't the next social app," Lucas said in the article. "Clinkle is a movement to push the human race forward by changing how we transact."

A group of a dozen Clinkle employees stayed up all night eating doughnuts and working like they were back in college until the article came out at 6 AM. For most, the college vibe felt familiar, as Clinkle was their first job after graduating from or dropping out of Stanford. Clinkle's office at the time was only a short drive down El Camino Real from Stanford, in Mountain View, in Google's complex of buildings known as the Googleplex.

In the summer of 2013, Clinkle's public relations staff reached out to over a dozen publications, from *The New York Times* to *TechCrunch*,* asking them to cover "the largest seed round in Silicon Valley history." While Lucas was happy to wax poetic about how Clinkle was going to change the world and how much money he had raised, he refused to talk at all about the product or technology behind Clinkle. Now, Lucas was attempting to keep the product and technology in stealth mode, while announcing the company to the world. It was a bizarre strategy.

Like most young founders in Silicon Valley, including Evan, Lucas looked up to Steve Jobs as his idol. He wanted to create a company like Apple, polished and ready to dazzle consumers. Lucas never wanted to talk to users or customers—he felt he should decide what was best for users and deliver them an amazing, innovative product that was a massive improvement over their current wallets. But hyping Clinkle to the press was one of Lucas's fatal errors, as he put inordinate pressure on the young company. Evan and Bobby shipped a minimum viable product in Picaboo—that is, the lowest-quality product that's still acceptable

---

* I was still a reporter for *TechCrunch* at the time and covered Clinkle's fundraising announcement. In my story, I also included details about the product and how it worked, much to Lucas's chagrin.

to early users, who will provide feedback to improve the product. It took Evan and Bobby years to add in all the features they wanted beyond the initial disappearing picture-sharing app only for iPhones. They were able to see how people used the app and iterate quickly. More than anything, what killed Clinkle was Lucas's refusal to ship a minimum viable product. Lucas killed Clinkle as much as Evan birthed Snapchat.

Clinkle got bogged down working through regulations and trying to bring a banking partner on board to legally process users' money. With $30 million in the bank and a talented, hungry team, Lucas indulged seemingly every idea he and his team of engineers had. Typically, early stage startups are so strapped for resources that they have to ship products that are worse than they'd like them to be. However, these constraints force the founders to focus on what really matters most to their product.

Clinkle never came close to feeling this sort of pressure. This long runway, combined with their insistence on perfection, became toxic as they spun their wheels, creating many products that never saw the light of day. The team created nine different sign-up processes but weren't able to test which one worked best with users because they hadn't launched.

Head designer Rob Ryan designed a beautiful app that looked and acted just like a real-world wallet, mimicking the motions of pulling dollars out and handing them to a friend. But Clinkle sat and waited and never launched the app. Eventually, the design world shifted away from skeuomorphism—the design concept of creating digital products that look and feel like the real-world products they are mimicking—and Clinkle's app looked odd and antiquated before it even launched.

Clinkle employees were constantly told by Lucas and his brain trust that they were just a couple months away from launching to consumers.

Being a startup CEO is a lot like being a quarterback or a goalie in sports—win and you get all the glory, lose and you get all the blame, whether you deserve it or not. In Lucas's case, he earned the blame for Clinkle's failure.

At Snapchat and other successful companies, employees are happy to experiment and work hard on products that may never see the light of day because those products that do get shipped have a major impact on millions of users. At Clinkle, no product had shipped, and no one knew when a product would ship. So engineers worked on products for months and had no idea what would become of them.

◉

In the summer of 2013, former Stanford classmates and Clinkle cofounders Frank Li and Jason Riggs both left the company after having issues with Lucas. Lucas became more secretive, refusing to show Clinkle's app to prospective hires and even some Clinkle employees. Some employees began to suspect that the demo they had been shown in their interviews was not the same as the company's actual product.

Later that summer, engineering head John Rothfels gathered the team and told everyone Clinkle's new plan: to send users debit cards. Clinkle's entire mission, the three words that they had repeated over and over to recruit employees and investors, was "eliminate the wallet." But the company's technology for making payments to vendors in a coffee shop or restaurant via sound waves wasn't working well enough. Clinkle could have released a peer-to-peer money-transfer app, like Venmo or Square Cash, while continuing to work on their merchant payment system. But they had already ceded significant ground to the aforementioned competitors by not launching eighteen months earlier. And Lucas was obsessed with launching a full peer-to-peer and merchant payments system.

In September, Lucas visited Clinkle investor and entrepreneur Richard Branson in London. The two posed for several photos with four wads of $10,000 in fake $100 bills and an iPhone loaded with Clinkle's beta app. For the final picture, to symbolize how Clinkle was going to destroy physical currency, the duo set the money on fire and smiled for the camera.

Back in San Francisco, Lucas made a key hire in October 2013, bringing on Netflix chief financial officer Barry McCarthy to serve as the proverbial "adult in the room" and bring some stability to Clinkle.

Later in October, Clinkle took its sales team out for a celebration after they had signed up 100,000 college students to a waitlist. Clinkle, with no live product, had twenty people emailing college students in fraternities, sororities, and student groups offering prizes and other promotions in exchange for sending over their group's email addresses. Clinkle would then add all these addresses to their waitlist, which they would theoretically sign up once the product launched. After the sales team had their big night out on Thursday, they were all laid off on Sunday. Some found out when they went to check their email and found themselves locked out. Lucas let Barry handle most of the layoff discussions.

The week after Thanksgiving, Lucas called an all-hands meeting to proudly introduce a new member of the team. Chi-Chao Chang had joined from Yahoo to be Clinkle's new vice president of engineering. Chang stood up and addressed the team, introducing himself and noting how excited he was to be joining Clinkle. The next day, Lucas called another all-hands meeting. He stood next to Barry McCarthy in front of about forty assembled Clinkle employees.

"Chi-Chao has left Clinkle," Lucas said.

Chi-Chao had arrived at Clinkle and learned that the company only had a demo—not a fully functional product. Lucas and the Clinkle leadership had spent so much time going back and forth over features and design that the system's architecture wasn't ready, key security features weren't ready, the sound for merchant payments still didn't work, and, oh, Lucas still wanted to make more aesthetic changes.

Barry McCarthy left the company in March, less than five months after joining. He had joined in October believing Clinkle would launch its product in November, but the product still had not launched. Clinkle had become such a laughingstock in Silicon Valley that its brand was toxic, so it attempted to rebrand to "Treats." Clinkle put a "Treat Bot" on campus one day at the University of California, Berkeley that gave students $20 bills. In theory, it was supposed to get students to talk about Treats, download Treats, and share it with their friends. In reality, it was burning money faster than Lucas did with Richard Branson.

Some investors asked for their money back, while others just quietly disassociated themselves from the company. In May 2015, the last remaining loyal employees walked out after yet more failed acquisition talks.

Clinkle died an ugly death. But its death illuminated some thorny questions for Stanford.

◉

"If the Ivy League was the breeding ground for the elites of the American Century, Stanford is the farm system for Silicon Valley," Ken Auletta wrote in a *New Yorker* profile of the school, dubbed "Get Rich U" in April 2012. Auletta's *New Yorker* colleague Nicholas Thompson later bemoaned, "The school now looks like a giant tech incubator with a football team." Thompson readily admits that he is also a Stanford graduate who founded a digital media startup, and when he needed funding, he raised venture from his former classmates.

Much like professional athletes, computer science students can perform ridiculously impressive tasks at equally young ages. But this is a far different time frame than traditional career paths. How does it change college if we need to be ready for our prime by age twenty-two? There was a shift at some point, from smart kids saying, "I want to solve X problem" to students going, "I want to start a startup. Now I just need a damn idea!"

The environment at Stanford could be fantastic for innovation—the number and quality of opportunities was, and still remains, unparalleled. But there are negatives to being in this echo chamber. While most people have some vague idea of a startup or product that they could make, at Stanford there is an air of hubris around new ideas. Some of this was positive, as students feel empowered to jump and commit to their ideas. But some is inevitably negative, as teenagers walk around talking about their weeks-old ideas as if they are the greatest things to grace the earth. The air people breathe in the Bay Area is innovation, entrepreneurship, and disruption. But overindulging in this bubble can get a founder too far away from regular users of their product, distorting their true north. Steve Jobs famously left Silicon Valley to travel in India. And soon, Evan Spiegel would very purposefully leave Silicon Valley to create Snapchat.

CHAPTER FIVE

LAWSUIT POSSIBLE

SUMMER 2011

THE STARTUP HAUS

PACIFIC PALISADES, CA

John Spiegel's house sits in a picturesque neighborhood in Pacific Palisades, a posh enclave that lies above Santa Monica and the beach in western Los Angeles. The quiet sidewalks are lined with manicured green lawns and skyscraping palm trees. Although it is just a short drive down the winding hill to the chaos of the city, it feels secluded and serene.

Inside the house, Reggie, Evan, and Bobby laid their plans for an internet revolution. While Evan's class hadn't loved the idea of disappearing photos, it was different from what other people were working on, and Evan thought that was important. The prototype they built in the spring was far too slow, and it would need to be scrapped and rebuilt entirely. This was Bobby's purview, as he was the only one with real coding chops. Evan, a product design major, worked with Bobby to create the new version of the app. While Reggie did not have Bobby's or even Evan's technical skills, there was plenty of nontechnical work to be done. After they rebuilt the app, Evan, Bobby, and Reggie would need to launch a marketing and public relations campaign to entice people to download and use Picaboo.

Reggie and Bobby stayed in Evan's sisters' old rooms, and the three of them commandeered the kitchen as their Picaboo headquarters. Evan dubbed the place the "Startup Hau5," their startup home's name written in the style of the popular DJ deadmau5. John Spiegel had a private chef keep the house stocked with food and meals for the boys. Given that the trio hadn't raised any funding, they were covering all expenses out of their own pockets—known as "bootstrapping" in Silicon Valley parlance—so the free rent was a big plus. Despite John's repeated urgings for Reggie to call him by his first name, Reggie, with his Southern manners, called him Mr. Spiegel the whole summer.

As they rebuilt the app, Evan talked Reggie and Bobby through the design choices and constraints he wanted to build into it. Picaboo would always open directly to a camera, so that users could quickly take a photo of whatever they wanted to share with friends. They realized users wouldn't want their impermanent photos to be screenshotted and saved forever; lacking a way to make it impossible for users to take a screenshot, they came up with a clumsy alternative: users would have to keep their finger on their phone to view a photo, making it more difficult to press two iPhone buttons and take a screenshot. They also worked out a way to notify a user if the recipient took a screenshot of their photo.

They would need a logo for the app, something that instantly enticed users to download and use Picaboo. Reggie and Evan sat together and created the logo over the course of a few hours, going back and forth on ways to symbolize the disappearing nature of the app. They settled on a friendly ghost who was smiling and sticking out its tongue. Evan drew the ghost in Adobe InDesign while Reggie tossed in ideas. Reggie named the ghost Ghostface Chillah, after the Wu-Tang Clan rapper Ghostface Killah.

Evan studied the hundred most popular apps in the app store and noticed that none had yellow logos. To make Picaboo stand out, he put the Ghostface Chillah logo on a bright yellow background. Reggie slapped the logo on Facebook and Twitter pages he made for the app.

While Evan worked hard on the design and vision for the product and Bobby coded, Reggie contributed less. Plenty of successful Silicon

Valley founders do not write code; but they play other roles, relentless hustling in the early days of their companies, dominating nontechnical jobs like marketing and user growth. Reggie simply wasn't doing that. Having recently turned twenty-one, he wanted to enjoy the Los Angeles nightlife, and he stayed out into the wee hours of the morning. While Evan and Bobby lived the plot of *Silicon Valley*, Reggie was more *Entourage*. Evan had always remembered and valued what Clarence Carter had told him when he worked at Red Bull, "When everyone is tired and the night is over, who stays and helps out? Because those are your true friends. Those are the hard workers, the people that believe that working hard is the right thing to do." His co-founders felt Reggie was not pulling his weight, and it was beginning to cause resentment.

By the end of June, they had a working beta version that Bobby emailed out to some technically inclined friends to test. Evan, Bobby, and Reggie went out and celebrated the milestone. Later that evening, they arrived back at Spiegel's house and Reggie and Evan got into a drunken argument about how much time and effort Reggie was—or wasn't—putting into Picaboo.

Reggie, having had enough of Evan's outburst, retreated upstairs. But hearing Evan and Bobby continue to discuss Evan's grievances in the kitchen, he paused on the landing, halfway up the staircase. He overheard them talking about getting rid of him and bringing in someone better, someone more experienced, to run marketing. Reggie's temper flared, and he thought about running back down the stairs into the kitchen and shouting at Evan, "What the hell are you talking about?"

But he knew Evan would fire back and things would escalate. So Reggie walked to his room, his head swirling with emotions, ideas, and cocktails. He took out his bound writing notebook and jotted down everything he had contributed to Picaboo, punctuating the note-to-self with a reminder:

Lawsuit possible.

The next morning, cooler, albeit hungover, heads prevailed. Reggie had gone outside and Evan and Bobby came out to join him. The three of them discussed the argument, apologized to each other, and agreed to move on. For the moment, at least, things were fine.

Putting the fight behind them, Bobby continued making improvements to the codebase, while Evan mocked up better designs and new features. Reggie typed up a Terms of Service, FAQ, and Privacy Policy for users based on templates Evan had found and sent him. Reggie organized receipts and records for when the company would eventually need to file tax returns. The three of them voted and changed the name from Picaboo to Pictaboo then back again to Picaboo.

Reggie struggled with the marketing, mocking up press releases for *Cosmopolitan*, announcing "First Timed-Picture Messaging Game Is Here: Picaboo." In another draft, Reggie positioned Picaboo purely as a sexting tool, writing, "Picaboo lets you and your boyfriend send photos for peeks and not keeps!"

In July, Picaboo was finally ready, and Evan began to move past the limited sexting use case, positioning Picaboo as a general picture-sharing app for friends. Apple reviewed Picaboo and approved it, allowing anyone to download the app from the App Store. Evan sent it to a Stanford group for students working on startups, telling them, "Our team just launched Picaboo on the AppStore and we'd love for all of you to check it out! Picaboo.me/dl the first epehemeral picture messaging app for iPhone :)."

Evan, Reggie, and Bobby went out to dinner to celebrate the launch and Bobby's birthday. After dinner, they tore into a cake Evan's dad had brought, complete with Picaboo-yellow frosting and Ghostface Chillah resting on top. A few days later, Evan, Bobby, Reggie, and their friend Joey from freshman year in Donner went to see the popular DJ Avicii perform in Hollywood. Evan had made bright yellow Picaboo tank tops with the Ghostface Chillah logo on them, and they all wore them to the show.

Evan used the analytics tool Flurry to track Picaboo's users and their activity, gaining information on where they were located, how often they opened the app, and how long they used it for. He hoped they could hit at least 30 percent retention with Picaboo—that is, have roughly one-third of people on the app come back and use it again a week later. If they could clear this hurdle, it would show they were onto something useful with Picaboo—that they were solving a need for users and were close to product-market fit.

The guys were getting some decent feedback on Picaboo from

friends who were downloading it and testing it out, but Evan knew he needed to make it more immediately appealing to his target market. Reggie's marketing and PR efforts weren't gaining much traction, so Evan stepped in. Picaboo needed to quickly capture people's attention when they landed on the App Store page, drawing them in to at least read about the app, and hopefully download it. A mutual friend put him in touch with Elizabeth Turner, an aspiring model who was living in Los Angeles for the summer. Turner and her sister Sarah agreed to model for Picaboo, which Evan described as a class project, for free.

The two sisters drove over to Evan's dad's house and did a photo shoot there, on the Santa Monica Pier, and on the beach. Evan and Bobby snapped pictures of Elizabeth, in a white bikini, and Sarah, in a pink bikini, smiling, splashing water at each other, and jumping on each other's backs in the ocean. Evan incorporated photos from the shoot to the screenshots of the Picaboo app for the App Store and website.

After the photo shoot, Evan emailed Bro Bible, a popular website among college fraternity guys, hoping the editor would cover Picaboo. In an email titled "Ridiculous iPhone app," Evan told the editor he had been reading Bro Bible for a while and that he was a "certified bro—our fraternity got kicked off last quarter." He then pitched Picaboo, explaining succinctly that "it's the fastest way to share photos that disappear." He briefly explained how to use the app, then mentioned his new marketing secret weapon—the Turner sisters. "The girl who modeled in our iTunes screenshots is from Duke and very good-looking," he wrote, including a link to download the app. The editor did not respond.

At the end of July, Reggie flew home to South Carolina to spend time with family and work remotely on the project. Ever paranoid that someone would steal their brilliant idea, Evan had become convinced that they had to file a patent to protect Picaboo.

"Hope you had a safe flight dude," Evan texted Reggie. "People know we don't have a patent so we gotta jump on that shit haha let me know if we can do anything to help."

Reggie replied, "In the car on the way to the beach working on the patent app, will call tonight and let you know progress."

"Awesome," Evan responded. "We've been hustling Picaboo to the max. This thing is a rocketship. Our 7 day retention is 60% right now (target is 30%) and we're growing."*

While Reggie worked on the patent in South Carolina, Evan and Bobby figured out a way to get rid of the animation that occurred whenever you opened the iPhone camera app. The friendly animation mimicked an old-school camera opening its gray lens. It only took a second or two, but this was too long for Evan. Eliminating this step made the camera for the Picaboo app load much more quickly than the standard iPhone camera app could. If the Picaboo camera loaded faster than the standard camera, some people might start using Picaboo as their default camera. Users might take all photos with Picaboo by default, then send them to friends and save (by taking a screenshot) the ones they wanted to save.

Evan's view of what Picaboo could be expanded beyond sexting as he realized how valuable and useful a general ephemeral app could be. Bro Bible chose not to cover Picaboo, but Evan persisted, emailing smaller outlets. He knew from Picaboo's strong retention that they had an interesting product—something far more interesting than just a sexting tool. With better PR and awareness, Picaboo could get a vitally important core base of early users. Eventually, they could hit a tipping point where Picaboo started spreading organically via word of mouth.

Evan reached out to a blogger he liked, Nicole James, who ran her own blog called *That White Bitch*. Evan started the pitch in a similar fashion to his Bro Bible attempt, explaining again how he, Reggie, and Bobby were "certified bros" whose frat had just been kicked off campus. This time, he adjusted his pitch slightly, calling Picaboo "a game for sending disappearing pictures with your friends." Evan urged James to download Picaboo, claiming, "If you get one of your girlfriends on it we promise you'll be obsessed."

"So it's like, the best way to sext, basically. Cuz you can't save the images?" James sent back.

"Some people use it for that . . . but it's also the best way to quickly

---

* Seven-day retention is the number of people who open the app and return to the app a week later. So in this case, six out of ten people who opened Picaboo were coming back and opening it again one week later.

share an ephemeral moment with a friend . . . it makes the images you send special. the most exclusive photos in the world haha," Evan replied.

"I like it," she said.

"Blog target #1 acquired," Evan wrote to Bobby and Reggie, forwarding his email chain with James.

A few days later, Nicole James posted on her blog:

> My internet friend Evan [Spiegel] created this app called Picaboo whereby you can send a photo to anyone else who has the app. . . . There is NO WAY for the person to save the photo. Imagine all the n00dz you'd get cuz people would feel so safe about it!!!! . . .
>
> For Evan's sake, as he's probs reading this, I should mention he is not my sexting partner—he sends me photos of like, the beach and tacos and other stuff people do in California, while I send him photos of Times Square and taxis. . . . You know, New York shit. Now we are photo friends! It's neat.

Back in South Carolina, Reggie sent Picaboo's documentation in to the US Patent Office and excitedly texted Evan, "#patentpendingbro djsjsjshhajsndkdjs fuck yes fuck yes you and Bobby need to celebrate this shiz tonight." Evan responded, "no chance we're celebrating without you bro!"

CHAPTER SIX

THE FIGHT

AUGUST 2011
THE STARTUP
HAU5

Evan and Bobby, both in the Startup Hau5, and Reggie, still home in South Carolina, hopped on a conference call to update each other on their progress.

Evan paced in his room, cellphone to his ear, while Bobby sat outside listening on his phone, as Reggie quickly started reading from the patent application:

> ### Timed, Non-Permanent Picture Messages
> ### for Smart Phone Devices
>
> We (Murphy, Brown, Spiegel) have invented a new method of transferring picture messages via smart phone device technology. Specifically, our software allows users to specify the amount of time for which they wish to send their picture messages, at the end of which the message will delete, leaving no trace of either the message or the image on the user's smart-phone device.

Recently in the media, we have seen the plethora of ways in
which the permanence of normal picture messaging has become
a tool by which recipients of picture messages . . .

Evan was livid. Murphy . . . Brown . . . Spiegel? Hadn't he told Reggie to list Bobby as the sole inventor? Bobby had written every damn line of code! He invented it! And why the fuck is Reggie ahead of me? In what world is Brown ahead of Spiegel? Reggie hadn't built a single piece of the fucking thing!

Evan cut Reggie off and started tearing into him. Reggie shouted back and the argument escalated. Three years of unaired grievances came spilling out over the phone line, as issues that had been brewing for years exploded to the surface. Evan demanded to know what Reggie had contributed that warranted Brown being placed ahead of Spiegel.

Reggie started listing his contributions to Picaboo, from the original idea to the marketing materials to the damn logo.

Evan interjected, furiously arguing that he had designed the logo, drawing it all in InDesign.

"I directed your talents," Reggie said.

Evan hung up.

Bobby stayed on and quietly listened to Reggie venting. Calming him down, Bobby asked Reggie how much equity he felt he deserved in Picaboo. Reggie acknowledged, as he had earlier in the summer, that he knew he didn't bring as much to the table as Evan and Bobby, so maybe he didn't deserve as much as them. Still, he felt he deserved 30 percent of the project. After all, it was *his* idea.

"That's not gonna happen," Bobby replied.

Later that night, Evan texted Reggie, "Hey man I honestly feel insulted so I wanted to make sure—I didn't want to overreact. I definitely want to continue the conversation but it's hard when I feel so attacked."

"I want to make sure you feel like you are given credit for the idea of disappearing messages because it sounds like that means a lot to you," Evan continued. Reggie didn't respond.

Four days later, Evan emailed Reggie, his tone terse and cold:

Hi Reggie,

I still haven't received a copy of the provisional patent application that was filed. Can you please send me everything that you submitted to the patent office?

Thanks,

Evan

Evan's note reads more like that of an exasperated supervisor than an email between close friends. Reggie fired back, seemingly frustrated: "Like I told you before Evan, I plan on sending you everything that I submitted to the patent office once THEY return it to me. This is a government office and most of the time these things take a few weeks to be processed. . . . I know it is difficult for you, but wait."

But Evan had no intention of waiting.

Evan and Bobby changed the passwords and locked Reggie out.

Picaboo was theirs.

CHAPTER SEVEN

SNAPCHAT

SEPTEMBER 2011
STANFORD, CA

In 1839, an American photography pioneer named Robert Cornelius* took a photograph of himself; because the process at the time—using an iodine-sensitized silvered plate and mercury vapor—was so slow, Cornelius was able to uncover the lens, sit in the shot for a couple minutes to get the photo, and then recover the lens. On the back of the photo, Cornelius scrawled "the first light Picture ever taken." It is believed to be the first American photograph taken as a self-portrait.

In 1914, thirteen-year-old Anastasia Nikolaevna, the grand duchess of Russia, attached a photograph of herself to a letter she sent to a friend. "I took this picture of myself looking at the mirror," she wrote. "It was very hard as my hands were trembling."

In 1943, Edwin Land was on vacation with his family in New Mexico when his three-year-old daughter Jennifer asked why she couldn't immediately see the picture he had just taken of her. Within an hour,

---

* In a funny coincidence, Bobby's full name is Robert Cornelius Murphy.

Land had a crystal-clear image in his mind for a camera and film that could produce these instant photographs. Land's Polaroid camera was released in 1948, and by the 1960s half the households in the United States had one. Land went on to run Polaroid for over forty years and held 535 patents.

Over the following decades, people took pictures of themselves and their friends using high-end Leicas and disposable Kodaks. After returning from vacation, my family would drop off film rolls and disposable cameras and dutifully wait for the pictures to be developed. There was a bit of wonder in this, as we relived a vacation the day we went through all the photos. But there were inevitably a few accidental pictures with a finger over the lens.

In the early 2000s, as we moved from AOL Instant Messenger (AIM) and dialup internet to broadband and Myspace, many young people started posting pictures of themselves online, whether on social media sites like Myspace and Facebook, founded in 2003 and 2004, respectively, or photo-specific sites like Flickr (started in 2004). Around the time we were all on Myspace, people began taking self-portraits, or "selfies," by pointing digital cameras into mirrors.

In 2007, I joined my high school classmates on Facebook as we dumped hundreds of photos into albums to share with friends on the site. Even when we first had flip phones, the cameras were so bad and memory was so low that people would go out to parties with both a flip phone and a separate digital camera. The next day they would connect their camera to their computer and upload a bunch of pictures to a Facebook album.

In 2010, Instagram launched, riding the wave of the iPhone's overwhelming success, as suddenly millions of people were walking around with an internet-connected camera phone in their pockets. The cameras still weren't ideal—a major part of Instagram's appeal was that the filters made low-quality photos look great—but they were good enough to ditch the separate digital camera in most cases. People shared photos as a way of sharing themselves—where they've been, who they are friends with, who they are.

All of these social networks developed their own cultures and aesthetics as we used each one in different ways, determined by the early primary use-case and the stage in our lives during which we joined them.

By the time Reggie had his epiphany, the tech world was embracing front-facing cameras. On October 14, 2011, Apple released the iPhone 4S, its second phone with a front-facing camera (making the iPhone 4, also with a front-facing camera, more affordable). Apple's front-facing cameras were mostly for its video chat feature, FaceTime, but were starting to be used for photographs as well.

Technology and art were converging as the iPhone created amateur photographers of everyone. Evan wanted to build Snapchat as an art and technology company, modeled after two of his heroes, Edwin Land and Steve Jobs. Jobs had also considered Land a personal hero and someone he modeled his career after.

There is an obvious connection between the three visionaries. Land created the first truly portable, instant camera in Polaroid, enabling people to snap a photo then almost instantly view it. Jobs created the iPhone, which put a high-quality digital camera into hundreds of millions of people's hands. Evan created Snapchat, which let people quickly trade pictures back and forth as a means of conversing, using Jobs's iPhone. But the connection goes a level deeper, to the way the men think.

In the 1980s, then-Apple CEO John Sculley and Steve Jobs went to see Dr. Land at his lab on the Charles River in Cambridge, Massachusetts. In a 2010 interview, Sculley recalled the visit:

> Dr. Land and Steve were both looking at the center of the table the whole time they were talking. Dr. Land was saying: "I could see what the Polaroid camera should be. It was just as real to me as if it was sitting in front of me before I had ever built one."
>
> And Steve said: "Yeah, that's exactly the way I saw the Macintosh." He said if I asked someone who had only used a personal calculator what a Macintosh should be like they couldn't have told me. There was no way to do consumer research on it so I had to go and create it and then show it to people and say now what do you think?
>
> Both of them had this ability to not invent products, but discover products. Both of them said these products have always existed—it's just that no one has ever seen them before. We were the ones who discovered them.

Like Land and Jobs, Evan was more of a discoverer than an inventor. He explored the world around him in college and pulled Snapchat out of it. He also didn't believe users could tell him what they wanted—he simply had to discover what was next and show it to them.

◉

Now just a two-man operation, Picaboo still had the user growth problems it had as a three-man job. Although it had less than a hundred users, most of whom were Evan and Bobby's friends, the people who did use the app were using it all day, every day. Bobby and Evan agreed to keep working on the app and get it into more people's hands in the fall. As Evan moved back into Stanford housing to start his senior year, Bobby searched for coding jobs in San Francisco so he could afford rent.

One day, they received a cease-and-desist letter from a photo-book company called Picaboo. They needed a new name; something fun and playful like Picaboo, but that better conveyed what the app did. Combining the idea of snapping photos to send to friends and chatting with them, they landed on Snapchat. On September 26, 2011, Evan and Bobby launched Snapchat, née Picaboo, in the App Store; they now celebrate September 26 as the official founding date of Snapchat.

Bobby moved into a studio in Nob Hill in San Francisco and started coding for an iPad point-of-sale company called Revel Systems. He worked on backend engineering for the small startup, which only had a couple dozen employees at that point. Frequently, the head of engineering or the CEO would walk past Bobby and see him working on Snapchat code at his desk and have to chastise him to get back to Revel work.

Reggie moved into a house on campus and picked out the creative writing and English courses he would take senior year, bummed about the falling out with Evan and frustrated with his lack of direction as his friends started receiving job offers and charting their courses for postgrad life. Reggie thought Picaboo was a cool idea but ultimately a dead-end student project.

Evan and Bobby knew better. Evan had a bigger picture in mind for what Snapchat could become. And Evan and Bobby could see on Flurry that Snapchat was growing in popularity—climbing to a thousand daily active users by November 2011. Evan moved into a single studio room in an on-campus dorm called Ujamaa. With the frat kicked off campus for the year, he focused the energy he used to pour into planning parties into making Snapchat work (and attending the occasional class he enjoyed).

Evan and Bobby needed to make Snapchat stand out and be more useful—it wasn't enough that the photos disappeared, it had to be more fun to send a photo via Snapchat than any other messaging app. They added photo captions to the app, so users could add a line of text over a photo, and let users draw on top of the photos they took.

Evan and Bobby knew Snapchat had value, because everyone who used the app used it all the time. They just needed to get it into more people's hands and make it grow, even if they had to force this growth at first. So they started showing it to people one on one, giving tutorials, explaining why it was fun, even downloading the app for them.

Evan and Bobby figured if they could get ten thousand people to use Snapchat every day, that would be proof that the app had traction and venture capitalists would fund them. They were nowhere near that, but the app was inherently social. If they could get a thousand dedicated users who loved the app, those people would tell their friends, who would in turn tell their friends, and the app could spread very, very quickly.

Evan was willing to try anything to get users. When he was home in Pacific Palisades, he would go to the shopping mall and hand out flyers advertising Snapchat.

"I would walk up to people and say, 'Hey would you like to send a disappearing picture?' and they would say, 'No,'" Evan later recalled.

Evan took a small seminar called "Silicon Valley Meets Wall Street" full of like-minded upperclassmen interested in working at startups and in venture capital. One day before the guest speaker arrived, he convinced the entire class to download Snapchat and try it out.

On campus, people talked about "Evan's app," as it was more commonly known, in a mostly mocking tone, wondering why anyone would admit to using a sexting app. Nonetheless, there was some buzz around it because of Evan's force of personality. Even though he was no longer a member of Kappa Sig and was mostly focused on Snapchat rather than partying, Evan was still a large figure on campus.

In October, Evan opened up Flurry, the analytics dashboard he was using to monitor Snapchat's users, and noticed that new users were signing up in Orange County, California, and their activity was spiking between 8 a.m. and 3 p.m. Evan's mother had told his cousin, a high school student, about Snapchat. She and her friends downloaded the app on school-distributed iPads, which blocked Facebook. They started using the app as a way to pass notes in class. Snapchat fed the high schoolers' desire for attention, as they could see when the recipient opened their snap.

Snapchat started catching on in small clusters at various high schools in Orange County and Los Angeles that fall. Then, these high school students went home for the holidays and many found iPhones with front-facing cameras in their stockings. Teenagers began taking selfies using the front-facing camera and sending them to each other via Snapchat, having entire conversations through images of their faces. From December to January, Snapchat's user base grew by a factor of ten, growing from just over two thousand daily active users to over twenty thousand. Snapchat broke out from a note-passing gimmick to a full-fledged communication tool, replacing texting for many teens.

I should note that I don't use the term "millennials" in this book to describe Snapchat users, as it's too broad and often inaccurate. Many millennials born in the 1980s are too old for Snapchat's core user demographic, especially the early demographic, and many Snapchat users are in fact too young to be considered millennials. Snapchat gained early popularity primarily among high school and college students. The demographic expanded as these early users grew up and their siblings and friends, both older and younger, joined the app.

As useful as texting and messaging had become, they had become boring for teenagers. You were now just as likely to get a text message from your parents as you were from your crush. There was no excitement to most messages. But with Snapchat, you could see what the other person was doing in a rich way, and you could capture funny moments—a friend asleep in class, your dog making a weird face—that didn't seem worthy of interrupting someone with a text message.

Facebook, too, had become boring for teens, as they and their friends posted less content, less personal content, and often, no content once their parents joined the social network. Facebook notifications, once a thrilling red marker signifying that you had your friends' attention, now came with a "mark all as read" button more reminiscent of an email inbox than a fun social app. Because people rarely deleted old posts and photos from Facebook and other, less popular social networks, their profiles became dusty collections of the mementos they had posted over the years. This wasn't as big of a problem for people who signed up after a certain point in their life—when they arrived to the Facebook party, they came as their mostly formed selves. Snapchat did not resonate much with this older crowd.

But for college and high school students, they had signed up for social networks at a time in their lives of enormous change and growth. So these profiles came to represent weird versions of themselves that they no longer wanted to be associated with. Like outgrown sneakers or clothes that had gone out of style, these profiles needed to be tossed out and replaced with something fresh and new.

And, of course, for people of this age, there was always the fear that something dumb they posted on social media would get them in trouble with their parents, college admissions officers, or their employers. Perhaps Katy Perry summed it up six months earlier in her June 2011 song "Last Friday Night," singing, "Pictures of last night ended up online, I'm screwed."

Teenagers also felt pressure to post the most glamorous representations of their lives on Facebook, Twitter, Instagram, and other social media sites to rack up likes. Evan designed Snapchat as an antidote to this obsession with likes and retweets. Snapchat was not meant to be a social network—it was designed as a small, private network, to share with your closest friends. Snapchat had no likes, no permanence, no social anxiety. You could just send whatever you thought was funny or cool or interesting, even if that was an otherwise unflattering image of yourself.

Evan and Bobby carefully set up Snapchat to maintain and promote this intimacy. While most other apps at the time let you find and add your friends via a Facebook login or by uploading your email contacts, Snapchat only let you add people if you had their phone number (or knew their Snapchat username). Because of this, most people had a smaller group of closer friends on Snapchat than on other social networks—at least initially. They managed to make Snapchat feel like a small, cool club to belong to. It was a welcome escape from the Facebook empire.

In the early days, if you sent a Snapchat to the "teamsnapchat" account, Evan or Bobby would occasionally reply with a selfie.

Additionally, they didn't let users upload photos from the camera roll. Any photos sent via Snapchat had to be taken in the app and immediately shared, giving it an unparalleled sense of real-time interaction. When you received a Snapchat, for ten seconds you were transported to where your friend was at that exact moment.

I remember personally being told to download Snapchat because some of my friends were goofing around sending each other dumb photos. Like most people, I had to be told a few times before I actually downloaded it. Snapchat's been on my phone's home screen ever since. There was something undeniably cool about being able to hold your phone in your hand, open the app, and say, "My friend built this."

I opened Snapchat for the first time and added friends from my contacts, all of whom were undergrads at Stanford with me. I quickly snapped a picture of myself making a goofy face and sent it to a few friends. We would snap each other photos of ourselves bored in class and pictures from around campus that reminded us of inside jokes. There was an understanding that we weren't sending each other *National Geographic*–quality photos of the campus scenery. We would send silly pictures and photos with funny captions meant to shock and provoke a reaction in our closest friends.

Because you could only reply with a photo, friends would send selfies of themselves reacting to photos. We talked through photos instead of posting them to garner likes. The cost of creating and sharing a photo dropped so much knowing that the photo would disappear. It wasn't just that taking and sharing a photo was essentially free; sending a photo to a friend no longer had the importance it once did with texting. You were just exchanging lightweight photos that were meant to be discarded immediately.

We sent and received dozens of photos per day, more closely mirroring our text message frequency than our social media posts. The speed and frequency with which we took and shared pictures was unlike anything we had used before. Open the app, snap the photo, send, share, view, delete, on to the next.

In order to view a Snapchat from a friend, you had to hold your finger down on the screen. If you lifted your finger off the screen, the photo would disappear, a feature that initially started as a way to make it more difficult to screenshot Snapchats. But it also served to make users feel hyperconnected. When you posted on Facebook or Instagram, you weren't sure who saw it unless they liked or commented, and you didn't know if they were paying attention to you or aimlessly scrolling through a feed while multitasking. With Snapchat, you could see when the recipient had opened your snap, and you knew they had held their finger down, touching your photo as they absorbed what you had sent. It was an addicting combination.

A March 2004 article titled "All the Cool Kids Are Doing It" in *The Stanford Daily* described Facebook's newfound popularity: "Classes are being skipped. Work is being ignored. Students are spending hours in front of their computers in utter fascination. Thefacebook.com craze has swept through campus."

In 2012, classes were not being skipped in favor of Snapchat—students were simply Snapchatting from class rather than paying attention.

Students would sit around during free periods at Crossroads talking about the newest apps they were using and games they were playing. By early 2012, Snapchat was the hot new toy. At parties, people would send Snapchats to friends who weren't there. If you didn't download Snapchat, you were missing out. Snapchat had a confusing interface, so users in high school and college frequently showed each other how to use new features and navigate the app. It's a very visual app that's often difficult to explain but easy to show to someone. People who knew the hidden features felt cool showing them to friends. Users delighted in discovering Easter eggs and features they didn't know existed. This in-person sharing helped Snapchat grow quickly among young people.

There were other apps at the time that erased your conversations, most notably TigerText. TigerText was founded in 2010 in Santa Monica. The company has done quite well, raising over $80 million in funding, as a secure messaging service for doctors and healthcare providers. But it has not done nearly as well as Snapchat. Two companies founded a year apart practically next door to each other in LA focusing on disappearing messages—how could their outcomes be so different? The difference is Evan. Evan was able to see this idea as much more than a messenger for secrets or naked photos. Snapchat wasn't for secrets. It was for everything.

As thrilled as Evan and Bobby were that Snapchat was taking off so quickly, it posed a big problem for them. It cost a lot of money to pay for the servers that processed all these pictures teenagers were sending to each other. Evan was able to cover some of the costs with money he borrowed from his grandfather; Bobby picked up the rest of the tab out of his paycheck from Revel Systems. But the monthly costs were soaring to $5,000 and increasing every day.

In February, Evan went to speak with Peter Wendell, his professor from sophomore year, and Raymond Nasr, Google's former director of executive communication who helped Wendell run the business school course Evan took. Evan explained that user growth was phenomenal, but they needed investment money badly. Wendell suggested going to a venture capital firm or angel investors.

"We don't want to lose control of the company," Evan replied.

Wendell offered to introduce Evan to executives at Twitter, but Evan worried they would steal his idea. Finally, Evan agreed to get advice from a mutual contact at Google Ventures, the company's venture capital firm, and eventually decided to raise seed funding.

But the first venture capitalists who met with Evan, including blue-chip firms like Sequoia Capital and Benchmark Partners, passed on the investment. Disappearing photos? It sounded like a sexting app at best, or a fad at worst. Or was it the other way around? Some, like Chris Sacca, who put the first checks into Uber and Twitter, declined even meeting Evan.

In March, Barry Eggers, a partner at Lightspeed Venture Partners, came home from work to find his daughter Natalie and her high school sophomore friends sitting around the table in his kitchen. They were all staring at their phones and laughing. Eggers asked Natalie what they were doing.

"It's called Snapchat," she said. "It's like funny and goofy stuff between friends. It's one of the most popular apps at school, along with Angry Birds and Instagram."

Eggers had obviously heard of Angry Birds and Instagram, but not Snapchat.

"How often do you use it?" he asked.

"I used to send five or six a day. Now I get thirty a day!" Natalie said.

Eggers relayed this story to his fellow partners at the firm. One of the partners, Jeremy Liew, decided to track down the Snapchat team.

Evan and Bobby hadn't included any contact information on the Snapchat website, and no one was listed as an owner or even employee on the Snapchat LinkedIn page. Liew had to track down the owner of the web domain for Snapchat.com to find Evan, who he finally emailed. No response. Growing impatient, Liew sent Evan a message on Facebook. Evan responded within minutes, agreeing to meet Liew and pitch him on Snapchat.

On March 22, senior quarterback Andrew Luck threw fifty passes to Stanford wide receivers in front of a throng of NFL scouts, media members, and even Stanford faculty members like former secretary of state Condoleezza Rice. This "pro day" was part of the evaluation process that NFL teams put prospects through, as they try to evaluate young college players' natural talent, as well as their motivation and drive to improve, to project how they will perform years down the road.

Across campus, Jeremy Liew was trying to perform a similar forward-looking analysis on Evan. Liew needed to evaluate three main things: product, market, and team. Most importantly, he needed to see how these could grow over the coming years. Could this photo-sharing app popular with teens blow up into the next Instagram and be worth a billion dollars in a few years? And were Evan and his partner Bobby the team to drive the company down that road?

Evan launched into his pitch, explaining to Liew that he wanted to be the camera for the world. If Instagram is the prettiest 1 percent of photographs, Snapchat would happily host the rest of the 99 percent. Evan seemed like the kind of relentless entrepreneur who would walk through walls to make his idea become reality. Then Evan pulled up Flurry and showed Liew Snapchat's numbers. One jumped off the page: daily active users. Snapchat had jumped from one thousand daily active users in late 2011 to *one hundred thousand* daily active users in April 2012. The number of people who had downloaded Snapchat once to try it out and were now using it daily was an order of magnitude larger than anything Liew had seen before. Just half an hour into the meeting, Liew knew he had to invest.

"There was no way that I could've organically understood what that engagement process looked like," Liew later said about that initial meeting with Evan. "What I could do was open up the Flurry analytics dashboard with Evan and look at the numbers and see 50 percent month-on-month growth and see engagement and retention metrics. There were multiples of what we might expect from other companies. Something was working. It didn't matter that I didn't understand it right away. It didn't matter that my intuition was bad.

"What mattered was the data," Liew continued. "The next question is, this is clearly working, why is it working? Evan could explain it, he had some really unique insights that said why Snapchat was taking off at the time and we listened. We said, 'That makes a lot of sense. You seem to have unique insight,' which is gonna lead not just to one good idea, but to many good ideas in the future and that's proven to be that case."

The engagement and retention showed an uncommon excitement around Snapchat. Uncommon excitement precludes uncommon growth. Snapchat had struck a chord. Just ten days after meeting Evan, Liew convinced his partners, and Lightspeed invested $485,000 in Snapchat, valuing the young company at $4.25 million.

Barry Eggers also sat on the board of his daughter's high school's investment fund. He convinced the fund, as well as Evan and Lightspeed, in which he is a partner, to invest $15,000 in Snapchat's round of funding. If the company did well, Saint Francis High school would make over $40 million off that investment.

Evan was thrilled. Snapchat had a fast-growing, dedicated user base. He and Bobby had the funding they needed to take the company to the next level. And now they had a wise advisor and investor in Jeremy Liew and Lightspeed.

Little did Evan know, it would be years before he and Bobby spoke to Liew amicably again.

CHAPTER EIGHT

SEXTING

APRIL 2012
STANFORD, CA

In the spring of 2012, I was a sophomore at Stanford and had just started writing for *TechCrunch*. I had been emailing with my new editor about two of the hot startups on campus—Snapchat and Clinkle. She urged me to get an interview with the Snapchat founders for my first story.

While Evan had dropped out of classes, he was still able to live on campus for the remainder of the academic quarter. I ran into him at a Cinco de Mayo party in the backyard of 680, one of the non-Greek row houses on campus where seniors lived. We had a number of mutual friends, and I had hung out with him several times before. He greeted me warmly, and I relayed what my editor had told me.

"That would sink us," Evan replied, imploring me not to write about Snapchat.

I was taken aback, but I agreed not to cover the company until he was ready. Most people on campus were excited to be interviewed for the school newspaper, let alone for an outside publication. Facebook had just bought Instagram for $1 billion, and photo apps were all any-one was talking about. How could an app that just shares pictures be worth that much? Surely we were in a bubble, right? I thought Evan would jump at the opportunity to share his story and get his company mentioned in the larger discussion. But he was already worried that too much of a spotlight too early would mess with the small, weird, cool community that Snapchat was nurturing. Evan was perhaps being some-what paranoid about how deleterious media coverage would be to Snap-chat. But he's always had a secretive side, often preferring to hustle on his side projects, from grand party schemes to Future Freshman to Snap-chat, until he was ready for the world to see them.

The next day, *New York Times* reporter Nick Bilton, unencumbered by a personal connection, published a short piece about Snapchat, writ-ing, "All of this sexting, as the practice is known, creates an opening for technology that might make the photos less likely to end up in wide circulation. This is where a free and increasingly popular iPhone app called Snapchat comes in." Bilton reported that Evan had declined an interview, saying he was too busy with schoolwork.

After Bilton's story went up, Evan realized the cat was out of the bag on Snapchat and media coverage was coming whether he liked it or not. He emailed me, "We're receiving a lot of inbound requests after the NYT post yesterday. Lmk when you want to talk-I'd be happy to give you the story." He'd had interview requests from much more sea-soned reporters from the *Times*, *The Wall Street Journal*, and elsewhere, but he gave me the story. He knew me, and, more importantly, he knew I understood the product and wouldn't jump to the conclusion that Snapchat was for sexting. As with every other aspect of his life, he couldn't have cared less about pandering to the norms and the more established players in the industry. He also probably thought he had a better shot at controlling the message with me than with another reporter.

We met up at the *Stanford Daily*'s building at the center of campus (I was running the paper's news department at the time and liked to use the building for my interviews). In a glass-walled conference room, Evan laid out his vision for Snapchat and a new way of interacting with friends digitally.

"It seems odd that at the beginning of the internet everyone decided everything should stick around forever," he said. "I think our application makes communication a lot more human and natural."

Evan fired off theories on the internet and communicating with friends at a rapid pace, at times wildly gesturing as he explained why he was so excited about Snapchat and what lay ahead. We talked about Bilton's article and the sexting narrative surrounding the company, which he dismissed in his typically brash way.

"The minute you tell someone that images on your server disappear, everyone jumps to sexting," Evan said, laughing and leaning his chair back against the wall. "I'm not convinced that the whole sexting thing is as big as the media makes it out to be. I just don't know people who do that. It doesn't seem that fun when you can have real sex."

Just as Snapchat rode a technological wave to early adoption, sexting, too, was taking advantage of the ubiquity of internet-connected smartphones.

The term "sexting" was first used in a 2004 *Globe and Mail* article dubbed "Textual Gratification," which covered text-based sexting. But as more and more people had cellphones with high-quality cameras and less restrictive data and text message plans, sexting took off.

In June 2011, when Snapchat was still called Picaboo and barely had a working prototype let alone users, *The New York Times* published excerpts from interviews with groups of teenagers focused on sexting:

> Q. Is sexting ever O.K.?
> Kathy, 17, Queens: There's a positive side to sexting. You can't get pregnant from it, and you can't transmit S.T.D.'s. It's a kind of safe sex.

> Q. How often do they go viral, really?
> Nate, 16, Lower Merion: About three photos go viral each year and a third of the school sees them. The kids who receive them are in the alpha social group, and they send it to their friends. But everyone hears about them.

> Q. Did you know that sexting under 18 is illegal?
> Saif, 18, Brooklyn: There's a law? I didn't know that. How would you catch somebody when everyone does it?

Social media scholar and Microsoft researcher danah boyd spoke at an industry conference in 2011, noting:

> So the mean girl behavior mixes with the slut shaming mixes with explicit image content. Put these [three] together and you've got a ticking time bomb. All of a sudden, prosecutors determined to "teach those kids a lesson" start prosecuting teenagers for creating, possessing, and distributing child pornography of themselves. The age-old practice of "slut shaming" takes on an entirely new meaning when photographs are used. Schools panic and just suspend everyone.
>
> Kids start committing suicide over the emotional costs of being shamed. Websites panic because they can't tell the difference between a 17-year-old and an 18-year-old, let alone determine the intention behind the posting of the images. Attorneys general cherry pick which companies they want to pick on. And the news media takes the most egregious cases out there and hypes them as the latest teen craze. In short, sexting has become a disaster for pretty much everyone involved.

A 2011 University of New Hampshire study that surveyed 1,560 people aged 10 to 17 found only 2.5 percent of respondents had sent, received, or created sexual pictures using a cellphone in the previous year. The researchers found that many of the 2.5 percent included photos in the study that would not even qualify as pornographic.

Another 2011 study sampling 744 college students found 54 percent had sent sexually explicit photos or videos to a partner at least once, with a third of the sample saying they did this occasionally. A December 2013 McAfee survey of 1,500 people aged 18 to 54 found 49 percent had sent or received sexts, although their definition included both email and messaging. Of McAfee's sample, 70 percent of 18-to 24-year-olds said they had received sexts before. Additionally, 77 percent of the sexters in McAfee's group said they sent content to their partners, while 16 percent said they sent it to stranges.

Of course, all of the information in these studies is self-reported and should be taken with a large grain of salt. The big picture is that a lot of people sext. And yes, they use Snapchat to sext. But they don't exclusively sext via Snapchat, and they don't exclusively use Snapchat for sexting.

While smartphones have caused a surge in sexting, my generation is hardly the first to experiment with naked photographs.

New York Magazine editor Christopher Bonanos wrote about the phenomenon in his book about Polaroid:

> We will never know exactly who first figured out that using a Polaroid camera meant whatever happened in front of the lens never needed to be seen by a lab technician. It is clear, though, that it happened early on. There are plenty of naughty first-generation Polaroid photos out there to confirm that instant photography's success was at least in part built on adult fun. At the time, "camera club" sessions were a popular fad: afternoons with a hired nude model, allowing amateur shutterbugs a few hours to indulge their artsy-prurient sides. Bettie Page, the 1950s pinup, got her start in these places, and pornography historian Joseph Slade has noted even frontal nudity in her Polaroid photos from these sessions. The Kinsey Institute has many such Polaroid pictures on file, too. By the 1960s, ads were appearing in certain magazines for a woman who would pose for nude Polaroid snapshots for a price.
>
> Did Polaroid itself know? Of course. Donald Dery, Polaroid's longtime director of corporate communications, puts it this way: "We didn't acknowledge it, but we always talked about 'intimacy.'" Sam Yanes, who succeeded him in the job, offers a little more detail: "There was a subject-photographer relationship that didn't exist with a regular camera . . . an intimacy, and we felt it was one of our main features. I never saw any research that said X percent of sales went for bedroom pictures, though.

Reggie originally thought of the idea for Picaboo as a safer sexting app. Evan and Reggie positioned it as such that first summer. Reggie emailed *Cosmopolitan* explaining how the app "lets you and your boyfriend send photos for peeks and not keeps," and Evan emailed a Stanford professor to ask him about his sexting research.

Evan quickly realized it could be much more and worked hard to change the narrative early, focusing on communicating that Snapchat was about lighthearted, impermanent communication between friends rather than sexting between lovers.

In my initial interview with Evan for *TechCrunch*, he pushed back against the sexting narrative, explaining that 80 percent of Snapchat photos were sent during the school day when students were bored in class, not late at night when they were home. He savvily introduced me to the mother of a college student, and in doing so he got me to accurately but positively portray the app in this light:

> Snapchat user Marilyn Feldman uses the app to keep in touch with her daughter, who attends college across the country.
>
> "It's subtly different even from taking a picture on my iPhone and sending that," Feldman said. "It's more immediate and even more casual. Almost like, 'thinking of you.' Picture of a red rose in the neighborhood. I didn't even send her a message, just a picture of the red rose, and she knew what that meant."

But it took a lot of time for the sexting narrative to die down. Snapchat had an image that it was *only* for sexting.

Ironically, perhaps the most famous sext ever sent was by then-congressman Anthony Weiner, via Twitter. And yet Twitter has no association with sexting. But there is far less of a generational gap on Twitter, and reporters are among its core users. Of course, it didn't help that Snapchat's main promotional photos for years were the Turner sisters in bikinis on the beach; in some versions they seemed nearly naked, as imposed images of the app covered their bathing suits.

In April 2013, Evan and Bobby appeared on *The Colbert Report*, where Stephen Colbert peppered them with jokes about sexting.

"Is this a sexting app?" Colbert asked as the crowd cheered at the salacious mention.

"You can always take a screenshot and you can always take a picture with another camera so it's not a great way to send inappropriate photos," Evan replied.

"Ok . . . is there a better way to send inappropriate photos?" Colbert retorted. " 'Cause I can't think of one!"

Since Snapchat started, there have been persistent scandals at high schools and colleges of X-rated Snapchats being saved (usually via a screenshot) and shared widely, fueling sexting concerns. These incidents have often had serious consequences with law enforcement and schools. One 2012 study found that teenagers were more worried about their parents finding out about them sexting than they were about legal consequences.

Snapchat doesn't officially allow children under thirteen to use the app, although the policy is merely enforced by a self-reported birthday. In 2015, Snapchat launched a Safety Center with information to help parents understand the app and keep their children safe.

danah boyd believes parents must give their children more room to potentially get hurt online. "Rather than helping teens develop strategies for negotiating public life and the potential risks of interacting with others, fearful parents have focused on tracking, monitoring and blocking," boyd argued in a 2014 *Time* article. "These tactics don't help teens develop the skills they need to manage complex social situations, assess risks and get help when they're in trouble. Banning cell phones won't stop a teen who's in love cope with the messy dynamics of sexting. 'Protecting' kids may feel like the right thing to do, but it undermines the learning that teens need to do as they come of age in a technology-soaked world."

Perhaps we should care less about sexting, at least for people over eighteen.

"It's time for the cultural norm that says nude photos are shameful or shocking to end," tech writer Mat Honan wrote in *Wired* in 2015. "There are simply too many naked pictures of too many people."

Like many problems for a startup, growth seemed to be the primary cure for Snapchat's sexting narrative. As the number of people who used Snapchat daily skyrocketed into the hundreds of millions, it became harder and harder to look at it as just a sexting app. And as Snapchat's user base grew into older demographics, more people used the app themselves and understood its purpose.

But that growth did not come overnight, and Evan and Bobby had to battle the sexting reputation for years.

CHAPTER NINE

BETRAYAL

APRIL 2012
STANFORD, CA

A few weeks after signing the term sheet with Jeremy Liew and Lightspeed, Evan sat in a machine-shop class, half listening to the professor drone on. He refreshed the Wells Fargo app on his phone again and again, staring at the red and yellow colors as they loaded. Nothing. Nothing. And then there it was! Finally, the cash from Lightspeed appeared. As soon as the class ended, Evan walked up to his professor and told him he was dropping out of Stanford.

While he had always wanted to follow in the footsteps of Jobs, Gates, and Zuckerberg as an entrepreneur, Evan didn't really have to follow in their footsteps as a college dropout. He was three credits and a few weeks shy of graduation. Actions like this would eventually lead people to look at Evan as cocky and arrogant. To him though, this was simply a radical expression of his beliefs. Evan had never cared about grades in classes he didn't enjoy or prestigious internships just because that's what his peers were doing. He had Snapchat and venture funding—in his mind, what was the point of continuing to put any effort, no matter how small, into getting a degree?

The spring was not as smooth a ride as Evan had hoped, though. In May, Evan opened his email and saw a new message from Reggie. Reggie started off praising Evan for his success with Snapchat thus far, but quickly brought up their falling out and his stake in the company:

> As I expressed to Bobby this past summer, I understood both then and currently that my role in the process was of a different nature, and was thus willing to accept a significantly less portion of equity than either of you. Unfortunately, these discussions lead [*sic*] to you changing the passwords to the accounts and servers, limiting any continued involvement on my part and cutting off communication.

Reggie went on to note that he had hired lawyers who told him he currently owned one third of Snapchat's intellectual property. Reggie threatened to contact Snapchat's current and potential investors, noting that this could be "incredibly detrimental" to Snapchat. Reggie said he would forgo suing Evan, Bobby, and Snapchat if they were able to come to an agreement on his equity stake.

Evan was furious. Now that things were finally taking off, finally working, Reggie comes back and wants a piece? Evan and Bobby promptly hired a major Silicon Valley law firm, Cooley LLP, to represent them. They fired back a strongly worded letter to Reggie, which read, in part:

> Though you have refused in the past to provide actual copies of the '897 Provisional Application to our client, a draft of the application reflects that you fraudulently claimed yourself as an inventor on the application. Having posed as one of three inventors of the '897 Provisional Application, you now claim to "currently own a third of SnapChat's IP." The claim is utterly groundless as a matter of law and fact. . . .
>
> The Company rejects your demand in its entirety because you contributed nothing to the Company's intellectual prop-

erty, and you cannot claim any ownership interest in the
Company. . . .

Your last demand for "equity" came in August of 2011 . . .
that demand was a transparent and desperate attempt to shake
down Mr. Spiegel and Mr. Murphy for a share in a company to
which you contributed nothing. Your demand of May 8, 2012
is no different, and it is devoid of merit.

The application Reggie submitted was very broad and attempted
to patent the entire idea for Snapchat rather than specific technical
features or inventions. A successful patent would have bound Evan,
Bobby, Snapchat's intellectual property, and Reggie together. But the
patent was never approved.

As May turned to June, Evan was still living in his studio on campus, although all his energy was focused on Snapchat. Evan had more
tank tops and beer koozies made with the Snapchat logo on them, and
Bobby quit Revel Systems to work on Snapchat full time. Evan celebrated
his twenty-second birthday at the posh Italian restaurant Il Fornaio in
Palo Alto with a few close friends. His dad brought Snapchat-themed
cupcakes. For the first time since freshman year, Reggie wasn't part of
the birthday dinner crew.

Back in March, a venture capitalist at General Catalyst Partners
named Niko Bonatsos had heard from mutual friends at Stanford that
Evan had exciting traction with Snapchat. Bonatsos met up with Evan
and listened as he described how he wanted to make communication
between friends much faster and more natural, and how he wanted
Snapchat to be the fastest camera app available. But by the time he met
Bonatsos for the first time, Evan was already close to completing the
deal with Jeremy Liew and Lightspeed. Bonatsos persisted, and he
stayed close to Evan over the coming weeks. Spiegel showed Bonatsos
Snapchat's analytics: the majority of the users were women, and 20
percent of the users were opening the app more than fifty times a day.
Bonatsos had never seen that level of engagement. And he figured if
teenage girls were using the app in droves, the boys would soon follow.

Snapchat's server costs continued to soar, so Evan considered raising
more funding. Other members of General Catalyst's team quickly got
involved, including partners Hemant Taneja, Joel Cutler, and Jon Teo.

Teo met with Evan next, listening as he railed against Facebook's stale, boring product and described how he wanted to make talking with friends feel light and fun again. Returning to his office, Teo searched for people tweeting about Snapchat and came across a teen girl tweeting about how it was finally OK for her to take an ugly photo of herself.

Teo offered Evan and Snapchat a term sheet to invest $2 to $3 million, valuing Snapchat at $22 million. A term sheet is essentially a promise between a venture capitalist and entrepreneur that agrees upon the price and stipulations of an investment. As they were discussing the deal, Evan told him, "I'm gonna make you a ton of money." After agreeing to the deal in principle, Spiegel and Teo started digging into the specifics, and hit a big roadblock.

When Jeremy Liew and Lightspeed had invested just a few weeks prior, Liew had included terms giving Lightspeed the right of first refusal to invest in Snapchat's next round of funding, as well as rights to take 50 percent of the next round. Essentially, Lightspeed controlled Snapchat's next round of funding and made Snapchat unattractive to other investors, who would want to take a larger stake in the Series A round. Evan was furious. He felt betrayed and taken advantage of. Liew had told him these terms were standard. Evan would warn other students about this betrayal for years to come, as he did in a keynote address at a Stanford Women in Business conference in 2013:

> One of my biggest mistakes as an entrepreneur involved a term sheet. This particular term sheet was our first. And when we talked to the venture capitalists, and we talked to our lawyers, they took refuge in the notion of Standard. When I asked a question because I didn't understand something, I was reassured that the term was standard, and therefore agreeable. I forgot that the idea of STANDARD is a construct. It simply does not exist.
>
> So rather than attempt to further understand the document, I accepted it. It wasn't until a bit later, when the company had grown and we needed more capital—that I realized I had made a very expensive mistake.

He also warned in a 2015 talk at the University of Southern California, "If you hear the words 'standard terms,' then figure out actually what the terms are, because they are probably not standard and the person explaining [them] to you probably doesn't know how they work."

Teo and General Catalyst put Evan in touch with lawyers who would help him escape the blocking structure with a new round of funding. Evan struck a deal with Jeremy Liew to sell Lightspeed a limited number of Snapchat shares at a discount in exchange for removing the onerous terms. Feeling stung by Silicon Valley venture capitalists, Evan then put the deal with General Catalyst on hold and put together a group of angel investors from Los Angeles, including his father, John Spiegel, and the CEO of Sony Entertainment, Michael Lynton.

Lynton's wife Jamie had noticed that their two older daughters were addicted to Snapchat. Like Evan, their children attended Crossroads, and Jamie recalled that some of her daughters' friends had their reputations hurt by things they'd posted online. Jamie Lynton, a major fundraiser for President Obama, invited Evan to their house for dinner. Within an hour, Evan was at the Lyntons' home in Brentwood, which neighbored Pacific Palisades. As Evan shared his vision for Snapchat and an impermanent internet, Jamie and Michael Lynton became more and more impressed. They soon became close, and Evan would frequently lean on Michael for advice and rely on him for introductions to major players in the entertainment world.

Michael Lynton would join the board of directors a year later. After graduating from Harvard with a degree in history and literature, Lynton worked in finance at Credit Suisse First Boston in the 1980s before earning an MBA at Harvard Business School. He worked at Disney, running Disney Publishing and Hollywood Pictures, before joining Time Warner as CEO of AOL Europe. In 2004, he took over Sony Pictures.

With the fresh influx of capital and an active, growing user base, Evan and Bobby needed to grow their team, particularly in engineering. Evan wanted the best and brightest from his class to join them, so he went in search of students who had been vetted by the computer science department to be teaching assistants. He knew that these students had already been screened to be very high performing and able to work on teams.

Evan met Daniel Smith during their freshman year when they were both in the same introductory product design seminar. The two became fast collaborators, working on countless product design projects together. It helped that Smith, who double majored in art practice and computer science, shared Evan's passion for music and photography—he played acoustic guitar and was an avid photographer, even developing his own pictures.

David Kravitz and Evan met during their senior year, when a mutual friend introduced them. As a teaching assistant for several computer science classes, Kravitz was popular among his students; he was friendly and easy to talk to, whether it was about hard, technical problems or life in general.

In a single conversation, Evan convinced Smith and Kravitz to drop out of Stanford and move down to his dad's house in Pacific Palisades to work on a disappearing photo app popular with teenagers. With Smith and Kravitz joining Bobby on the coding end, Evan was confident they would have the technical horsepower they needed. But they needed help in other areas, too. The users would need support when they lost their passwords or whatever else they messed up. And they eventually would have to grow Snapchat into a real company, with offices and structure.

Dena Gallucci, an extroverted junior from one of the sororities that Evan frequently hung out with, had worked with Evan and Bobby on Future Freshman during its brief run. She had proved herself to Evan as a hard worker, even on the menial tasks like data entry for college information. They got along well, and, most importantly, Evan knew he could trust her. He hired Dena to be the community manager for Snapchat.

On June 17, 2012, robed students, faculty, parents, and friends gathered in Stanford Stadium for the school's commencement ceremony. Reggie Brown filed into the stadium, set to receive his English degree. Evan's friends from Donner and Kappa Sigma and product design classes walked in and waved to smiling friends and family. While Evan wasn't graduating, he chose to walk for the ceremony and receive a blank diploma rather than skip the celebration where all his friends were. After all, he was never really there for the grades anyway. It was a strange final act of conformity for Evan before fully departing Stanford and returning south to Los Angeles to build Snapchat. Three years later,

Evan delivered a commencement address at USC's Marshall School of Business, reflecting on how he later regretted walking:

> It only recently occurred to me, while preparing this address, how totally absurd this whole charade was. It reminded me that oftentimes we do all sorts of silly things to avoid appearing different. Conforming happens so naturally that we can forget how powerful it is—we want to be accepted by our peers—we want to be a part of the group. It's in our biology. But the things that make us human are those times we listen to the whispers of our soul and allow ourselves to be pulled in another direction.

CHAPTER TEN

A NOT-SO-INNOCENT TOY

JULY 2012

STARTUP
HAU5

John Spiegel's dining room had once again been transformed into a startup headquarters. Evan and Bobby were joined this time by new hires fresh from Stanford, David Kravitz, Daniel Smith, and Dena Gallucci. The group sat around the dining room table, charting a course for Snapchat's product improvements. With laptops, notepads, and drinks covering the table and wireframes* taped up on the walls and windows, they discussed their two main goals for the summer: make the app run more smoothly and crash less and build an Android version. It had only been a year since Picaboo launched in the App Store. When Facebook was one year old, there was no News Feed, no tagging, and no Like button. Likewise, there was much ahead on Snapchat's product roadmap.

Evan, Bobby, David, and Daniel lived in the Spiegel house in Pacific Palisades. Daniel got the short straw and lived in Evan's sister's room,

---

* Wireframes are depictions of what the finished product will look like.

which was covered in orange and pink polka dots. Bobby would often push changes to the app's code late at night before going to sleep, causing the others to wake up in the morning in a panic as they checked for bugs. Bonatsos and the other General Catalyst Partners would stop by the house to give advice and feedback on product development and take Evan and Bobby out for dinner.

More than ten thousand people—primarily teenagers and twentysomethings—were downloading and joining Snapchat every *day* that summer. Snapchat grew by a factor of ten, from one hundred thousand daily active users to a million in just six months. While the front-facing camera on smartphones helped Snapchat gain early traction, smartphones' address books may have done even more to drive viral growth. Before smartphones were ubiquitous, Facebook (and others) had to work extremely hard to build a social graph on the web. But with smartphones, people had a computer in their pockets with a complete social graph—their address book. This allowed Snapchat, Instagram, WhatsApp, and others to quickly build enormously valuable services.

Snapchat's existing users were also sharing more and more photos. This put a heavy strain on Snapchat's infrastructure, as they had to deliver millions of photographs in real time. Because users saw Snapchat as a texting replacement, they expected messages to be sent and received within seconds; if Snapchat failed to do this too often, Snapchatters would abandon it, which could cause the app to start bleeding users and spin into a death spiral. This famously happened to early social network Friendster: the website was regularly down, and people jumped ship to Myspace and then eventually Facebook.

The team also needed to develop an Android version of the app. Unlike iOS, which only has a few different screen sizes for various iPhones, Android has been developed across thousands of devices with varying screen sizes. So when they first completed an Android build and tested it on different devices, they found many phones were putting black bars at the top and bottom of the screen for picture previews, which made Snapchat look weird and ugly. It took them over six weeks to rebuild the camera function for Android to get rid of the black bars. All the while, Snapchat wasn't available on Android, limiting its growth to iPhone users.

Finally, Snapchat launched an Android version of the app on October 29, 2012; I covered the launch for *TechCrunch*. Evan and I spoke about the technical difficulties behind the Android development and how users had sent over a billion images through Snapchat since it had launched. But most interesting were his comments when I brought up the possibility of selling the company: "There's no way I'm going to work for anybody else," Evan said. "I don't think you're going to see us selling any time soon."

Evan wasn't interested in a quick payday or a steady job at a big tech company. And Marc Zuckerberg would soon give him good reason to rule out working at Facebook. But most of all, Evan wanted to be a founder and a CEO—the captain of his own company that he could grow to be the next Apple. Evan's attitude and Snapchat's traction made the company's next fundraising, a Series A round, the hottest deal on Sand Hill Road. There were plenty of questions surrounding Snapchat: Is this really a full-fledged company or just a feature that Facebook, Apple, Google, or someone else can copy? Isn't every other company in the Valley moving toward collecting *more* data, not zero data? How will they make money? And, of course, isn't this for sexting?

But the other side of the fear/greed coin was even more compelling: teenagers were using this app with a frequency investors hadn't seen since Instagram or Facebook. An early investment in a breakout company like that could return billions to a venture capital firm, making the partners personally wealthy and professionally respected. General Catalyst was still keen on doing the A round as the "lead" investor, meaning they would put the majority of the money in, receive a large ownership stake (typically 15 to 20 percent of the company), and would likely receive a seat on the company's board of directors. But they had stiff competition from the best venture capital firms in the world.

On a Monday night in October, Evan was as a guest speaker in a class Niko Bonatsos, the venture capitalist who had been persuing Evan and Snapchat since March, was running at Stanford's entrepreneurship-themed dorm. During his speech he again suggested to the students that if a venture capitalist offered "standard" terms, they should in turn offer merely standard performance. Afterward, he went to dinner with General Catalyst's contingent (Bonatsos, Jon Teo, Hemant Taneja, and Joel Cutler) at the Dutch Goose, a dive bar and burger joint in Menlo

Park that is as popular with venture capitalists as it was with Stanford frat guys.

The evening went so well that the General Catalyst group left the Dutch Goose thinking they had won the deal. But the next morning, Evan called and told them he was going with Benchmark as the lead investor. Several partners from Benchmark, primarily Peter Fenton and Matt Cohler, had maintained a relationship with Evan and Snapchat since they passed on the seed round the previous winter. They introduced Spiegel to Benchmark partner Mitch Lasky, who lived in Los Angeles, unlike most of the Bay Area venture capitalists vying for the deal. Benchmark invested $13.5 million in Snapchat, valuing Evan and Bobby's nascent company at over $70 million.

Some readers may wonder if there was any backlash or resentment to Snapchat choosing Benchmark over General Catalyst for their Series A round. Even the very best firms get turned down by entrepreneurs sometimes; if they're smart, like General Catalyst was, they seek to maintain a relationship with the founder and try to invest in the company's next round.

As part of the deal, Lasky joined Evan and Bobby on Snapchat's board, which would soon also include Sony's Michael Lynton. Like Lynton, Lasky had as many, if not more, ties to the entertainment industry as he did to the tech industry. After earning a BA in history and literature at Harvard in 1984, Lasky went to law school at the University of Virginia. He briefly practiced law before joining Disney and video game publisher Activision. He then joined mobile gaming company JAMDAT as CEO, taking the company public in 2004 and then guiding it to a $680 million acquisition from Electronic Arts. In 2007, he started investing, primarily in gaming companies, as a partner at Benchmark. Evan, ever the showman, wanted to align Snapchat much more closely with Los Angeles, Hollywood, and entertainment than with Silicon Valley and its nerdy tech culture.

Evan was very intentional about building Snapchat in Los Angeles; he loved growing up there and didn't feel like the usual suspects in Silicon Valley understood the real world and real users, and thus weren't good at building products that delighted consumers (with a few notable exceptions, particularly Apple). Once the company had outgrown his dad's house in Pacific Palisades, Evan decided to move Snapchat to

Venice, a funky beachfront town in western LA just south of his hometown Pacific Palisades and Santa Monica, where he attended Crossroads. Evan, Bobby, David, Daniel, and Dena moved the company into a low-slung powder blue bungalow on the beach in Venice; the new office featured a big yellow Ghostface Chillah out front.

In 1891, a real estate developer named Abbot Kinney and his partner bought and developed a 1.5-mile tract of land on the beach in Santa Monica and put in a pier, horse-racing track, golf course, and boardwalk. Kinney's partner died shortly thereafter, and Kinney did not get along with his partner's successors, so they agreed to divide the land—Kinney won a coin flip and chose the marshy southern half of land. He built several miles of canals to drain the marshes and filled them with gondolas and gondoliers from Venice, Italy. He called it Venice of America.

It quickly became a major tourist attraction, with three piers full of amusements and paid aviators performing aerial stunts over the beach. Following Kinney's death in 1920, Venice fell into disrepair, as a fire to one of the piers and Prohibition crippled the town's tax revenue. By 1926, Venice was annexed to Los Angeles. The city felt the town needed more streets and paved over many canals.

The city subsequently fell into neglect, and by the 1950s it was referred to as the "Slum by the Sea." But the low rent and beach would attract young counterculture artists, actors, poets, and writers. In 1965, Ray Manzarek and Jim Morrison founded The Doors in Venice; in 1980, another rock band—Jane's Addiction—got their start in Venice. In the 1990s, the town was overrun by gang violence, but it has been significantly gentrified in the time since then—so much so that in 2012, *GQ* named its central road, Abbot Kinney Boulevard, "the Coolest Block in America."

Venice has always attracted an interesting mix of creative types. A few blocks from Snapchat's bungalow office sat the Binoculars Building, designed by Frank Gehry, which features a massive, eponymous pair of binoculars over the entrance. It now serves as Google's Los Angeles office, but it was built for the famous advertising firm Chiat/Day, which created the "1984" ad for Apple and Steve Jobs that introduced the Macintosh. Google relocated its Los Angeles office from Santa Monica to the Binoculars Building in 2011, a move that began the migration of

the Los Angeles tech scene to Venice. But Snapchat is the most prominent homegrown startup, serving as the tentpole for Venice. Evan chose
Venice because Snapchat is primarily an entertainment company, not a
technology company. And Southern California is the perfect place to
start a popular entertainment company.

"Because consumer technology has become popular culture, you
really need to understand popular culture to be able to have an insight
about it," early Snapchat investor Jeremy Liew later said. "Then to be
able to drive new innovation from that. I think Silicon Valley is such an
isolated bubble, our reality is not the reality of a normal American in
normal America. That is what is preventing as much insight and there-
fore innovation happening here."

Just as venture capitalists had watched Snapchat's ascent with great
interest, so did another group of wealthy, bright technologists in Menlo
Park. On November 28, Mark Zuckerberg, having purchased Instagram
just eight months prior, emailed Evan, saying he was interested in Snapchat and what they had built and would love to have them over to Facebook's campus. Evan responded coolly—he wasn't sure when he would
next be in the Bay Area—delivering the not-so-subtle message that he
wasn't going to plan a special trip just to see the Facebook billionaire.
Zuckerberg noted that he would be in Los Angeles soon and they could
meet then.

Days later, Evan and Bobby traveled to a private apartment in Los
Angeles to meet Zuckerberg in secret (Zuckerberg had obfuscated the
purpose of the trip, saying he was going to meet architect Frank Gehry
to discuss Facebook's new headquarters). Zuckerberg asked probing
questions about Snapchat and their vision for the product and company. He then wondered aloud what Snapchat might look like as a
Facebook-owned company, with Evan and Bobby still at the helm, able
to take advantage of the social giant's resources and funding to grow more
quickly, as Instagram had. And indeed, Zuckerberg had an impressive
story to tell there: following its acquisition, Instagram's daily active users grew almost 1,200 percent in just six months. Perhaps Facebook
would be interested in acquiring Snapchat for $60 million, instantly
making Spiegel and Murphy millionaires in their early twenties.

Evan explained that they weren't interested in selling the company.
In response, Zuckerberg showed them something new that his team

had been working on. Poke, a new Facebook app, would be released in a few days. What was it? A messaging app for disappearing photos and videos.

The message was clear: join us, or we will crush you. Leaving the meeting, they returned home and ordered a book for each of their employees: *The Art of War*. Written in the fifth century BC by Chinese military strategist Sun Tzu, it is considered a seminal book on strategy and tactics, not just for the military but also for business. One aphorism from the book was particularly relevant to the challenges the upstart Snapchat faced:

> Victorious warriors win first and then go to war, while defeated
> warriors go to war first and then seek to win.

CHAPTER ELEVEN

POKED

DECEMBER 2012

STARTUP

HAU5

On December 14, 2012, Snapchat released its most significant product update yet, adding video recording and messages to the photo-sharing app. Users had already been plenty addicted to Snapchat, sharing twenty million photos per day on the app as of October; these new features made Snapchat even more alluring. When users opened the app, it still went directly to the camera. But this time, if users pressed and held the circular button at the bottom of the screen, it started taking a video. When a user released the button, the video stopped recording. It was a brilliant user experience, simple but useful and effective.

At the time, messaging using videos was neither seamless nor easy from a user perspective. Most video recording user interfaces at the time required you to tap the screen twice—once to start recording, and once to stop. Evan constantly sought to minimize the number of touches required on Snapchat. Other apps like Instagram and the standard iPhone camera app had separate buttons that you had to toggle to for photo versus video. While the difference may seem trivial, Snapchat became the fastest and easiest way to open an app and immediately start capturing a funny or interesting moment to share with friends. Snapchat as simply a photo-sharing app may have been a quick fad that was soon overtaken by the myriad other ways to share images with friends. But this smooth, fast way to share videos gave users multiple options to interact with friends.

The excitement from the launch did not last long.

On December 21, Evan received a one-sentence email from Zuckerberg.

> I hope you enjoy Poke.

Evan had deactivated his Facebook account, so he couldn't even access the app. In a panic, he called Bobby, who downloaded Poke and made an account.

It was an exact replica of Snapchat. An unabashed copy, Poke even stole Snapchat's user interface for recording video. And in addition to sending disappearing photos and videos, users could send disappearing text messages, and even just "poke" each other to get their attention, like in the earliest days of Facebook, when it was fun and weird.

But there was nothing fun about Poke. This was a show of might from Zuckerberg and his team up north. Veteran Facebook director of product Blake Ross had led a small team in developing Poke in just twelve days. Zuckerberg, who invented poking years prior, even wrote some of the code for Poke, even though he rarely programmed at Facebook anymore. If users dragged their message list all the way up in the Poke app, the text "I'll find something to put here" appeared, which is the same text Zuckerberg left at the bottom of Facebook.com in its earliest days. And finally, the notification that said "Poke" to users when they received a message? It was a recording of Zuckerberg saying "Poke." Designers Mike Matas and Sharon Hwang created the app's icon; Zuckerberg changed the imposing sign outside Facebook's campus from the Like symbol to the rightward-pointing hand for Poke.

"If you're trying to help convince people that they want to join you, helping them understand all the pain they would have to go through is a valuable tactic," Mark Zuckerberg later said when asked about Facebook's acquisition strategy. Now, he intended to show Evan and Snapchat the pain they would have to suffer to compete with Facebook.

Reporters were quick to call Facebook out for the blatant ripoff. The *Next Web*'s Matthew Panzarino wrote, "Note, as well, that when I described Poke as 'Snapchat-like' above I really meant 'complete clone'. This is essentially a Facebook skin on the Snapchat app. Fairly blatant copy of a popular app by Facebook here."

Many journalists who had not gotten over their initial impression that Snapchat was for sexting covered Facebook's Poke from that angle, including "Here's Your First Look at Facebook's New, Sexting-Friendly Poke App" from *Business Insider*'s Kevin Smith; "Test Driving Poke, Facebook's New 'Safer Sexting' App for Tweens" by *ReadWrite*'s Taylor Hatmaker; and "Poke for Mobile: Facebook's New Sexting App" from *CNET*'s Donna Tam.

When I called Evan to get a comment from him on Poke's release, he sounded nervously energetic. Evan, Bobby, and the team had known this moment was coming since their meeting with Zuckerberg a few weeks prior. But now it was here and they had to put on a brave public face and hope the Snapchat community stayed loyal to them. Evan wanted his statement to be just three words: "Welcome, Facebook. Seriously." It was an homage to Steve Jobs and Apple taking out a full-page ad in *The Wall Street Journal* saying, "Welcome, IBM. Seriously," when the much larger computer giant started competing with Apple in the personal computer business. It also mentally conjured the image of a young Jobs standing below an IBM logo giving it the middle finger.

Most rational people would have needed heavy odds to bet on Snapchat to beat Facebook's Poke. Facebook launched the app right before the holidays—the same time of year that had given Snapchat its early liftoff just a year prior—when everyone was getting together with friends and family, sharing photos galore, and trying out new apps. Facebook also had the advantage of its *billion-plus* user base, allowing anyone who downloaded Poke to send a Poke message to any of their Facebook friends; if the recipient hadn't downloaded Poke, they would receive a notification from the main Facebook app urging them to do so.

On the day it launched, Poke shot up to the top spot in the iOS app store, pushing Snapchat down to ninth. But just a week later, Poke had dropped to thirty-fourth, while Snapchat rose back up to third. Influential tech blogger and venture capitalist Om Malik wondered,

> How is that Facebook, which has some of the smartest folks in the room, can't really invent any new single online behavior that would keep people addicted to Facebook?
>
> Why does it have to look at others to come up with new user behaviors and new features? For instance, checkins came from Foursquare, while the short status updates were a direct response to Twitter. Facebook Answers were nothing but a variation on Quora's offering. Poke is yet another example.

Why did Poke fail? It failed to solve any problems for young users, who were more than happy with Snapchat, and it solved a problem that didn't exist for older users, who still didn't get the appeal of disappearing content.

Facebook's strategy with Poke was to have a family of separate, highly successful apps filling different user needs: Facebook, Messenger, Instagram, and Poke. Instagram, by far Facebook's coolest property, was still just single-photo posts at the time, and had much more on its immediate product roadmap than adding impermanence.

Poke was further hampered by the fact that teens were drawn to Snapchat because it explicitly was not Facebook, which was populated by their parents and collected everything they posted forever. Most of their friends were either on Snapchat or signing up by the day. They had no interest in Poke messaging with their Facebook friends who they weren't friends with on Snapchat already. So why would they all pick up and leave Snapchat to share pictures on Poke when half the reason they had migrated to Snapchat was to escape the Facebook empire?

Within weeks it became clear that Poke hadn't just failed—it actively helped Snapchat.

Searches for and mentions of Snapchat skyrocketed in the weeks following Poke's debut. More importantly, Zuckerberg's flailing attempt at an acquisition and then clone validated the ephemeral messaging space and helped change the sexting narrative that had been dogging Snapchat.

Despite users sharing over a billion images through the service, Snapchat struggled to be taken seriously. Many people, particularly those over twenty-five, still thought of it as a sexting app or a toy.

An internet revolution was going on, but all anyone wanted to talk about was sexting. By having the dominant, respected social network take impermanent photo sharing seriously, Poke helped change the narrative, and Snapchat benefited enormously. The logic changed from "The photos disappear—Snapchat must be for sexting" to "Facebook made a disappearing photos app—disappearing photos must be the next big thing!"

Evan would later call Poke "the greatest Christmas present we ever had."

Evan, Bobby, David, Daniel, and Dena had every reason to celebrate. In a single year they had gone from an unknown app with a couple thousand users to over one million daily active users; they had rejected an acquisition offer from Mark Zuckerberg himself and then beat his Snapchat clone head-to-head. So they threw a Snapchat New Year's Eve party at their beachfront office. Stanford was playing Wisconsin in the Rose Bowl on New Year's Day, and the city of angels was filled with Stanford students and alumni. In a move seemingly antithetical to the company's mission, Evan had put "no photos please" on the party invites, hoping the lack of documentation would let everyone loosen up and have more fun. This illuminated an interesting contradiction in Evan: he wanted to throw big, inclusive parties, but he was also a very private, often secretive person.

As the start of the party drew nearer, a crowd formed at the entrance to the house, eager to get in and indulge in the open bar. The usual suspects from the Stanford Greek scene milled around greeting each other. Evan strode out and soaked in the scene, walking down the steps to say hi to a few friends. He was back in his element, where he had been since high school, entertaining a huge group of people. As everyone streamed into the house, the music blared and the liquor flowed. All of the furniture in the house had been taken out and replaced with bars or dance floors. The outside deck was covered in people, bars, and heat lamps. People who hadn't been lucky enough to be invited snuck into the party through a hole in the fence. Inside, partygoers talked with old classmates, danced, and scoured the crowd for a midnight kiss.

Upstairs, Evan had created a sectioned-off VIP area, with more bars and friends. It was a house party on steroids, with one hundred, maybe two hundred people crammed into Snapchat's new headquarters to sip champagne and ring in the New Year.

John Spiegel stopped by the party, saying hi and congratulating Evan, Bobby, David, Daniel, and Evan's girlfriend at the time. He chatted with some of Evan's friends he had met over the years, sharing a sense of bewilderment over how quickly his son's crazy scheme had taken off. John had worked his way up a very traditional ladder, climbing from the law review to a Supreme Court clerkship to becoming an extremely successful litigator. Evan had eschewed a bachelor's degree from Stanford to focus on his seemingly quixotic business.

Everything seemed to be going perfectly.

CHAPTER TWELVE

REGGIE'S RETURN

FEBRUARY 2013
SANTA MONICA, CA

On February 25, Reggie filed a lawsuit against Evan, Bobby, and Snapchat, seeking one-third of the company that he'd been kicked out of. Seeing Evan take his idea and turn it into a multimillion-dollar company infuriated Reggie. Instead of running the company together, Reggie sat on the sidelines watching Evan soar past Poke and Zuckerberg.

Reggie hired James Lee, an up-and-coming partner at Lee Tran & Liang, as his lawyer in the case. Lee had begun his career as an LAPD detective; when he started studying at Stanford Law School, the Palo Alto campus was so quiet it gave him insomnia. Evan and Bobby still retained Cooley LLP, who responded to Reggie's letter in May 2012, as their lawyers for Snapchat. The ensuing discovery and depositions cost Snapchat significant time and money, but perhaps most importantly it weighed heavily on Evan at a pivotal point for the company.

On April 5, Evan, Bobby, and their attorneys from Cooley, along with Reggie and his attorneys from Lee Tran & Liang, filed into a conference room in Cooley's offices in downtown Santa Monica. Outside, tourists strolled up and down Santa Monica Boulevard, stopping in the trendy neighborhood's upscale shops, restaurants, and bars; they might walk down the palm-tree-lined street to the beach or the famous pier. Inside the conference room the temperature was more frigid.

Cooley's Mike Rhodes began deposing Reggie, attempting to establish that Reggie had accomplished little since graduation:

> "What is your current employment, if any?"
>
> "Well, currently I'm working in the South Carolina attorney general's office."
>
> "And how long have you worked there?"
>
> "I guess about a month at this point."
>
> "And what is your position?"
>
> "It's basically an intern/clerk position."
>
> "Is that a nonpaying position?"
>
> "Yes, it is."
>
> "And again, what was your approximate start date?"
>
> "A few weeks ago. Probably about a month."
>
> "So early March?"
>
> "Yes."
>
> "And what were you doing, if anything, for employment prior to that date?"
>
> "Well, I was applying to law school."
>
> "Were you working?"
>
> "No."

Reggie became distracted midway through answering a question about which lawyers he had spoken with. A naked man had chosen the sidewalk across from the Cooley office as his performance stage for the day and was gesturing at Reggie through the window. The lawyers hastily closed the blinds and continued the deposition much less eventfully.

Two days later, Bobby was deposed in the same office and had some trouble with his memory. James Lee asked Bobby if he had ever referred to Reggie Brown as an employer at Picaboo. Bobby said he hadn't. Lee showed him an automated email from Facebook, reading "Bobby Murphy tagged you in Picaboo under Employers." Bobby's eyes darted, his head tilted down, and he twitched his mouth nervously. Glancing up at Lee, he sheepishly replied "Uh . . . Well it looks like here that I did something to that effect," Murphy said. "I don't have a specific recollection of this happening . . . although I would say that it would have been unclear to me what . . . tagging someone as an 'employer' under Facebook would mean."

The following Monday, it was Evan's turn in front of the deposition camera. Like Bobby, Evan got tripped up a few times. After getting Evan on the record that Reggie had not been building an application with Evan and Bobby, Lee showed Evan an email he sent to Nicole James, the blogger who wrote about Snapchat, in which he wrote, "I just built an app with two friends of mine (certified bros.)" Evan reluctantly admitted that the two people he was referring to were Bobby and Reggie. The deposition continued:

> "Did you come up with the idea for deleting picture messages?"
> "No."
> "Did Bobby come up with the idea?"
> "No, he did not."
> "Who came up with the idea?"
> "Reggie did."
> "Do you think Reggie deserves anything for the contributions he made on the project?"

Evan paused for seven seconds. The room was dead silent.

> "Reggie may deserve something for some of his contributions."
> "Do you have any regrets?"

Evan sat still for thirty seconds. Again, the room was noiseless. Evan searched for the right words.

> "That's a really hard question for me because it's pretty clear
> that I lost a good friend."

Evan looked tired and miserable, his shoulders slumped in the chair,
his eyes sullen and searching for the ground.

> "I regret inviting him to my house. I regret spending that time
> with him at my house. I regret giving him so many chances. He
> exploited my attempts at generosity . . . the generosity was giv-
> ing Reggie an opportunity to work on something like this . . .
> for experience that he didn't have."

> "Do you regret Reggie sharing his idea with you?"

There was no pause this time. "No."

These depositions did significant damage to Snapchat, both in the
case and in the court of public opinion. Someone leaked videos of the
depositions to *Business Insider*, making Evan and Bobby look bad for
cutting Reggie out of the company and inconsistencies in response to
deposition questions about Reggie's level of involvement.

After these disastrous depositions, Evan and Bobby replaced Cooley
with David Quinn and the team at Quinn Emanuel Urquhart & Sullivan,
the same firm where Lee and his partners got their start. It was also the
firm that represented the Winklevoss twins in their infamous suit against
Mark Zuckerberg and Facebook. David Quinn was tenacious in and out
of the courtroom, running Ironman triathlons in his free time. Evan and
Bobby were convinced Quinn Emanuel could use their experience from
the most infamous startup lawsuit of all time to help them defeat
Reggie.

Quinn Emmanuel was much more aggressive than Cooley had been.
They filed a sea of requests for documents, depositions, and subpoe-
nas. They tried to dismiss the case and remove it to federal court, and
they sought contempt sanctions and a restraining order against Reggie
and Lee Tran & Liang.

Lee Tran & Liang tried to have Quinn Emmanuel thrown off the
case, as Reggie had tried to get another Quinn Emmanuel lawyer to
take his side of the case before he went to Lee Tran & Liang. Ultimately,

the judge ruled against Reggie and said the waiver Reggie had signed and the ethical wall Quinn Emmanuel erected were sufficient for them to continue representing Evan, Bobby, and Snapchat. Lee Tran & Liang also tried to sue all of Snapchat's investors, claiming their shares were diluting Reggie's one-third stake. They even lined up a tell-all interview for Reggie with *GQ* magazine, but he backed out at the last minute. At one point, Lee's partner Luan Tran took a copy of *Forbes* magazine with Evan on the cover, scrawled red devil horns over his head, and pinned it to the wall in his office.

The combative trial would wage for months, and each side had plenty more cards to play. Reggie claimed he owned one-third of Snapchat's intellectual property since he filed the original patent (which, again, was never approved). He also claimed that they had entered into an oral partnership agreement when he and Evan initially agreed to split everything 50/50 (before they brought Bobby in).

Evan and Bobby claimed Reggie was merely working with them on a project, and they never agreed to an equity split; because they used the Limited Liability Company (LLC) structure that Evan and Bobby had set up for Future Freshman rather than a whole new one, they claimed Reggie should know he had no equity in the venture.

One of the most difficult parts of the case was that Snapchat's valuation continued to soar throughout the lawsuit, climbing from $70 million when Reggie filed to $800 million in a matter of months. Soon, the company was worth billions. If Reggie was owed something, what was a fair amount? If a picture is worth a thousand words, and Evan's disappearing pictures company was worth millions and then billions, how much was Reggie's idea worth?

The lawsuit had a significant effect on Evan; he was already secretive and a bit paranoid by nature, but the lawsuit, combined with Snapchat's growing public profile, made him retreat further into the bunker—he preferred to take walking meetings so that others wouldn't overhear him, and he noted that iMessage and emails are permanent records. The stress was clearly getting to him. He would frequently blow up at his lawyers, screaming at them in the hallways in between depositions and settlement talks. It would be many months before the lawsuit reached a conclusion.

CHAPTER THIRTEEN

THE PHENOMENON

MAY 2013

VENICE, CA

Snapchat kept growing in users and in frequency of use. It had become a verb: Snapchat me that; Snap me. Users had grown from 3 million in the fall to 10 million in the spring, while photos shared per day shot up from 50 million in December 2012 to 150 million in April 2013 and again to 200 million in June 2013.

Most social networks track users by daily actives—that is, how many people visit the website or use the app on a given day. Other businesses with less frequency of use—like Amazon or Airbnb—focus more on monthly active users. In Snapchat's case, teenagers were so addicted to the app—opening it and sending and receiving snaps dozens of times per day—that the company started focusing on hourly active users.

Poke's failure had provided convincing proof that Snapchat had built an app that was defensible—a bigger company couldn't just copy it and wipe them out, which made it extremely attractive to venture capitalists. Evan reopened conversations with many of the venture capitalists who had been chasing the company. These VCs quickly began seeing

Snapchat in a similar light as Instagram when the photo-sharing app raised its Series B, a $50 million round at a $500 million valuation right before it was acquired by Facebook.

Snapchat's Series B valuation started in the low hundreds of millions, with many blue-chip backers like General Catalyst Partners, Greylock Partners, Charles River Ventures, and Institutional Venture Partners trying to get in the round.

Evan took advantage of Snapchat's strong negotiating position to extract favorable terms from investors. When he met with Institutional Venture Partners' Dennis Philips, Evan told Philips he would not accept IVP's standard investment terms.

"If you want standard terms, invest in a standard company," Evan told Philips.

The valuation climbed and climbed as backers offered higher valuations to win the deal. When the dust settled, Evan had driven the price up to an $80 million raise at an $800 million valuation. General Catalyst finally got their meaningful stake, while SV Angel joined the round and previous backers chipped in.

As part of the deal, Evan and Bobby each sold a small portion of their equity in exchange for $10 million apiece in cash. For the venture capitalists, this was great—they got to buy more stock in a red-hot company, and it aligned the founders' incentives with the VCs; venture capital firms see their returns follow a power law, where one investment makes them the majority of their money while most of their investments fail. If the founders have $10 million sitting in their pockets, they will be more likely to aim the company for the bigger, longer-run exits or IPOs rather than selling for less.

Amazon CEO Jeff Bezos summed up this idea in a letter to his shareholders, writing, "We all know that if you swing for the fences, you're going to strike out a lot, but you're also going to hit some home runs. The difference between baseball and business, however, is that baseball has a truncated outcome distribution. When you swing, no matter how well you connect with the ball, the most runs you can get is four. In business, every once in a while, when you step up to the plate, you can score 1,000 runs. This long-tailed distribution of returns is why it's important to be bold. Big winners pay for so many experiments."

An $800 million valuation for a two-year-old company that wasn't generating revenue, combined with the young founders each receiving $10 million in cash, soon generated a backlash. Media pundits, tech industry experts, and bankers screamed that Snapchat was the canary in the coal mine showing that the whole tech industry was in a bubble. It was threatening to people's world order that a disappearing photo app with no revenue and no plans to start making money could go from college dorm idea to $800 million in two years.

"The round, which values the photo-sharing company at $800 million pre-money, means that Snapchat is now an $860 million company in the eyes of venture capitalists—a staggering valuation after less than two years of operations and not a cent of revenue" wrote *Forbes*'s J. J. Colao.

"What Snapchat doesn't have yet, however, is revenue. Nor does it have easily identifiable paths to revenue," added *Fortune*'s Dan Primack.

Snapchat has been consistently underestimated in part because it is difficult to wrap one's head around the idea that a simple, free, photo-sharing app can tap into such a large market. It seems silly to think that this gimmicky entertainment device in our pockets could be worth so much, but the fact that it *is* in our pockets and used daily, if not hourly, sheds light on why. The number of smartphones in the world is an order of magnitude larger than the number of PCs, and the gap is growing. And unlike desktop computers, mobile phones are with us nearly 24/7.

Previously, time spent on media, whether browsing on a PC, watching TV, reading the newspaper, whatever, was very intentional. You sat down to read *The New York Times* or to watch *Friends*. But now we're primarily filling empty space when we take our phones out of our pockets—we're bored waiting in the checkout line, we're bored riding the subway, we're bored by the commercial on TV.

As naturally social creatures, we spend a lot of time on our phones with other people—messaging, liking, hearting, and retweeting things until our thumbs bleed. And there isn't a fixed amount of time for this—as pages load faster and Facebook and Snapchat and Instagram add more and more features, the time on mobile eats into everything else—time spent watching TV, using a PC, reading, staring at the sky, and, yes, sadly, probably talking to other humans. Be honest with yourself—how many times have you put this book down to check something on your phone? *That's* why mobile offers such an enormous opportunity.

Take a look at your phone. How many apps have you used today? How many have you opened every day for the last week or so? Of those apps, how many are not owned by Apple, Google, or Facebook? Most people will find that final list to be quite short. The average smartphone user has about ninety apps on their phone, but uses only seven or eight on a daily basis. According to market-research firm Verto Analytics, Apple, Google, and Facebook-owned apps account for 60 percent of users' time and 80 percent of advertisers' dollars spent on mobile.

For most kids in high school and college, Snapchat has become one of those daily-use apps, if not their top app. Having someone's attention is incredibly valuable. Whether a bar is advertising its happy hour, Walmart is selling toothpaste for mere cents (as it did in its early days), or Taco Bell is running a publicity stunt claiming it had sponsored the Liberty Bell, if you have someone's attention—whether they are in your physical store or in your digital world—you can make money.

Meanwhile, the media still portrayed Snapchat as primarily a sexting app. A lengthy February 2013 *New York Times* feature read, "The Snapchat service, which started two years ago but has steadily gained users, has been painted as a popular way for people, especially teenagers, to send naughty pictures." Growing popularity and competition from Facebook helped change this sexting narrative some, but reporters still leaned on it, as sexting headlines earned plenty of clicks.

Many people outside the company wondered aloud how it was possible or fair that Snapchat could be worth $800 million. As popular as Snapchat had become with the high school and college crowd, it still had very few users older than twenty-five. So older people, like these media talking heads, only saw a disappearing photo app that they didn't understand. They didn't yet realize that kids weren't simply using Snapchat to share pictures.

"People wonder why their daughter is taking 10,000 photos a day," Evan later said. "What they don't realize is that she isn't preserving images. She's talking. . . . It's not about an accumulation of photos defining who you are. It's about instant expression and who you are right now. Internet-connected photography is really a reinvention of the camera. And what it does is allow you to share your experience of the world while also seeing everyone else's experience of the world, everywhere, all the time."

Of course, it didn't help that Evan and Bobby spent the money like, well, young rich kids in LA. Evan bought a red Ferrari and started learning to fly helicopters, although he still lived at his dad's place in Pacific Palisades. Bobby bought a modern, concrete-and-glass-styled $2 million house in Venice, a block from the beach and a five-minute walk from Snapchat's office.

But the press and money did not distract Evan. Having grown up around Hollywood and wealth, he knew when to have a good time and party and when to focus on work. He was single-minded about his vision for the future of the world, and he was focused on doing everything in his power to bring that to fruition.

As fun as the blue bungalow on the beach had been, it had become very distracting to work there. People would constantly take selfies in front of the big yellow Snapchat logo and peer in to catch a glimpse of the team. Plus, an influx of young talent was making the beach house crowded—the long table packed with monitors, sodas, and coffees where the engineers built the future of social media wouldn't hold the entire team for much longer. Evan moved the company a few blocks away to a former art studio near the Venice boardwalk. This time, they skipped the big yellow Snapchat sign and inscribed a small, barely visible outline of the Ghostface Chillah logo on the wooden front door.

With their new larger office and more funding in the bank, Evan and Bobby decided to expand Team Snapchat, tripling the team from ten to thirty in 2013. Every one of a startup's early employees is a crucial hire. A players tend to attract and hire more A players, propagating a virtuous cycle that fills the team with talent; on the flip side, B and C players attract their peers, filling even the most promising young companies with mediocrity. Evan and Bobby had hit the nail on the head with their initial hires: David, Daniel, and Dena are all still at the company as of this writing, and all had played crucial roles in the company's success. But Snapchat was becoming too large and needed too much help to keep the team this small.

Chloe Drimal, a gregarious lacrosse player at Yale University, caught Evan's attention with her funny, insightful, and fearless columns for the *Yale Daily News* that were unafraid to touch on taboo subjects. In "Profile of a SWUG," she described a Senior Washed Up Girl (SWUG):

> She's the girl who promised she would never hook up with someone younger than her but now finds herself texting sophomore boys who unavoidably turn her down. She thinks this is funny. She thinks about getting a vibrator; she may already have a vibrator. It may be better than that sophomore boy.

Her social commentary frequently touched on social media, including a piece called "Newest Diet: Facebook Cleanse." But the article that caught Evan's attention was from December 2012, titled "Snapchat: The Phenomenon":

> I was first introduced to Snapchat on the patio of Box 63 during Camp Yale this year. "You have to download this app—it's so fun," said an already proficient snapchatter.
>
> I thought it was stupid. I didn't get the point of taking a picture that would inevitably disappear. But I did start sending "snaps" of my friends and me, mimosas in hand, to the few users that showed up from my contacts. Then I kept using it. Every day. Then new friends started Snapchatting me. Then my daily Snapchat notifications jumped from five to 35. Then, my friend started referring to his iPhone as his "Snapchat machine." And then, yesterday, my friend was invited to DKE formal through a Snapchat.
>
> Snapchat stopped being just an app and turned into a culture, a phenomenon. It's basically Twitter combined with texting combined with crack. Twitter gives you 140 characters to say your thought or what you are currently doing; Snapchat gives you 31. A text is permanent; a Snapchat is gone within 10 seconds.
>
> Anyone who has you in his or her contacts can Snapchat you. I doubt that you would refer to everyone in your contacts as a friend, and I am positive that you wouldn't text most of them at 11 a.m. on a dreary Monday just to say, "I hate Spanish," or "All I want for Christmas is you." But these are just

two of my Monday Snapchats from people that I would never text, and who would never text me at 11 a.m. on a Monday. But now, because of Snapchat, I'm receiving a picture of their face during a lecture on a dreary Monday, and you know what? I like it.

And I'm not the only one. I'm not the only one that feels legitimately closer to some junior guy because I receive a Snapchat every time he moves from the eighth to the fourth floor of the Stacks.

Because of Snapchat, we feel more connected to the girls and guys we used to know solely in terms of bars and fraternities. We know who has a lot of work and who doesn't. We know who is hung over and who is on a walk of shame. Best of all, we can see it. We see the aftermath of that looming senior thesis or that Zeta late night.

I think Evan Spiegel, the founder of Snapchat, understood our generation when he put a time limit on a picture message. Maybe he didn't mean to, but he took technology backwards a bit, bringing us a little closer to what real human interaction is supposed be. It's supposed to be a memory, not something tangible.

A conversation with a friend at Flavors is not transcribed and then published on the Internet, searchable by future job prospects. It is simply left as a memory. And when we retell the story tomorrow, we might misquote our friend or forget some details—but that's OK. That's what human interaction is about.

That's what Snapchat is about. You see it for a few seconds, then it's just a memory.

By taking out the forever part of a picture or text, more people want to share. They aren't afraid to put themselves out there, to send an ugly picture that may turn someone off or a beautiful picture that may seem narcissistic. They know it will eventually disappear.

We are a generation of the "Like" button, of the comments box and the anonymous comments box. Of statuses and tweets. We post things online, aware that anyone can see them. Aware

we are being judged and almost always looking for approval—
for that "Like."

Snapchat is different. It's fun without the terrifying permanence of the rest of our technology.

Hopefully this is just the beginning. Hopefully our culture
can go back to a time when we weren't scared to share too much.
But for now, my username is Chaoticklowy, and I accept silly
faces, hungover stares and, of course, formal invites.

Few people had better articulated why Snapchat was resonating so
strongly with its users. So when Drimal graduated Yale in the spring of
2013, Evan hired her to join the small team and work on a soon-to-
be-created content section of Snapchat.

Next, Evan turned his attention to Nathan Jurgenson, a PhD student at the University of Maryland. In 2011, Jurgenson, writing on a
social sciences blog called Cyborgology, introduced a term he called
"digital dualism," arguing that the distinction between the virtual
and real worlds is a fallacy. He rejected the distinction between "real"
and "virtual" worlds, or the notion that we live and act one way in person but build and create a separate identity online. In Jurgenson, Evan
found a provocative thinker who managed to capture and describe Snapchat's core ethos before he'd even heard of the app. Jurgenson would go
on to influence Evan's thinking and Snapchat's strategy in a deep way.

In February 2013, Jurgenson wrote about Snapchat: "The tension
between experience for its own sake and experience we pursue just to
put on Facebook is reaching its breaking point . . . that breaking point
is called Snapchat." After reading the piece in *The New Inquiry*, a nonprofit digital magazine, Evan reached out to Jurgenson and convinced
him to join Snapchat as a researcher. It is rare for a startup to hire someone so early just to focus on research and new thinking that may not be
directly relevant to a product. Jurgenson would speak with Evan often,
and Jurgenson's thoughts and writing eventually had a significant impact on the way Evan thought about Snapchat, social media, and the
internet more broadly. Evan would frequently quote Jurgenson and discuss his ideas in interviews with journalists.

Snapchat also needed more engineering firepower, so they hired seven new engineers, almost all from Stanford, and two designers to work with Evan; like Evan, Bobby, David, and Daniel, most were interested in art or music as well as coding, and many had been involved in Greek life at school.

All these young engineers needed more experienced leadership, so Evan recruited longtime Amazon engineer Tim Sehn to become VP of engineering. Sehn had joined Amazon in 2001 as an intern and quickly rose through the ranks; at one point he was responsible for the performance of Amazon's main website, and later he moved on to maintaining Amazon Web Services. Sehn's recruitment was crucial, and his willingness to join Snapchat showed the hiring power Evan and Bobby enjoyed as the hottest new startup in the tech world.

Phillippe Browning next joined the team from CBS Mobile to head up monetization at Snapchat; Evan had been redirecting every email he received from marketers to a dead-end mailbox. Now, at the very least, Browning would handle them. Although Snapchat ignored marketers, companies were beginning to test the app's capabilities.

On New Year's Day, 2013, the frozen yogurt chain 16 Handles ran the first promotion on Snapchat. The company's community manager noticed that Snapchat had gained traction with 16 Handles's core demographic of pre-teen through early twenties consumers. He suggested to his boss that the frozen yogurt chain run a promotion on the nascent app. If customers added 16 Handles on Snapchat, a 16 Handles employee would take a picture of a coupon code with a discount of 25 to 100 percent off, and send it to that customer. The customer would then show it to the cashier right away (before it disappeared in 10 seconds) and receive the discount. The promotion, dubbed "Snappy New Year," was only tested for a few hours across three stores, but 16 Handles estimates that it drove about $1,500 in sales. While a small moneymaker, 16 Handles had shown that businesses could convert captive audiences on Snapchat into real dollars.

In May 2013, Taco Bell became the first major advertiser to create a Snapchat account and interact with customers. Taco Bell had poached the 16 Handles community manager who came up with the "Snappy New Year" campaign. On May 1, the company tweeted "We're on @ Snapchat. Username: tacobell. Add us. We're sending all of our friends a secret announcement tomorrow! #Shhh."

The next day, Taco Bell sent their Snapchat friends a photo of a burrito; they had used Snapchat to draw "Hi Friend" and "5-23-13" over the photo in lime green ink. The ad suggested that Taco Bell's new burrito would hit stores on May 23.

"People are obsessed with Beefy Crunch Burrito so Snapchat seemed like the right platform to make the announcement," Taco Bell director of social and digital media Tressie Lieberman said at the time. "Sharing that story on Snapchat is a fun way to connect with the fans that we are thrilled to have. It's all about treating them like personal friends and not consumers."

Soon, Taco Bell would have a much more powerful way to advertise on Snapchat, as Evan prepared to unveil a storytelling tool that he, Bobby, and the rest of the team had been debating for almost a year.

CHAPTER FOURTEEN

STORIES

SEPTEMBER 2013
VENICE, CA

Whenever Evan, Bobby, David, Daniel, or anyone else at Snapchat asked users what additional features they wanted, the response was universal. From Oslo to Santa Monica, users wanted group messaging. Tired of combing through their lists of contacts to send a funny picture to everyone in their clique, users wanted to be able to create a group the way they could in text messages and other messengers.

But Evan and the Snapchat team worried that group messaging could kill the magic of Snapchat. If users could easily fire off mass Snapchats to big groups of people all the time, it might destroy the vibe they had worked so hard to create. Was there a better way to create a one-to-many sharing tool than group messaging?

Evan and his team knew what they didn't want to create. One of Evan's strengths is his ability to see issues in his social feeds and circles and extrapolate them broadly to get into the heads of his users. When users first signed up for Facebook, it was amazing. All their friends were on it, and they could post funny things and goofy pictures. But all these posts built up over time and started becoming representations of people—their so-called "personal brand." It turns out it was a lot of work to curate a personal brand that spanned many years and was cool to your peers and acceptable to parents and work colleagues—not to mention future friends and colleagues who might want a different you.

At some point were you supposed to go back and unlike Sean Paul? Or would your friends understand that ten years ago the song "Temperature" was just that good? What about seventeen "new phone, need numbers" groups? Is there a button for deleting every photo of you before 2011? Why did you think that haircut was a good idea? And so users started posting less frequently and started sharing news articles instead of silly pictures. The spontaneity, goofiness, and lightness of social media was replaced; instead of throwing Polaroids at friends across the room, you were curating a gallery of professionally framed, high-gloss photos.

A Snapchat rebuild of the newsfeed would obviously have to be impermanent—all of the content would disappear at some point, like the disappearing messages. That way users would feel comfortable posting whatever suited their mood in the moment without worrying about how it would look months and years later. To get away from the manicured photos filling Instagram and Facebook competing for likes, Snapchat's feed would do away with likes and comments. Users could post whatever they wanted, and if their friends really wanted to respond, they could send them a reaction Snapchat.

And so, in October 2013, nearly a year after they had seriously started discussing the idea, Snapchat Stories was born. If users tapped to the right after opening the app—it still opened straight to the camera, as usual—they would see a list of their friends, with a circular thumbnail on the right side of each name. Holding their fingers down on a friend started a slideshow that played content in the order that it was posted rather than in reverse chronological order, like many feeds. Evan, having studied journalism at Crossroads, was obsessed with Stories being able to show a narrative, as users could really tell rich stories mixing photo and video rather than just posting a couple photos from their night out. Content would appear for twenty-four hours then disappear. If a friend's story was dull or too long and dragged on, users could just tap it to skip ahead. With no likes and comments, there was no need for a sorting algorithm, like those found on Facebook, Instagram, and Twitter. Content would just appear based on who had posted most recently—an added incentive to post more often.

Without likes and comments, Snapchat's new feature needed a different way to reward users for posting and capture its users' psychological craving for attention. With Snapchat messages, the sender could see when the other person opened it (I have their attention!), and the recipient knew the sender had scrolled through a list and manually touched their name to send it to them (they chose me!). With Stories, users could see a list of names of everyone who viewed their story.

Evan argued that it was awkward and insincere when people pretended in real-world interactions that they hadn't been watching their friends' lives unfold via social media; so, he argued, why not just show people who's watching their stories. There was some concern that this would deter people from watching as many friends' stories, but ultimately they decided this risk was worth taking for the tradeoff of addicting users to seeing all of their friends who had watched their story. This list turned out to be psychological candy for users, as they could scroll through and see exactly who had watched their story. This phenomenon was by no means new—Myspace founder Tom Anderson said the number-one feature that Myspace users begged for was "who's viewed your profile."

Even though Evan, Bobby, and the team had debated, prototyped, reworked, and iterated for a year on Stories, there was still a significant risk when they launched that it would flop—or worse, that it would hurt Snapchat's growth and success with messages.

"Snapchat may not look much like Facebook, but with Stories, the company is taking its first steps toward competing with Facebook's most important product: News Feed," Ellis Hamburger, who would later work for Evan at Snapchat, wrote about Stories' launch for the *Verge*. "Behind Stories is a deep understanding, or perhaps loathing, of the way social apps work today. Spiegel claims to have no special knowledge of the way we work as social organisms aside from what he learned as a college student, but has thus far proven himself and his colleagues to be surprisingly thoughtful about our hidden social behaviors and desires. Stories is the next big piece of how Snapchat thinks social media should work, and everybody's watching."

Much like Snapchat's ascent in early 2012, Stories caught on slowly at first as users played around with it and learned the new medium; but once they had grown comfortable with it and accustomed to their friends posting and watching this still-disappearing content, Stories caught on in a big way.

The brilliance of Stories was everything that wasn't in it; with no permanence, fancy editing, likes, follower counts, or comments, users could post whatever they wanted. No one else's Stories were these amazing, manicured productions, so most people felt comfortable sharing silly videos and selfies. It was also easier to pull Snapchat out of your pocket, record a video of your friends, and post it to your Story—much easier than taking the perfect picture in the most attractive lighting and picking the best filter and writing a witty caption. The cost of sharing was incredibly low, both mentally and socially. So people shared a ton of content on Stories.

Because users couldn't upload photos or videos from their phone to Snapchat—they had to record them in Snapchat and immediately send them to friends or post them to their story—it became the best way to see what your friends were doing in close to real time. As my friends started using Stories more and more my senior year at Stanford, I started to have an ambient sense of where people were on campus. I would watch friends' stories and see that a dozen of my friends were drinking by the Arillaga pool while Sam and David were on the golf course, and Zach was bored to tears sending goofy selfies from the library.

Stories made young people feel like reality TV stars and celebrities; they'd go to class or out to a party or on vacation and post a bunch of photos and videos and be able to see how many dozens or hundreds of people were watching their life. It became an easy, lightweight way to stay in touch and see what friends at other colleges and in other cities were up to and, at times, to live vicariously through them. You could see—even *feel*—a Kanye concert without even going to the show. College students studying abroad would take a whole series of Snapchats with their phone on airplane mode and then post them all when they connected to a WiFi network (Snapchat saved uploads that wouldn't post due to cell service for up to twenty-four hours, but the content still expired twenty-four hours from when it was taken).

Stories and messages created a powerful double-piston engine for Snapchat. Messages pulled people in—your friend has sent you a Snapchat. Stories filled a boredom void—what are your friends up to? This made it much, much harder for companies like Facebook, Google, or Apple to simply add ephemeral elements to their messengers or copy the app to wipe out Snapchat.

And both pistons drove growth in a big way. Snapchat had these little features, like being able to turn the colored pen to white or black or changing the size and color of text. Like In-N-Out Burger's secret menu, these attributes were well known to the regulars and the cool crowd, but there was no text or help from Snapchat alerting the average user to its presence. So teenagers would ask, "How did you do that?!" and show each other how to use new and hidden parts of the app. They would also talk about who had good Snapchat stories and whose were bad, what cool things people did, and *Oh did you see what happened on Caitlin's story?* Once again, it all added up to a simple fact: if you didn't have Snapchat, you were missing out.

Snapchat looked like an insignificant toy when it launched, but was actually a big improvement in communication for many people. The more you used it, the more fun and addicting it became. Quickly, it started replacing conversations and content that previously took place via text messages or on social networking sites. As its user base and community grew larger and more devoted, Snapchat was able to build out Stories and gain a larger share of content that users previously posted elsewhere. Like Facebook, Snapchat had boundless ambition flowing down from its founder down through the ranks of the employees. But people only had so many photos to post and so many hours in a day to watch.

On October 30, Facebook chief financial officer David Ebersman noted during the company's earnings call that Facebook "did see a decrease in daily users specifically among younger teens."

It was the first time the company had told investors it was having any trouble with its young teen users.

Zuckerberg realized he had to take one more shot at acquiring Snapchat.

CHAPTER FIFTEEN

HOW TO TURN DOWN
THREE BILLION DOLLARS

NOVEMBER 2013

VENICE, CA

As the Neon Trees song "Everybody Talks" blares over the set of CNN's *New Day*, host Michaela Pereira greets her audience, "I'm thinking back to when I was twenty-three, would I have turned down THREE BILLION DOLLARS? That's precisely what Evan Spiegel—he's the young CEO of Snapchat—has done."

"We turn to a made in America success story with a twist," Diane Sawyer said on *ABC World News*. "Imagine you're living with your parents when you have a great idea. An idea so good that Facebook offers you billions in cold cash to buy it. So how is it possible the two guys turned the money down?"

Weeks earlier, Mark Zuckerberg had reached out to Evan again with an offer: join us at Facebook. Build your vision of Snapchat with our resources and enormous userbase. The total package Facebook offered, if Snapchat hit certain performance targets, would be well north of three billion dollars.

Evan and Bobby, each of whom owned about 25 percent of the company at the time, would have received hundreds of millions of dollars apiece if they had sold. They also maintained the majority of voting rights in the company. Evan and Bobby went back and forth on the decision, sometimes favoring the exit, other times wanting to see how big they could make Snapchat on their own. Snapchat still had zero revenue and didn't even have a proven business model.

Behind the scenes, Zuckerberg called Matt Cohler, one of the first five employees at Facebook and now one of Snapchat board member Mitch Lasky's partners at Benchmark, to see how he could influence Snapchat's decision. Lasky had an interesting parable to draw upon—Benchmark was an early investor in Instagram, and many thought Instagram would have been worth far more in a short time had it remained independent instead of selling to Facebook. As Evan wavered on their decision, Lasky wondered aloud to fellow board member Michael Lynton about "how much of [Evan's actions are] window dressing for me and how much of this is real," meaning Lasky wasn't confident that Evan was being fully truthful with him.

At the end of the day, could Evan really see himself working as a Facebook employee, heading to the Menlo Park campus every day to work for Zuckerberg? Wouldn't it be more fun to run Snapchat on his own down in Venice? If he turned down Facebook and ran Snapchat poorly, he would probably never get an offer this big again. But if he sold Snapchat, he would probably never again have an idea this great. Once again, Evan and Bobby turned Zuckerberg and Facebook down, opting to stay independent in Venice.

As he was talking with Facebook, Evan was wooing investors for a Series C round of funding, seeking a high price tag. These acquisition and fundraising conversations often happen simultaneously, as the two processes are not too dissimilar; Instagram closed its large Series B round just days before it agreed to sell to Facebook. Evan scared off several firms from this round, as he was seeking a $4 billion valuation just months after the company had been valued at $800 million.

Evan proposed one deal with Chinese e-commerce company Tencent and Russian investment firm DST Global that would include a sale of $40 million of Evan and Bobby's shares, just months after they each unloaded $10 million of their equity. These terms made investors uneasy

lar role to the one Sandberg held at the nascent Facebook: advising the younger wunderkind CEO and turning the hot social property into a thriving business.

Legendary tech journalist Kara Swisher called it a "major talent grab," noting that "the hiring is a clear signal that Snapchat intends to remain independent and grow its business, which is likely to include another large investment round of several hundreds of millions of dollars. . . . It vaults White to one of the more high-profile roles in the Internet space."

The hiring spree would continue into 2014, as Peter Magnusson, a former engineering director at Google, left Google App Engine to become a VP of engineering at Snapchat. Mike Randall followed White from Facebook to become Snapchat's VP of business and marketing partnerships. Randall had spent four years at Facebook running the Preferred Marketing Developer program, helping brands run ads and publish content through Pages.

So why did all these veterans leave cushy, high-paying jobs to go work for twenty-three-year-old Evan Spiegel? They bought into Evan as a visionary leader who would make Snapchat the Next Big Thing. They believed what Evan had always believed about himself.

On November 18, 2013, two weeks after the Facebook rejection hit newsstands and the Tencent funding round hit the skids, board member Mitch Lasky emailed Evan about the road ahead. Lasky's email was a long memo, and Evan replied with an equally long memo, but for our purposes we will look at the exchange as a back-and-forth point-by-point. First, Lasky:

> Here are some of the things I think we should have on the agenda:
>
> 1) Financing. At this point, we can take a couple of different paths:
>
> On the one hand, we could pull back and attempt to "prove it" to the market to get the higher valuation. I'm not exactly sure what that "proof" would be. We always run the risk that overall froth in the market declines, and we end up filling a

leaking bucket—doing everything right to "prove it" while macro valuations decline. I'm not that valuation-focused anyway, so this matters less to me.

If we think we are going to change the market's perspective through revenue generation, I think that is quite dangerous to assume. Right now it's all about users and growth and engagement, which we know will go up and to the right for a while. Once you introduce revenue, that becomes the dominant paradigm. Take subscriptions: if you got ~2% monthly active user conversion to subscription at $1.99 for the balance of the year with no churn, which would be pretty good, it's $25–30 million post Apple/Google tax.* It's going to take a while to come up with a cluster of monetization schemes that get you to the point where you want to be judged on revenue/earnings multiples. We have to assume there is no AdWords-like magic bullet.† I want us to be able to be really, really patient and get it right.

Lasky warned Evan that starting to generate revenue would change the lens through which investors evaluate Snapchat from user growth–focused to revenue-focused. He went on to suggest that Snapchat raise $50 million at a multibillion dollar valuation to give Snapchat a longer runway.

Just an hour later, Evan replied:

1) I 100% understand your perspective on the raise. That said, I would prefer to keep the valuation of the co at $800 million going into a potentially turbulent time in the market. We have 13 months' runway, and with a minimally successful monetization

---

* If Snapchat decided to start monetizing by charging a fee to use the app, only a small percentage of the user base would pay, and Snapchat would have to pay 30 percent of that revenue to Apple and Google, which levy an app store tax. For Snapchat, $30 million a year will not cut it revenue-wise, so they would likely need to look at a combination of in-app purchases, advertising, or other revenue.

† Google's AdWords is considered the best revenue model in the history of startups; Snapchat cannot plan to stumble across an advertising model that good.

scheme we will be able to comfortably extend that. I don't think that monetizing the business will affect our ability to raise at high valuations—Facebook was bringing in money in the very early days and didn't have any problem attracting high valuations. If anything, we need to monetize the business in order to create leverage for future financings as needed. In the next two weeks I want to focus on the monetization product rather than a potential financing. It's almost there and it's really awesome. If we have a business that is sustainable over the next 2–3 years we will be in a much stronger position . . .

We will benefit from having lower strike price* as we hire over the next few years. Especially if that price becomes based on revenue rather than VC valuations. I don't think $3bn valuation for fundraising is going to go away—esp because Tencent and others are already pricing in market volatility. You've seen the data—we have high engagement and high retention product with tremendous growth ahead of us. Monetizing the business now only makes a stronger case for the permanence of our product. I think the most important thing I want to communicate to you is that this is not an emotional decision and is not about "proving it"—this business needs to make money. The argument of grow now, monetize later doesn't make sense because we have reached abnormal levels of growth and our monetization product is value-added. I'd rather not burn another $100 million of other people's money before we find out whether or not we have a business. If we can build profitable biz with Twitter-scale, 30-person headcount,† and major growth ahead we are not going to have a problem attracting additional capital. (This does not preclude necessity of building a much larger team).

---

* The price employees must pay to exercise their stock options and buy the underlying common stock in Snapchat.
† Snapchat's current number of employees.

At a young age, Evan would listen in on his father's long legal calls, which he credits for giving him early business exposure that helped develop his critical thinking and business accumen. He can often become obsessed with ideas, hungrily learning everything he can about them at a rapid pace. Evan is constantly curious and is learning and getting better at being a CEO very quickly. But his two superpowers are (1) his ability to get inside his users' heads and think like a teenage girl and (2) his knack for attracting brilliant, powerful mentors. Evan loves picking other people's brains over a walk or a meal. Over the years he has attracted an A-list roster of mentors, including SoftBank's Nikesh Arora, Twitter's Jack Dorsey and Google's Eric Schmidt. He doesn't just limit these brain dumps to tech luminaries, though, as he often walks and chats with fashion designers, politicians, documentary filmmakers, and other intriguing peers. Often, these impressive people will come speak to Team Snapchat at their Venice headquarters.

Lasky continued his memo:

> 2) Hiring. If we are going to go for it and build the big company you want to build, we need to accelerate the hiring of the executive team. The IVP* guys said they introduced you to Zander as a potential COO. I think of him as more of a business development type but he's a good guy and very smart. Is Daversa [a head-hunting firm] formally retained on the COO search? We should get our general counsel search rekindled, too. We've passed on some good options and I want to make sure we aren't looking for a unicorn. And if we are planning to generate revenue early in 2014, we really need a CFO or at least a VP of Finance. Let's discuss.

Venture capitalists frequently push young, inexperienced founders to bring on more seasoned executives to build out a team that can take

---

* Institutional Venture Partners, another venture capital firm.

a high-growth company to the next level. The most crucial hire for Snapchat would be a COO who could serve as Evan's number two.

Evan replied:

> 2) I completely agree. Not interested in Zander. I am working with Daversa on CAO/COO role and meeting with 4 terrific candidates this week. Will report back on those meetings. As far as general counsel goes, I have my dream candidate and I think we can make it happen. I am calling him today to discuss but don't feel comfortable bringing him on until we are making money. We will be able to attract best (and risk-adverse) candidates if we can show a path to real revenues. I am moving Philippe to internal operations (we can discuss this on the phone, please do not discuss with him as I have not yet had this conversation with him) and I think he will be able to monitor cash flow while we look for CFO or VP Finance. We're not doing anything fancy—we just need to know if the amount of money in our accounts is increasing or decreasing.

Evan again pushed for generating revenue, framing it this time as a way to attract a better team.

Back to Lasky, who advised Evan to apologize to Zuckerberg in order to stay on good terms:

> 3) FB. Confidentially, Zuck pinged Cohler during the peak of the news cycle on the acquisition leak. He was disappointed that the deal didn't get done, but also believes that you leaked this to the press in order to bolster your fundraising efforts. Cohler told him that he could easily make the argument that FB leaked it to put pressure on Snapchat, or that it was leaked by a third party. Regardless, my advice is to be the bigger person and call Zuck and apologize for the leak (even though it wasn't your fault) and deny any culpability. I know you have no interest in selling to him, but you want to keep on good terms with the enemy. :)

Evan again:

> 3) [Re: Zuckerberg] We texted last week, planning on calling
> him today.

Lasky concluded by informing Evan that Lightspeed partner
and early investor Jeremy Liew wanted to sell part of his stake if
Evan sold some of his own shares in a funding round, and advising
Evan to make sure everyone on the Snapchat team was on the same
page:

> 4) Lightspeed. Finally talked to Jeremy late yesterday. He
> clarified his position on selling. Said that he's a seller if you are
> a seller—if you do any secondary he wants to sell pro rata.*
> He denied that he's a seller into a 100% primary deal, but who
> knows—that could just be VC posturing.
>
> 5) All Hands Meeting. You've probably already done this,
> but if not you may want to consider getting your staff together
> briefly and telling them what's going on—well, maybe not
> everything, but these are key moments to communicate. They
> are reading about all this in the press and are probably wondering
> what's happening. It's totally natural. Good opportunity
> to remind everyone that you plan to build a big company
> together.
>
> Anyway, I wanted to get this to you now because we may
> not talk until later in the week. Sorry for the long email.
>
> —Mitch

Evan quickly responded to Lasky's main points before adding on
a lengthy note about his thoughts on the macroeconomic environment and why he wanted to generate revenue sooner rather than
later:

---

* Jeremy Liew, the Lightspeed partner in the seed round, here wants to sell an equal
amount of Lightspeed's stake if Evan sells some of his stock in the round, but he will
not sell his stake if Evan doesn't sell his own.

4) [Re: Lightspeed] Talked to David this AM, sounds like Jeremy will be following up with Tencent later in the week. David seemed to think the deal could get done. As I mentioned earlier, I don't care either way but we would probably have to offer it to all shareholders to avoid potential lawsuit down the road. Could be more trouble than its worth.

5) [Re: All Hands Meeting] Happened at 10am.

As a note: my view of the market is as follows—

Fed has created abnormal market conditions by printing money and keeping interest rates low. Investors are looking for growth anywhere they can find it and tech companies are good targets—at these values, however, all tech stocks are expensive—even looking at 5+ years of revenue growth down the road. This means that most value-driven investors* have left the market and the remaining 5–10%+ increase in market value will be driven by momentum investors.† At some point there won't be any momentum investors left buying at higher prices, and the market begins to tumble. May be 10–20% correction or something more significant, especially in tech stocks. Facebook has continued to perform in the market despite declining user engagement and pullback of brand advertising‡ dollars—largely due to mobile advertising performance—especially App Install advertisements.§ This is a huge red flag because it indicates that sustainable brand dollars have not yet moved to Facebook mobile platform and mobile revenue growth has been driven by technology companies (many of which are VC funded). VC dollars are being spent on user acquisition despite unknown Life Time

---

* Investors who seek to invest in a company they believe is trading at a price below what the company's true worth is.

† Investors who look to invest in a company they believe will be trading at even higher prices tomorrow because the stock has momentum.

‡ Advertisements from major companies that are meant to build up a brand's value, like a billboard for Budweiser. Much more on this later.

§ Advertisements to install mobile apps; usually app developers pay per click or per download.

Value* of users—a recipe for disaster. This props up Facebook share price and continues to justify VC investment in technology products based on abnormally large market cap companies (i.e. "If this company attracts just 5% of users that FB has, it will be HUGE"—fuels spend on user acquisition as user growth is tied to values). When the market for tech stocks cools, Facebook market cap will plummet, access to capital for unproven businesses will become inaccessible, and ad spend on user acquisition will rapidly decrease—compounding problems for Facebook and driving stock even lower. Instagram may be only saving grace if they are able to ramp advertising product fast enough. Total internet advertising spend cannot justify outsized valuations of social media products that derive revenue from advertising. Feed-based advertising units will plummet in value (in the case of Twitter, advertising spend may not move beyond experimental dollars) similar to earlier devaluing of Internet display advertising.

That said, we are still in very early days in mobile application market. I remember growing up wishing I had been a part of PC revolution—and I feel very fortunate to have the opportunity to watch smartphones take off. Snapchat has become one of the top 5 mobile phone brands with Facebook, Twitter, YouTube, and Instagram.

For Snapchat to capitalize on market conditions in next 3 years, it is imperative that we become a revenue-generating company. That will allow us to attract the best talent and prosper despite extreme scrutiny on traditional social media that will have failed to deliver on $$$dreams. Team is working overtime to drive revenue and innovate on core product—we have a solid 3-year roadmap that we intend to follow.

As a profitable growth company with a focus on mobile we will not suffer from opportunities to raise capital at outsized

---

* The Life Time Value (LTV) of a customer is how much a company expects to earn from a customer over a certain period of time (often the average amount of time customers stay with the company). Calculating this LTV can be important in knowing how much to spend on advertising to acquire users or customers.

valuations despite market conditions. Strategically it is important for us to keep expectations low with an understanding that Snapchat may be valued on revenues going forward and that $800mm valuation for a two-year-old company is remarkable and already more than enough to grow into. With 13–15 months of runway extended by minimally successful revenue generation activities, I think we are positioned to capture the mobile communication market.

I disagree wholeheartedly with the notion that mobile will be forever fragmented—we are the only differentiated messaging service in the United States and we will continue to provide a unique and innovative product experience. Snapchat is not valuable in the long-term because it is used by teens or because it is a threat to Facebook. It is valuable because it has fundamentally changed the nature of digital communication in <2 years and will continue to do so for the life of the Company (may it be long and prosperous).

Our focus in the immediate term is revenue generation, growth and product development.

The clarity of Evan's response showed how much he had learned. Evan began with the world at large, then narrowed to the tech world, then his main competitor, then Snapchat, considering this entire stack now and in the future. He understood where his main adversary, Facebook, was weak and where it was strong, at least product-wise. He understood his users and what they liked inside and outside of Snapchat.

The key paragraph in his email began with "THAT SAID," in which he describes how Snapchat was fortunate to be in the very early days of the mobile market. Snapchat was a top five mobile brand as an enormous new opportunity developed. This vision was how Evan attracted and retained talent to make Snapchat a great company.

Unlike many founders, Evan wasn't aiming for the highest possible valuation right now. He was worried about the hurdles standing in Snapchat's way and thinking strategically about how his moves now set up his options down the road on the way to a Snapchat IPO.

He was as obsessed with Snapchat being a permanent company as he was with Snapchat being an impermanent product. This is the best idea Evan will ever have. He will not sell it to someone else. And he will not screw it up himself.

CHAPTER SIXTEEN

HAPPY NEW YEAR!

DECEMBER 31, 2013
LOS ANGELES, CA

While they didn't have $3 billion, Evan and Bobby felt like they had billions of reasons to celebrate 2013. Stanford's football team was again playing in the Rose Bowl, so they would throw another New Year's Eve party. The company had outgrown the beach bunga-low for a working space, and the guest list had certainly outgrown it for a party venue. And the company had grown too mature to throw a party at the new office.

I stepped out of the Uber with a half dozen friends from Stanford and straightened my jacket, staring at the inconspicuous entrance to a big, lofty warehouse on a deserted street. Unlike the previous year's bash, where they simply asked that you not take photos, this year secu-rity confiscated everyone's phones at the doors. Evan's desire for pri-vacy had risen right alongside Snapchat's heightened profile. Deciding our phones were a good trade for the open bar, we entered the party.

Hundreds of people, mostly from Stanford and Crossroads, as well as friends of Snapchat employees, mingled around the big circular bar in the middle, throwing back shots and toasting to a great year. The couches and low tables to the rear of the main bar were mostly unused as people gathered in the front on the dance floor.

Past the bar and dance floor was a big alley filled with a huge inflatable slide, food trucks, and, of course, more open bars. There I joined a circle of friends sharing a contraband phone to call our significant others and wish them a Happy New Year.

Throughout the party, people wondered aloud, "How had one of Evan's schemes become this?" "Weren't they nuts to turn down $3 billion?" "What would you do with $3 billion?" "First, I'd throw a party like this." And on and on it went.

The VIP area this year was significantly, and literally, elevated. Suspended on a narrow bridge above the main bar and rest of the party, Evan and Bobby mingled with friends, coworkers, and dates. Evan's date for the evening was one of the biggest stars on the planet: Taylor Swift. One of her famous pals, *Modern Family* star Sarah Hyland, also hung out upstairs. Swift's presence seemed to simultaneously lend an air of credibility to the event and make it seem like an even more far-fetched fairy tale. An enormous pop star was Evan's date—clearly Snapchat had proven it was much more than a sexting app. And yet, how was it possible that I, a mere college senior, was partying in the same room as Taylor Swift? Nights like this can seem absurd in the moment, only to fade with time. The surreal nature of that night has only grown with time. Evan and Taylor, both stars, would grow to become even bigger stars.

It had only been two short years since Snapchat took advantage of front-facing cameras on iPhones to explode from an unknown startup to one of the fastest-growing tech companies on the planet. As Snapchat grew, the selfie tipped over into the mainstream. President Barack Obama made worldwide headlines when he joined Danish prime minister Helle Thorning-Schmidt and British prime minister David Cameron in a smiling selfie during a memorial celebration for Nelson Mandela in Johannesburg, South Africa.

And the trend would only continue. At the start of 2014, Academy Awards host Ellen DeGeneres walked down the aisle of the Dolby Theatre in Hollywood with her phone out, taking a selfie with Liza Minelli and talking about it like a teenage Snapchatter. She stopped by

Meryl Streep and said she wanted to pay homage to Streep's record eighteen Oscar nominations by breaking the record for most retweeted picture ever. As she and Streep started crouching for a selfie, DeGeneres urged surrounding celebrities to join in. Julia Roberts, Channing Tatum, Bradley Cooper, Kevin Spacey, Angelina Jolie, Brad Pitt, Lupita Nyong'o, Jared Leto, and Jennifer Lawrence joined the picture, which millions of people retweeted.

While the picture itself wasn't taken on Snapchat, the influence of the selfie can certainly be directed back to the ephemeral messaging app. Mobile photography was already enormous thanks to smartphones, Facebook, Twitter, and Instagram. But Snapchat threw gasoline on the fire with the selfie and pushed us into taking so many pictures of others and ourselves that the cohost of the Oscars felt the need to take selfies mid-broadcast. Selfies had come a long way since Robert Cornelius's 1839 self-portrait. You can take a selfie using any camera or app, but Snapchat was *the* app to do it with, becoming nearly synonymous with taking a selfie, the way Kleenex had become synonymous with all tissues.

Snapchat was the belle of the ball. On New Year's Day, the Stanford band formed the Ghostface Chillah logo on the field at halftime of the hundredth Rose Bowl Game.

That New Year's Eve was a beautiful evening of contradictions. A picture-sharing company throwing a party that confiscated your phones. Newly famous youngsters celebrating an iconic holiday out of the limelight. There was a sense of wonder, looking back, at how quickly and awesomely this product and company had been built. But a taste of bittersweet, looking forward: the team would never be this cool, small, and tight knit again. It's very rare that you realize you are living in the "good old days" when they are happening; but that night, it was clear. This was a special period that would never be the same again. Snapchat was already huge; the world just didn't know it yet.

Part II

TOYS ARE PRELUDES TO SERIOUS IDEAS

CHAPTER SEVENTEEN

HANGOVER

JANUARY 2014

VENICE, CA

In August 2013, researchers at Gibson Security, a security research group, reverse-engineered part of Snapchat and found security holes that could allow malicious hackers access to usernames and phone numbers. They notified Snapchat, but the company did not respond.

On December 25, 2013, Gibson Security published the code they had used to find security holes in Snapchat, hoping the public pressure would force Snapchat to patch the flaw. On December 27, 2013, Snapchat wrote a brief blog post, downplaying the significance of the security flaw: "Theoretically, if someone were able to upload a huge set of phone numbers . . . they could create a database of the results and match usernames to phone numbers that way."

On January 1, 2014, a different set of hackers used Gibson's method to do just that, posting the phone numbers and matching usernames of over 4.6 million Snapchat users in an online database dubbed SnapchatDB. They published it to publicly pressure Snapchat to fix the flaw, telling the media that "security matters as much as user experience does."

On January 3, Evan was interviewed by Carson Daly on *Today* about the hack. "Technology businesses in general are susceptible to hacking, and that's why you have to work really, really hard," Evan said. "The key is striking a balance between providing [the] utility of a friend service and preventing abuse, and that is something we are always working on. . . . I believe at the time we thought we had done enough. But I think in a business like this and a business that is moving so quickly, if you spend your time looking backwards, you're just going to kill yourself."

The media skewered Snapchat for the hack—and Evan for not apologizing to users who had their information stolen and published. Journalists believed Evan was far too cavalier about users' privacy in refusing to patch the security hole, arguing that he was unfit to be CEO if he did not apologize to users. Evan and his team must have believed the flaw was not significant, but they could have patched it with very little effort. By choosing not to, they recklessly let millions of phone numbers and usernames, many of which are the same across various online accounts, become public.

Later that day, widely read *Fortune* editor Dan Primack wrote a column titled "Does Snapchat's CEO Need to Go?" in which he argued that either Evan should be fired or Evan should fire whoever was advising him not to apologize for what Primack called a "massive violation of user trust." Primack continued:

> It's about doing right by the millions of people who use the service, in large part, because it is designed to offer a more private social networking and sharing experience than do sites like Facebook or Twitter.

The hack and public fiasco made Snapchat seem amateurish. Effectively zero users deleted Snapchat because of the breach, and it did not slow Snapchat's wild user growth. But the breach did attract the attention of the Federal Trade Commission, which looked into the incident.

In May, Snapchat agreed to settle charges with the FTC that snaps did not disappear the way they promised. The agency charged that Snapchat told users messages could not be saved, but users could easily use third party apps or technical workarounds to save snaps. The complaint also stated that Snapchat used location information and collected contacts from address books, despite telling users that it did not do that. And finally, the FTC noted that lax security policies led to the January 2014 SnapchatDB breach.

Under the terms of the deal, Snapchat had to start a privacy program, agree not to misrepresent just how completely Snapchats disappear, and agree to be monitored for twenty years. While Snapchat did not have to pay any fines at the time, future privacy breaches could cost the company millions in penalties. Many tech companies, like Google and Facebook, have also entered into similar agreements with the FTC due to similar issues.

As all of this was happening, Evan appeared on the cover of *Forbes*'s January "30 Under 30" issue. An accompanying article promising "The Inside Story of Snapchat" ran on January 6, just three days after Primack said that Evan should be fired for the hack and refusing to apologize. The article began with an anecdote about Mark Zuckerberg emailing Evan to meet and Evan brashly responding "I'm happy to meet you . . . if you come to me."

Business Insider reporter Alyson Shontell tweeted her summary of the story with a caption, "If you didn't think Spiegel was arrogant before, his email to Mark Zuckerberg will convince you." Evan took to Twitter and replied with screenshots of his emails with Zuckerberg, showing that while he hadn't agreed to rush right up to Facebook, he hadn't played it quite as brashly as the *Forbes* story portrayed:

> Hey Evan,
>
> I'm a big fan of what you're doing with Snapchat. I'd love to meet you and hear your vision and how you're thinking about it sometime. If you're up for it, let me know and we can go for a walk around Facebook HQ one afternoon.
>
> Mark
>
> Thanks :) would be happy to meet—I'll let you know when I make it up to the Bay Area
> Sent from my iPhone

Sounds good. Do you have any trips planned for the rest of this year?

Nothing planned—let's shoot for something in the new year :)

Are you guys based in LA? I'm going to be down there in a couple weeks so I might be able to stop by if you're around then.

Yep, we're here. Let us know when you make it down—hopefully we can conjure up some good weather for you!

Forbes editor Randall Lane was furious and quickly published a retort, "Snapchat's Evan Spiegel and the Antics of a 23-Year-Old Novice," in which he skewered Spiegel: "Bill Gates, Michael Dell and Mark Zuckerberg have proven that you can be in your early 20s and have the wisdom to run a transformative billion-dollar company. Snapchat CEO Evan Spiegel seems intent on proving the opposite."

Many at Snapchat felt the news coverage and media takes were overblown. But many outside the company felt Snapchat, and particularly Evan, were arrogant and needed to be taken down a notch. Evan was quickly learning that after brashly turning down Zuckerberg, Snapchat was going to be under the microscope in the coming year like never before.

CHAPTER EIGHTEEN

THE MORE PERSONAL COMPUTER

FEBRUARY 2014

VENICE, CA

On February 19, 2014, Facebook shocked the world by spending $19 billion to acquire WhatsApp, the company behind its eponymous, free messaging app. It was one of the largest acquisitions in the tech industry's history.

The move both strengthened Facebook and seemed to shut the door on a possible future landing spot if Evan and Bobby did want to sell after all. Snapchat let users message their friends privately and share photos and videos with friends in a feed. Facebook had now spent $19 billion on a messaging company in WhatsApp and another billion on a feed-based social media company in Instagram. Would they want to shell out billions more on a photo-sharing/messaging company in Snapchat?

On the day the deal was announced, WhatsApp cofounder Brian Acton spoke to *Wired*, making it clear that he both despised Snapchat and didn't really seem to understand it:

It's not 100 percent clear to me what's working about Snapchat. Great, teenagers can use it to get laid all day long. I don't care. I'm 42, essentially married with a kid. I don't give a shit about this. I'm not sexting with random strangers. I send the "I love you's" in text. She's sending me photos of our baby. These are memories. It's not clear to me that being goofy with Snapchat necessarily creates that level of intimacy.

Clearly Evan Spiegel only has his pulse on one part of the world. We have a whole wall of stories about people who got to know each other long distance and eventually got married. You're not going to do this over Snapchat. And people want chat histories. They're a permanent testimony of a relationship.

There was no love lost on the Snapchat side of the war either. Bobby emailed Lynton and Evan about the acquisition, noting that it was a "pretty absurd price nonetheless, and indicative that FB is failing to innovate where it matters. WhatsApp is fairly uninteresting too except for their size."

Facing Instagram and WhatsApp united under the giant blue Facebook banners, Evan and Bobby would need to execute swiftly on a clarion vision. Instagram had a captive audience that overlapped significantly with Snapchat's young, North America–centric core user base. WhatsApp was wildly popular in much of the rest of the world, where Snapchat would one day look for growth. The two popular apps, backed by the Facebook empire, were a formidable opponent.

The manner in which Facebook decided WhatsApp's value was equally worrying. In 2013, Facebook acquired a Tel Aviv–based mobile-analytics company called Onavo. Onavo made a free app called Onavo Protect that creates a virtual private network, or VPN, to encrypt internet traffic. Because Onavo Protect handled users' internet traffic, it could create a log of users' action on Facebook's servers; Facebook's product teams could then look at detailed information, like how frequently and for how long people are using specific apps, from this aggregated data. If apps didn't encrypt their data, Facebook could see user behavior as granularly as the number of photos the average user likes per day.

Apple and Google have the ability to monitor user activity in a similar way because they own the mobile platforms in iOS and Android. This is just one of the major advantages that comes with owning the platform, which is why Facebook and Amazon have both tried to make phones. With Onavo, Facebook managed to capture this data advantage without owning the operating system.

From Onavo's data, Facebook saw that WhatsApp was installed on 99 percent of Android phones in Spain; this unique data helped drive its aggressive pursuit of WhatsApp, and promised to inform its acquisitions and product strategy in the future.

Having rejected Facebook's enormous acquisition offer, Evan and Bobby were prepared to blaze their own path to an IPO, keeping Snapchat independent. Evan delivered a speech in January 2014 that showed his grand vision for Snapchat. First, he talked about how Steve Jobs tied man to machine with the creation of the iPhone, letting users bring computers with them wherever they go, tied uniquely to them by a phone number. He argued that this should be called "the more personal computer" era, rather than "post-personal computer" era. Then he unveiled his framework for Snapchat through which everything—acquisitions, new features, and revenue—was developed:

> Internet Everywhere means that our old conception of the world separated into an online and an offline space is no longer relevant. Traditional social media required that we live experiences in the offline world, record those experiences, and then post them online to recreate the experience and talk about it. For example, I go on vacation, take a bunch of pictures, come back home, pick the good ones, post them online, and talk about them with my friends.
>
> This traditional social media view of identity is actually quite radical: you are the sum of your published experience. Otherwise known as: pics or it didn't happen.
>
> Or in the case of Instagram: beautiful pics or it didn't happen AND you're not cool.
>
> This notion of a profile made a lot of sense in the binary experience of online and offline. It was designed to recreate who I am online so that people could interact with me even if I wasn't logged on at that particular moment.

Snapchat relies on Internet Everywhere to provide a totally different experience.

Snapchat says that we are not the sum of everything we have said or done or experienced or published—we are the result. We are who we are today, right now.

We no longer have to capture the "real world" and recreate it online—we simply live and communicate at the same time.

Communication relies on the creation of media and is constrained by the speed at which that media is created and shared. It takes time to package your emotions, feelings, and thoughts into media content like speech, writing, or photography.

Indeed, humans have always used media to understand themselves and share with others. I'll spare you the Gaelic with this translation of Robert Burns, "Oh would some power the gift give us, to see ourselves as others see us."

When I heard that quote, I couldn't help but think of self-portraits. Or for us Millennials: the selfie. Self-portraits help us understand the way that others see us—they represent how we feel, where we are, and what we're doing. They are arguably the most popular form of self-expression.

In the past, lifelike self-portraits took weeks and millions of brush strokes to complete. In the world of Fast + Easy Media Creation, the selfie is immediate. It represents who we are and how we feel—right now.

And until now, the photographic process was far too slow for conversation. But with Fast + Easy Media Creation we are able to communicate through photos, not just communicate around them like we did on social media. When we start communicating through media we light up. It's fun.

The selfie makes sense as the fundamental unit of communication on Snapchat because it marks the transition between digital media as self-expression and digital media as communication.

And this brings us to the importance of ephemerality at the core of conversation.

Snapchat discards content to focus on the feeling that content brings to you, not the way that content looks. This is a conservative idea, the natural response to radical transparency that restores integrity and context to conversation.

Snapchat sets expectations around conversation that mirror the expectations we have when we're talking in person.

That's what Snapchat is all about. Talking through content, not around it. With friends, not strangers. Identity tied to now, today. Room for growth, emotional risk, expression, mistakes, room for you.

If 2011–13 was when Evan managed to turn down a three-billion-dollar offer, 2013 onward would need to be a lesson in how to make that a smart decision. Evan, Bobby, and their little team built a wildly popular app worthy of a three-billion-dollar offer. Evan had the vision for what differentiated Snapchat and why its core philosophy was unique. He believed a radical shift was taking place, from permanent posts and profiles to a new world where impermanence and ephemerality allowed users to be their true selves at any point in time. By making everything delete by default, users would post more personal content, and Snapchat would rule this new kingdom. Now, Evan and Team Snapchat needed to execute on both their product and their business in order to avoid being relegated to the history books as a footnote of notable foolishness.

Just as he thought at a high level about how to position Snapchat against Facebook, Evan also needed to understand more about Facebook's business and its path moving forward. Snapchat was incredibly popular, but Evan and Bobby wanted to build it into a real business. To do that, they wanted to know what their main competitor's potential weaknesses were and how well positioned they were to strike.

Evan wasn't an expert in this, so he befriended an expert. In April, Evan received advice from Anthony Noto, the co-head of Goldman Sachs's Global Tech, Media, and Telecom Investment Banking division, and an expert on the way Wall Street valued social media companies. A few months after emailing Evan, Noto joined Twitter as chief financial officer.

On April 24, Noto emailed Evan to discuss Facebook's future prospects. Facebook could tell Snapchat a lot about the mobile advertising market and what lay ahead for Snapchat. Noto explained that Facebook ad impressions had declined year over year but were offset by revenue per impression increasing. Ad impressions were declining because people were increasingly accessing Facebook on their smartphones, which had less space for ads than desktops.

Noto explained that although ad impressions were declining, mobile ads were earning more than desktop ads. Because Snapchat only exists on mobile, the question of why mobile monetizes better than desktop was enormously important to the company. Noto wondered aloud whether this was due to higher prices per click (the amount an advertiser pays when a user taps on an ad) or higher clickthrough rates (the rate at which users actually tap on said ad). This was a crucial question—were advertisers spending in a manner that was likely to continue and lead to long-term value or were they merely trying out a new ad format and then abandoning it? Noto explained that if the cause was to achieve higher clickthrough rates, this would be very positive for Snapchat, as higher clickthrough rates are highly correlated with better ROI, which leads to ad spending.

Next, Noto expanded upon this idea of higher clickthrough rates, noting that if this was driving spending on ads, it bodes well for all companies that focus on mobile advertising.

> If ads on mobile are more engaging for the consumer and more relevant than desktop ads then the addressable ad market for mobile will be bigger than desktop ad market and the valuations of mobile companies will be greater than desktop, all else equal on audience, size. . . .
>
> If Facebook knows this to be true it would result in them being willing to pay higher valuations for mobile companies than other acquirers because Google won't know nor will Yahoo Microsoft etc. because none of them have the scale in mobile to understand these powerful secular trends and in essence they undervalue mobile vs FB, and thus under invest and fall farther and farther behind.

Noto finally commented on Facebook's mobile user growth, noting that its number of monthly active users on mobile grew 34 percent year-over-year to 1 billion, and positing that it was a "remarkable and a clear indication that Facebook is still in early days on mobile penetration and there is a lot more room for growth in mobile MAUs for everyone in mobile. This is great news for Snapchat as you are mobile first and mobile only and if the user base on mobile is bigger than desktop (which I think it is by a magnitude or more) then you will be valued more favorably than before in absolute terms, and long term at scale you will be more valuable than desktop companies at scale."

Facebook's success boded well for Snapchat in absolute terms—the two companies were playing in a highly lucrative and growing market. Snapchat was an addicting, high-frequency app in a very attractive mobile market that was looking better and better by the day. To capitalize on this, Evan set out to raise more money to spend on new hires and acquisitions.

Between Evan's desire to challenge conventional wisdom and his bad experience with Lightspeed, he didn't see the value in raising venture capital the traditional way just because that's what everyone else did. Typically, startup CEOs would set out to raise a certain amount of money at a target valuation, both within reasonably narrow ranges. They'd talk to a number of venture capitalists and other backers, see who was interested, get all the investors on the same page for the same valuation, and close the round at a certain date. They would raise these rounds every six to twenty-four months (provided they stayed in business that long).

Evan and Snapchat were frequently able to raise funds on favorable terms because the company was doing extremely well with user growth and retention. They were also riding a major wave in the broader startup ecosystem that my former boss called the "steroid era," an homage to the 1990s and early 2000s in baseball when seemingly every player had inflated stats and was hitting every baseball for a home run (mostly because they were taking performance-enhancing drugs).

From 2014 to 2016, Snapchat, which had already raised roughly $150 million, raised an additional $2.485 billion from private markets. Uber tapped the private markets for over $14 billion over that period. By comparison, Amazon went public just three years after its founding, in a 1997 IPO that raised $54 million (valuing it at $438 million). Google's

2004 IPO, which came six years after its founding, raised just $1.67 billion (valuing it at $23 billion). Facebook went public eight years after Zuckerberg started it, at a $110 billion market cap.

In 2014 alone, Snapchat raised almost $500 million from investors, helping it to offset the $128 million it was in the red for that year. Tech startups were staying private for longer and were raising far more private capital with less oversight and scrutiny. This let Evan build his empire in secret.

CHAPTER NINETEEN

SNAPCHAT EVERYWHERE

MARCH 2014

VENICE, CA

In 2012, Snapchat had fewer than ten employees; in 2013, the number jumped to thirty. In 2014, it would soar past one hundred, and Evan and Bobby needed to put more structure in place.

Part-time jobs that were once done by a full-time person (in addition to their other responsibilities) were now handled by small teams. Entire new divisions sprung up as the team created new features and expanded supporting functions like HR. Evan and Bobby worked hard to align the culture and org chart with their strategy. Evan still liked to have his hands on every feature the company shipped, even as the pace of releases dramatically increased in 2014.

Snapchat employees are very loyal to the company and to Evan. While many think he is too stubborn and can be too hands-on, they admit that he is usually right about strategic and product decisions. If you look at the sum of major decisions Evan has made, from rejecting acquisition offers to introducing features, he has been right far more than he has been wrong. More importantly, when Evan's been wrong, the errors have been fairly minor, and they were corrected quickly. But when he's been right—rejecting Facebook twice, Snapchat Stories, and Live Stories come to mind—he's been right in a big way. And while it's frustrating for employees to have their features rejected because they don't load fast enough on Evan's phone or he doesn't like the look of something, most believe he's looking out for the best interests of Snapchat's users.

Evan strongly opposes running tests on users and collecting data to make decisions. Like Land and Jobs before him, he believes Snapchat should creatively think of what people will want next, then build that. He believes data, focus groups, and market research cannot successfully deliver an innovative leap large enough to meet his goals for Snapchat.

Snapchat exec Sriram Krishnan later wrote about this Snapchat core belief after leaving the company, explaining how most companies measure a proxy metric for actual human behavior, since the latter is nearly impossible to measure perfectly.

> You convert a nebulous human emotion/behavior to a quantifiable metric you can align execution on and stick on a graph and measure teams on. Engineers and data scientists can't do anything with "this makes people feel warm and fuzzy." They can do a lot with "this feature improves metric X by 5% week-over-week." Figuring out the connection between the two is often the art and science of product management.

Krishnan explained how these metrics often have unforeseen side effects, as people focus on simply making the metric increase, but not in the way the original system designers intended:

> For example, in terms of what designers wanted, what they built/measured and what they unintentionally caused:
>   Quality journalism→Measure Clicks→Creation of click-bait content

Marissa Mayer once tested forty-one different shades of blue on Google users to see which one would be most effective. Product managers at Facebook and Twitter regularly run tests on users to decide which feature or design they should roll out. "Data wins arguments" is a frequent mantra around Silicon Valley.

Unlike at most tech companies, engineers aren't rock stars at Snapchat. The designers are. Evan, a product design major, ran the design team as a flat team of twenty until 2016, when they began reporting to new VP of Product Tom Conrad. This small, tight-knit team is the core of Snapchat, with the most responsibility and the closest proximity to the leader. The design team works out of a secretive, unmarked office on Abbott Kinney Boulevard in Venice. Evan works out of that office a couple days a week, keeping the design team informed of the happenings of the company and working on product issues. Designers will jam on ideas with Evan, and he'll get deep in the weeds product-wise, often staying with designers until one or two in the morning in order to get a feature to display the right way. Evan's energy was infectious to the rest of the design team as they threw themselves into new products.

On many projects, designers simply tell engineers what they want them to build rather than collaborating together to decide what they should create. Many product designers function more like product managers—a well-named role that essentially gives the person domain over a team and specific product. At many tech companies, product managers come from an engineering background rather than a design one.

The engineering team was organized around products. Team Snapchat was growing so quickly that it was in a near-constant state of flux, but the core engineering teams consisted of camera, monetization, identity, security, broadcast, and messaging. There were also smaller groups, like engineering support, and a few subgroups, like a data team that was under monetization, and acquisitions that were allowed to remain independent under another group's umbrella. Tim Sehn, Snapchat's head of engineering, had a weekly meeting with each engineering sub-team rather than the entire engineering team at once.

The biggest and fastest growing team was monetization, a very broad team that handled anything Snapchat could use to make money. The messaging team worked on the actual process behind sending Snapchat photos, videos, and the chat product to make it the best possible way to communicate with friends. The broadcast team handled Snapchat Stories. The identity team focused on users' little profiles and created gamification features like emojis next to a friend's name that denoted if they were your "best friend" on Snapchat (based on who you snapped the most) or how many consecutive days you two had a "streak" (sending Snapchats back and forth).

The camera team focused on making Snapchat "the world's camera" by adding enhancements like zooming on video and fun creative tools. Their goal was to make users choose Snapchat as their default camera over the iOS and Android standard cameras (or any other camera).

Armed with a vision and a war chest, Evan made three key acquisitions in 2014. One was for the "right now," one was for the medium future, and one was a moonshot for the distant future.

Many tech companies "acquihire" startups—that is, they pay out a small but still typically multimillion-dollar figure to acquire a startup whose technology and product they have no intention of using; they simply want to hire the talented people at that startup. Evan had no interest in acquihires. If Snapchat was going to shell out cash for a company, it was going to use their product. Evan and Bobby leaned on a pair of longtime members of their Snapchat inner circle for help with acquisitions: Steve Hwang, who joined Snapchat from Cooley, one of Snapchat's law firms, and Dena Gallucci, who started working with Evan on Future Freshman and joined Snapchat back in 2012.

Evan was also fairly stingy with the purse strings. In the fall of 2014, Evan visited the anonymous messaging app Secret during their retreat in Las Vegas. A lot of bright people in Silicon Valley at the time believed anonymous apps, like Secret, the college-targeted Yik Yak, and the even younger-skewing app Whisper, would be the next wave of big social trends. In many ways, anonymous apps were similar to impermanent ones, as they thrived by rejecting the identity and permanence of Facebook and other entrenched social networks. But it was much harder to build a long-lasting community when everyone was anonymous. Evan didn't want to pay more than $60 million for Secret, which had been valued at $120 million, so a deal was never reached. Less than a year later, Secret shut down.

In April 2014, Evan set his sights on a startup that Snapchat needed immediately, spending $30 million to acquire AddLive, a company that provided the backend infrastructure for a high-quality video chat.

In early 2013, Evan and the small Snapchat team started talking about what a Snapchat phone would look like; not a hardware device, but the core features of a phone: messaging and calling. Evan had been an instant-messaging addict in high school and yearned for the early days of instant messaging when both people were engaged in the conversation, online at the same time and typing back replies instantaneously. As instant messaging moved from AIM and other desktop apps to mobile texting, it became more transactional and moved farther and farther from how people talked in real life.

By not allowing users to message unless they were sending photos or videos, Snapchat had taught users to communicate through media rather than around it. Photos became both the medium and the message. Users could send pictures back and forth with tons of context, feeling as though they were hanging out in the same room and offering friends a window into their present lives. Adding video chat to Snapchat would take that a step further and make it even more powerful.

"What does a phone look like without a ringer?" Evan later said to a reporter. "The biggest constraint of the next 100 years of computing is the idea of metaphors."

Evan challenged his team to think beyond mere comparisons to other video-chat apps like FaceTime and to simply think about how friends should hang out through Snapchat, with its focus on impermanence and fun. For many young people, Snapchat had replaced a series of text messages asking a friend what they were doing and then receiving a description in response. What if Snapchat could replace the action of picking up a phone, dialing a friend, and connecting, and just cut right to the core idea behind those actions—I want to talk with my friend.

On May 1, 2014, Snapchat rolled out a new update to users, letting them text and video call each other. Once you left a conversation, the messages disappeared (although you could tap to save them in the thread). Users could decide whether to let any Snapchat user who added them message them, or restrict it to only people who they mutually added as a Snapchat friend. Video calls were not placed like normal; rather, if both friends were in a chat thread simultaneously, a small circle would glow blue. If you pressed and held that button, you would start sending a video chat to your friend. They did not have to pick up or decline your call—they would immediately start seeing your video stream. They could hold their blue button to join your call, just watch your end of the call, or leave the chat to end your call.

Once you lifted your finger off the screen, your video chat ended—similar to how lifting your finger stopped recording a video or stopped a friend's Snapchat or story from playing. Holding your finger on the bottom half of the screen used your front-facing camera to send your friend a video chat of your face; moving it up to the top half flipped around to use the front camera to show them where you were. These features and the design were natural and intuitive for longtime Snap-chatters who only had to grow accustomed to one new thing at a time—they went from pictures only to video to Stories to messaging, and more and more got baked into the product. But these functions were much more confusing for people who joined later, as everything got dumped on them at once.

Snapchat notifications didn't differentiate between a photo Snap, video Snap, or text message—a universal notification simply appeared that your friend had sent you a Snapchat. This uniformity and users' learned behaviors helped keep the emphasis on communicating through photos and videos.

While AddLive and Snapchat's new chat feature led existing users to be more active on Snapchat, Evan found another app that would help users add friends—and potentially much more. In September 2014, Snapchat paid $50 million to acquire Scan, a Provo, Utah, startup that specialized in QR code (a type of barcode) scanning.

Garrett Gee started Scan as a student project at Brigham Young University, where he captained the varsity soccer team. Gee, Kirk Ouimet, and Ben Turley became obsessed with QR code scanners and the idea of using your smartphone to interact with the physical world. But every QR code scanner they had downloaded and used was terrible.

So they built Scan, a simple, intuitive way to use your phone as a remote control for the physical world. Users could hover over an advertisement and pull up a one-pager on a product and purchase it. People could create their own QR code for their website or social media accounts. When the three founders were at a party at BYU, someone mentioned they had cracked twenty-seven downloads. That seemed nice, but not very spectacular, until they realized he meant twenty-seven *thousand* downloads.

Scan's intuitive name and design prompted millions of downloads. In February 2014, Gee appeared on ABC's *Shark Tank*, where entrepreneurs pitch their startups to a panel of expert investors, including billionaire Mark Cuban. *Shark Tank* prohibited contestants from displaying URLs on camera but allowed Scan to use a big presentation board featuring a QR code for a demonstration. Before the show aired, Gee changed the end address that the QR code would lead to from a dummy URL that they'd used for filming to Scan's Instagram page. While Scan ultimately did not receive funding from the Sharks, over three thousand people watching the show scanned the QR code, hundreds of whom followed their Instagram.

A little over a year later, Gee was in Hawaii when Evan reached out to him about bringing Scan into the fold. He hopped on a flight to LA, met Evan on the beach in Venice, and explained his vision of using Scan to bridge the physical and digital worlds. They quickly struck a deal for $50 million. After selling the company, Gee, his wife, and their two young children sold most of their belongings and started traveling the world together, living out of two backpacks and two carry-on bags and posting about the adventure on their blog, The Bucket List Family.

Snapchat quickly incorporated Scan's QR scanning feature to make it very easy for users to scan each other's codes to add someone as a friend. The Snapcodes, as they were called, were reminiscent of Black-Berry Messenger (BBM), where you could hold your phone over a friend's BlackBerry and instantly become BBM contacts. This was another of the team's great talents—taking an old technology or feature that had fallen out of fashion and making it cool again. The earliest versions of Snapchat had a public list of your top three friends akin to a Myspace top-friends panel.

Snapchat is working on way to use Scan to realize its vision of bridging the digital and physical world. In its vision, you would tap on the barcode or QR code of an item in a store—say, a book like this one—and instantly receive a short page of information on it. You could learn more about the item and even buy it, potentially from Snapchat or through partners like Amazon.

In March 2014, Evan rolled the dice on a company that had a chance to be a true game-changer for Snapchat. Snapchat paid $15 million to acquire a small hardware startup called Vergence Labs. Vergence made a Google Glass–like product they called Epiphany Eyewear that could record video and upload it to a computer.

Erick Miller had begun working on the idea while studying for his MBA at UCLA in 2011; he was initially working on a set of virtual reality goggles, but when Google Glass was announced, he realized he could make something more fashion-forward that wasn't as awkward to use and look at. Although Miller raised $70,000 on Indiegogo (a popular crowdfunding platform), he was still remarkably persistent in searching for funding, often walking around outside Facebook's campus trying to catch Mark Zuckerberg walking to his car to pitch him.

While researching other projects on crowdfunding platforms, Miller ran across Jon Rodriguez, a Stanford student who was looking to build virtual reality hardware and software for x-ray vision. Miller convinced Rodriguez to team up with him on Vergence Labs. When they eventually sold the company to Snapchat, it was a reunion of sorts, as Rodriguez had lived with Evan (and Reggie) in the Donner dorm at Stanford back in their freshman year.

Evan set up a new division of the company, dubbed Snap Lab, and filled it with the ex-Vergence team and engineers with experience working on computer vision, gaze tracking, and speech recognition. Over the next year, Snapchat recruited a dozen wearable technology experts, industrial designers, and people with experience in the fashion industry. Members of the Snap Lab team took frequent trips to Shenzhen, China, to prepare a potential supply chain for a Snapchat hardware product.

Snapchat never announces its acquisitions. One day the startup is fully functioning independently; the next, employees are telling their friends that they are moving to LA and can't say any more. Even in this secretive culture, Snap Labs is particularly notable for its clandestine operations. When Vergence agreed to sell, Miller called their first investor, early Facebook executive Charlie Cheever, and said, "We sold the company. We can't tell you who. You'll get a check in the mail."

The division's future depended just as much on its technical progress as it did on Evan's evolving view of wearable technology. In September 2013, Evan spoke at the TechCrunch Disrupt conference, when Google Glass was near the height of its hype; he said Snapchat was not even considering building an app for Google Glass, saying it felt "invasive," like "a gun pointed at you." It remained to be seen if Vergence would ever launch a real product into the world or just stay hidden as an internal Snapchat experiment.

CHAPTER TWENTY

GOODBYE REGGIE

MAY 2014
RIO DE JANEIRO,
BRAZIL

luau fucking raged.

Thanks to all of you.

Hope at least six girls sucked your dicks last night. Cuz that didn't happen for me.

Thanks again for everything.

Champions.

Fuckbitchesgetleid

Spiegel

I n May 2014, someone leaked thirteen emails Evan had written to his fraternity brothers in his freshman and sophomore years in 2009 and 2010. Worse, they had leaked the emails to Valleywag, a Gawker blog whose mission was to poke fun at Silicon Valley. The emails, nearly all of which were sent when Evan was heavily intoxicated, seemed to confirm the worst caricature of Evan as an obnoxious frat bro.

Another message read:

> do not touch the stripper pole inside
>
> its going to live in the house for a few days while I try to figure out how to save it.

None of us would want our college missives released, but these were truly horrifying, ranging from merely idiotic to downright homophobic and misogynist. The leak was devastating for Evan's public image at a time when he was trying to build Snapchat into a serious, respectable company.

Evan and Bobby scrambled to respond. Evan was in Brazil preparing for a special content project Snapchat was working on for the Summer Olympics that were quickly approaching. Evan's main confidant on the board, Michael Lynton, was several time zones away in Tokyo. As they did during the hacking scandal, media pundits again called for Evan to be fired. Some wondered aloud how many companies would be willing to advertise with Snapchat or how many high-powered women would be willing to serve on the company's all-male board given Evan's comments.

The Washington Post's Jena McGregor tied Evan's emails to wider industry problems in a column titled "Snapchat, Sexism and the Reason Women Don't Stay in Tech."

"I'm obviously mortified and embarrassed that my idiotic emails during my fraternity days were made public," Evan eventually said in a statement to the press. "I have no excuse. I'm sorry I wrote them at the time and I was a jerk to have written them. They in no way reflect who I am today or my views towards women."

Jordan Crook, my former *TechCrunch* colleague, responded in a piece dubbed, "Confirmed: Snapchat's Evan Spiegel Is Kind of an Ass": "He's right to be embarrassed, the emails display the worst of the 'bro' mentality that continues to contribute to the marginalization of women in Silicon Valley."

"I think he needs to go a lot further than just apologizing and I think he needs to step down," online reputation consultant Eric Schiffer said to Bloomberg. "Is a Coca-Cola or a Procter & Gamble or a Pepsi, which has a female CEO, going to want to put millions of dollars into a company when the senior leader talks about women like cattle?"

Two days later, Stanford provost John Etchemendy emailed the entire student body, saying, "Like most of you, male and female, I found those messages abhorrent. I am writing now to convey clearly that the sentiments expressed in these emails do not reflect what we, as members of the Stanford community, expect of one another."

Evan had gone from the sterling example of a bright young Stanford student striking it big with an original idea to a looked-down-upon outcast.

Many people I spoke to for this book went out of their way to explain that the emails don't reflect who Evan is now. As a freshman and sophomore in the fraternity, Evan was constantly planning outlandish parties and writing ridiculous event descriptions trying to one-up his friends and his past efforts. Immature and superficial, he was trying to get attention in the worst way. Many say he has matured and grown since writing those emails as a nineteen-year-old. But he still wrote those emails. Unlike a Snapchat, the emails can't be erased, and Evan's own words stain his reputation.

◉

The email leak and Reggie's ongoing lawsuit combined to pose a major distraction to Evan and the Snapchat team. It was quickly becoming clear that Snapchat needed to settle the suit with Reggie at almost any cost just so they could move on and focus on more important issues.

Since he filed his lawsuit, Reggie had changed his mind about law school and ended up attending a master's of management studies program at Duke University. In June 2013, he began a one-year master's program that covered most of the first-year core classes of an MBA. He was still the same old personable, affable Reggie, making friends in his sections and camping out to get tickets to the Duke men's basketball team's games.

While his classmates would sometimes take Snapchats of each other falling asleep in class or making silly faces, Reggie never told anyone of his involvement with the company. His classmates found out through the grapevine, though, and word quickly spread through the program.

When he wasn't in class, Reggie was working with James Lee and his legal team on his ongoing lawsuit.

The two sides failed to reach a settlement in several conferences during the spring and summer, and for a while it looked like the case could go to a trial by jury. This outcome would surely drag things out longer and could get much uglier. Each side had released a lot of incriminating evidence about the other party throughout various filings and motions. And each side had plenty of dry powder left in the cannons. The lawsuit was also a major distraction to Evan, Bobby, and Snapchat, during a time when they needed to focus more than ever.

Finally, they reached a settlement. Reggie would receive $157.5 million and sign a gag order to never speak about Snapchat, the founding, or the lawsuit. Snapchat would acknowledge Reggie's contributions to the company.

Like Facebook's multiple lawsuits with the Winklevoss twins and Eduardo Saverin, it's difficult to neatly arrange the characters into winner and loser columns. Reggie Brown likely could not have built Snapchat into the multibillion-dollar company it is today. But he did not simply toss an idea out there for anyone to take—he recruited Evan, the best person he knew for the task, to join him and start the company. So what is fair for each side to receive? Snapchat's valuation soared so high and so quickly during the lawsuit that it was hard for each side to wrap their heads around it, let alone arbitrate what each side deserved.

This question isn't going away. *The Social Network*, featuring courtroom scene after courtroom scene of friends hurling accusations at each other through expensive lawyers, spurred scores of young college students to pursue startups. Evan's massive success with Snapchat has only increased the startup fervor on Stanford's campus. And Reggie's lawyers' firm, Lee Tran & Liang, has become the hot law firm for ousted startup cofounders to sue young tech companies.

In some ways, these lawsuits seem structural and inevitable: companies like Snapchat start on college campuses as part-time projects and change rapidly from a half-baked idea to a startup with real potential. There are dramatic differences in the talent of team members and the effort individual people are putting in while balancing school and other commitments. At first, they begin as silly, light projects between friends.

But when there are millions of dollars at stake, people sue each other. And friendships are quickly thrown aside.

◉

On September 9, 2014, Snapchat put out a press release about the settlement, writing, "Reggie Brown originally came up with the idea of creating an application for sending disappearing picture messages while he was a student at Stanford University. He then collaborated with Spiegel and Murphy on the development of Snapchat during its early and most formative days." The company buried the news, releasing it one minute before Apple kicked off its live event announcing the Apple Watch and iPhone 6 and 6 Plus.

Three years after being kicked out of Picaboo and eighteen months after suing Snapchat, Reggie finally settled with his old friends and was formally recognized by the company.

The release included a quote from Evan, stating, "We are pleased that we have been able to resolve this matter in a manner that is satisfactory to Mr. Brown and the company. We acknowledge Reggie's contribution to the creation of Snapchat and appreciate his work in getting the application off the ground."

SNAPCHAT LIVE!

JUNE 2014
MENLO PARK, CA

Eighteen months after Poke cratered, Facebook had not given up. Its new app, Slingshot, took another crack at copying Snapchat, with a slight twist. It forced users to send back a photo to the sender in order to unlock the picture they had received. This would ideally create a virtuous cycle in which people sent each other picture after picture in order to see what the other person was sending.

Again, Facebook's effort failed. The forced reply meant that people had to try to react to pictures before they saw them, or simply send an irrelevant photo. It wasn't a fun, organic conversation like Snapchat, but a weird, forced Facebook game. Six months later, Facebook released a new version of Slingshot that copied Snapchat's Stories feature; it also showed reactions to those Stories in a feed. Like the previous version of Slingshot, it failed. Facebook continually tried to copy Snapchat features without understanding the Snapchat community and why users were obsessed with the app's focus on impermanence.

In order to understand why Facebook failed to copy Snapchat, it's helpful to look back at Poke. On November 8, 2012, more than a month before Facebook launched Poke, Snapchat filed a patent: "Apparatus and method for single action control of social network profile access." The patent describes the way users view content in Snapchat Stories, which only shows you content you haven't seen yet (e.g., if you post a breakfast photo, an afternoon photo at the park, and an evening video from a bar, and I've already seen the breakfast photo, when I tap your story later on, I only see the latter two).

So when Facebook was gearing up to build a clone of the disappearing photo and video messenger, Snapchat was thinking ahead with Stories. Within a year, Stories passed Snapchat messages for daily views as users watched more than a billion Snapchat Stories per day. And on the same day that Facebook launched Slingshot, Snapchat added a new dimension to Stories that made the app an even greater hit.

In the spring of 2014, the illusionist David Blaine visited Snapchat's offices in Venice. Snapchat's head of content, Nick Bell, thought he might be able to figure out Blaine's magic if he watched all his colleague's Snapchat Stories, and was thus able to see the performance from dozens of different angles. This idea, which closely aligned with a product Snapchat had been working on internally, ended up being much more valuable than cracking Blaine's secrets. An individual's Snapchat Story showed their life from their point of view. But a group story, if done around a collective event like a concert or game, could show an engaging, interesting evening from everyone's point of view. Or, better yet, from the very best points of view. Instead of My Story, it would be Our Story.

And so, Emily White, Evan, and the rest of the team headed to Las Vegas for Electric Daisy Carnival (EDC), an electric dance music festival, to oversee Snapchat's first foray into content with Our Story.

Any one of the 140,000 at the Las Vegas Motor Speedway for EDC could add to Our Story. Snapchat set up a geographic "fence" around the festival grounds so that only people inside had the option to add to the story. Users would take Snapchats the way they normally would, and then choose whether to add the content to their individual story or to the communal Our Story.

Users who added the friend "EDC Live" could watch the event unfold via Snapchat. Unlike clicking through a photo album or searching a hashtag, all of the content was submitted by people physically at the event, and it was curated for users in a tight narrative by Snapchat employees. Over 100,000 people watched the first Our Story from the Electric Daisy Carnival. The format was unlike any other coverage of a live event, especially a music festival. All of the coverage came from first-person accounts on smartphones, so it had a very real, raw aesthetic; but the story was curated to show only the best videos, from the best angles, and often with backstage or other special access. This combination offered users the best of both worlds. Snapchat had once again caught lightning in a bottle.

Users would need to be told what they were watching, though. Snapchat didn't use much text on the screen, so it wouldn't just show a little text box denoting where a story was happening. No, this would be like a TV broadcast on your phone, complete with overlays giving you added context like location.

After snapping a photo or video, users could swipe right on their phones to add geofilters, small graphic stickers that display users' locations. Geofilters could pop up for events, like Coachella, to show Our Story viewers what they were watching. But soon Snapchat released permanent ones. The initial geofilters started in neighborhoods in New York and Los Angeles, as well as unique spots like SoulCycle and Disneyland. The latter two weren't paid advertisements, but they quickly let everyone see what geofilters could grow into as a business.

Over the next six months, Snapchat designers added geofilters for neighborhoods, cities, college campuses, coffee shops—there was even one at Facebook's campus in Menlo Park: a Ghostface Chillah logo pointing and laughing. Snapchat then opened geofilters up to anyone who wanted to make one. Users submitted designs for their schools, neighborhoods, favorite hangouts, and Snapchat vetted them and added them to the appropriate location. The unique visual stickers stuck out much more than a simple text location on an Instagram photo, and let users brag to their friends about the exotic places they were traveling to—or bemoan the opposite. Geofilters built upon and expanded Snapchat Stories's feeling of ambient awareness of where your friends were. Previously you would squint to recognize the skyline or some other detail grounding where your friend was. Now you could identify their location with an alluring headline.

As geofilters caught on, Snapchat's Our Story picked up steam as well. The two built off one another's momentum; users watched Our Story, became educated about geofilters, and used them more in their own snaps and stories. Snapchat then invested more resources in creating more Our Story programming. Our Story expanded to daily college campus and city stories, which you could only watch if you were at those locations, and global stories covering sports games, concerts, and other events. Snapchat renamed it to Live Stories, as all the content had been shot within the previous twenty-four hours, giving it an almost-live feeling. Snapchat figured out a way to take an age-old question—What is happening around me?—and reinvent the medium in a gripping, addictive way.

The college stories became a twenty-four-hour billboard on campus, showing everything funny, interesting, and dramatic happening on certain college campuses. Snapchat communicated with students through geofilters, encouraging them to post to the campus story and telling them when the stories would stop running as classes ended for holidays. Students would post each other stranded outside their dorms during a late-night fire drill or goofing off in the library while studying for midterm exams. Getting featured on the Live Story meant fifteen minutes—err, seconds—of campus fame.

And of course, college students used Live Stories plenty for flirting. At the University of Wisconsin, a twenty-two-year-old senior named Abby posted a video of herself in the library—complete with a "Memorial Library" geofilter—saying, "Guy wearing the Vikings jersey on the U-Dub Snap Story, I am seriously in love with you. Find me!" The guy in the Vikings jersey responded, and "Mystery Girl" and "Vikings Fan" started communicating through the campus-wide Snapchat story. Their classmates started posting videos all over campus cheering them on, hoping they would meet, and chiming in on the drama. Snapchat created a geofilter, "Help Vikings Fan Find Mystery Girl" to cover the campus phenomenon. Finally, happy ending, the pair met up at a campus bar, the Kollege Klub or, the "KK."

City stories featured young college graduates and summer interns adjusting to life in the big city, typically in New York and Los Angeles. All the stories tried to follow a narrative arc. They might begin with someone grabbing coffee or running early in the morning, progressing through office hijinks, and ending with a sunset or evening drinks and shenanigans. Most stories were only a few minutes long, but they were packed with original content, as each individual Snapchat was ten seconds or shorter.

These daily stories were only available to other people in that same city, but Snapchat also published city stories about specific places like Reykjavik, Iceland, and Nairobi, Kenya. These one-off stories let anyone in the world watch and vicariously travel to that city for a day through Snapchat. They also displayed just how far and wide Snapchat had spread and let young people around the world peer into each other's lives. Students could still Snapchat each other during free periods at Crossroads—but now they could also take a minute and see what a Wednesday looked like in Riyadh, Saudi Arabia.

To ring in the New Year at the start of 2015, Snapchat did a global Live Story that let users contribute from cities around the world like Dubai, New York, and St. Petersburg, Russia. As usual, anyone with Snapchat could watch the story. But the company also broadcast the story on video screens in Times Square, so revelers could watch it (and, presumably, download Snapchat) while waiting for the ball to drop.

Live Stories was an incredibly rich way of telling a story: the very best first-person, on-the-ground accounts, curated into an entertaining narrative. And users loved it—millions started regularly tuning in to watch. Most impressive about Live Stories is that Snapchat itself created it. Twitter users created the hashtag, and users on both YouTube and Twitter had a major impact on the platform's aesthetics. But Snapchat and its content team created Live and the medium's vibe.

Chloe Drimal, the Yale graduate who Evan hired after reading her column about Snapchat, was tasked with heading the Live Stories team. Drimal and Evan quickly became close colleagues and even friends, frequently walking around Venice together discussing the future of Live Stories, and the company more broadly. Evan rarely interacted with the content team as a whole, preferring to spend time with Drimal and Nick Bell and then letting them run their departments. Occasionally, Evan would share parts of his high-level vision with the entire department.

Drimal assembled a small team whose members had a deep background in film production and narrative storytelling, including stints in movie studios, book publishing houses, and liberal arts colleges' English and film studies departments. Snapchat engineers built the content team a custom backend to manage submissions for Live Stories. Content analysts flagged interesting content first, then came back and rearranged the flagged photos and videos and edited them down to the ones they wanted to use in a Live Story.

Drimal encouraged content analysts to approach Live Stories like a piece of fiction, with a linear chronology and no jarring jumps—if the story needed to get across a college campus or city, Snapchat should show footage of a user walking there or getting on the subway. Analysts typically aimed to add "chapters" of three to four new Snapchats every couple of hours to move the story along at a digestible pace. So if the story covered an awards show like the Emmys, it would start with celebrities getting dressed up and preparing for the big night, then walking the red carpet and mingling, then a few chapters covering the actual show, then A-listers celebrating at the afterparties. If users sent in a snap with no filters over it, the analysts could add a filter over it to give more context; some were simply to show the location, others were custom made for the concert or holiday, and still others were updated to show real-time information like sports scores and election results.

Analysts favored content that was "Snapchatty." Posts that utilized Snapchat's features, like drawing, captions, and geofilters, were favored. Photos and videos that were descriptive and moved the story along or showed a unique aspect would more likely be accepted. Nothing offensive or negative would be allowed; nor would any posts with nudity, drug usage, or smoking (even cigarettes). These behaviors were against the young, healthy, and positive image Snapchat wanted to portray. Drinking would be allowed on stories if it was in a responsible way and the person didn't look underage.

As Live Stories grew, the company broadcast increasingly diverse subject matter, from a Mecca story to covering gay pride parades and celebrations after the Supreme Court legalized gay marriage. The sheer quantity of content, and the department, grew too as Snapchat users ate up all the Live Stories that Snapchat could produce. The early hires

Snapchat's interface circa 2012, when the app's only feature was self-deleting pictures.

Billy Gallagher/TechCrunch

Engineers and early hires Daniel Smith and David Kravitz (top, left to right) celebrated Snapchat's first birthday with cofounders Bobby Murphy and Evan Spiegel (seated, left to right) in September 2012. At the time the team was riding high, as they had just finished building an Android version and were close to adding video messaging. They didn't know that they'd soon face a competitor in Facebook's Poke.

Snap Inc.

Bobby Murphy/Snap Inc.

(Left to right) Daniel Smith and David Kravitz visited Norway with Bobby Murphy and Evan Spiegel in October 2012.Norway was one of the young company's fastest growing markets; the team flew there to learn what was appealing to so many early adopters.

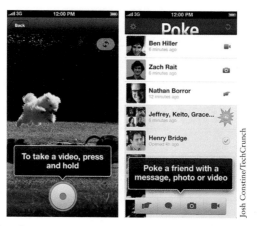

The interface for Facebook's Poke app, released in December 2012, bears an uncanny resemblance to Snapchat. Upon Poke's release, Mark Zuckerberg emailed Evan, writing, "I hope you enjoy Poke." The audio notification for the app featured Zuckerberg's voice saying "Poke."

Snapchat's first real office, a bungalow painted baby blue, spilled out onto the Venice promenade. Not long after they moved there in 2012, Snapchat fans began taking selfies in front of the logo. It quickly became so popular and distracting that Evan and Bobby moved the company—by then struggling to fit inside the house—down the beach to larger, subtler offices. Years later, they bought the house to preserve Snapchat's history.

J Emilio Flores/The New York Times/Redux

Bobby and Evan pose for a *New York Times* profile in Snapchat's new beachfront office in Venice, California, in early 2013. Just weeks before, they had thrown an epic New Year's Eve party in the still-unfurnished office. In the year that followed, they would turn down a multibillion-dollar acquisition from Facebook, get sued by their cofounder, and launch their most important feature, Stories.

Josh Constine/TechCrunch

After failing to copy Snapchat with Poke, Facebook tried again in June 2014 with Slingshot, which required users to send a picture back before they could view photos in their inbox. While this was a more unique spin on ephemerality than Poke, it lacked the conversational nature of Snapchat and also failed to catch on.

Snapchat introduced geofilters, visual overlays showing where a user was, in 2013. They started out in neighborhoods in New York and Los Angeles, as well as unique spots like SoulCycle and Disneyland, but eventually covered locations around the world. The geofilter for Venice, where Snapchat's headquarters is located, was one of the earliest created.

Soon after introducing geofilters, Snapchat designed one of its mascot, Ghostface Chillah, pointing and laughing at Facebook's headquarters in Menlo Park. Snapchat would later post specific geofilters at Uber, Airbnb, and Pinterest's locations, urging their employees to come work at Snapchat.

In December 2015, a shooter killed fourteen people and injured seventeen more in San Bernadino, California. As the tragedy unfolded, Snapchat created a live story, bringing viewers photos and videos from the scene as well as narrative developments and statements from authorities. This potent format, aggregating the best clips from citizen journalists and adding professional narration, led some to believe that Snapchat could be the next big platform for journalists. But the hype was short-lived, as Snapchat decided to favor more lighthearted content.

In January 2016, Republican senator Ted Cruz mocked fellow nominee Donald Trump for skipping the final Republican debate with a geofilter asking, "Where is Ducking Donald?"

Snapchat frequently advertised without using the word "Snapchat." This billboard was part of a March 2016 campaign in select cities around the country showing Snapchat geofilters for different localities.

In May 2016, a 22-year-old University of Wisconsin senior named Abby posted a video from the school's library to its campus Snapchat Live Story, saying, "Guy wearing the Vikings jersey on the U-Dub Snap Story, I am seriously in love with you. Find me!" The guy, dubbed by classmates as "Vikings Fan," responded, and the two started using the Live Story to coordinate a meet-up. Their classmates chimed in with Snapchats of their own, cheering them on and offering color commentary. They finally met at a campus bar, The Kollege Klub.

Evan and his then fiancée, model Miranda Kerr, attended a State Dinner at the White House in May 2016. Two months later, Kerr posted a photo of her engagement ring on Instagram with a Snapchat-owned Bitmoji cartoon laid on top, showing Evan proposing to her. The two married in a small, private ceremony at their home in May 2017.

Snapchat launched a pop-up store in New York, just off Fifth Avenue, in November 2016 to sell their new video-recording sunglasses, Spectacles. The Spectacles logo, set against Snapchat's bright-yellow coloring, loomed behind the picturesque glass box of Apple's flagship store, almost like a watching eye. The pop-up store was a plain, small storefront with a simple sign reading "Spectacles," with no mention of Snapchat.

Fitz Tepper/TechCrunch

After announcing Spectacles in late September 2016, Snapchat made it quite difficult to buy the $130 sunglasses. Prospective buyers had to seek out the location of vending machines called Snapbots, which started in Venice and moved around the country. Even in the New York pop-up store, customers, some of whom waited in line for hours, had to buy the glasses through Snapbots rather than human salespeople.

Business Insider

Longtime Snap employees Dena Gallucci, Nick Bell, and Juan Barrero stand on the floor of the NYSE on Snap's IPO day. $SNAP was priced at $17 a share, but opened at a much loftier $24. Standing nearby on the trading floor, Snapchat CFO Drew Vollero watched the stock jump and exclaimed, "That's crazy!" When the market closed, Snapchat had a market cap of $34 billion, on par with Marriott and Target, although $SNAP would struggle in the months to come.

working under Chloe put in long work weeks, but she quickly needed to bring on a bigger team to keep up with demand.

The team made processes more regimented and started planning out event coverage further in advance. The team was broken down into subgroups depending on the type of events they would cover: sports, life and culture, and entertainment. Designers were assigned to the content team to build specific geofilters and creative assets for Live Stories. Once a month, the team would sit down and plot out the upcoming content calendar: the who, what, when, where, why, and how of covering these stories, from the Oscars to the NBA Finals.

Like an international news channel, Snapchat had to have content up 24/7, and they covered stories all over the globe. This meant that the content team in Venice had to work some strange hours. Employees would come in early on weekends to work on a story and find a group midway through coffees and Snapchats, having started their shift at 2 AM.

Chloe and her early team set the tone for the department, working long hours and exuding passion about the stories but goofing around and still enjoying themselves. Because Snapchat had a series of buildings throughout Venice rather than one contiguous campus, the content team was a ten-minute walk down the Venice boardwalk from the main Snapchat offices—including the cafeteria with amazing food. There was an odd melting pot of cultures happening on the boardwalk and in the alleyways of Venice, as Snapchat security guards, homeless people, software engineers, surfers and locals smoking weed, content analysts, and tourists taking pictures walked among each other.

The content team's buildings were technically zoned as live-work lofts, so Snapchat put a bed in the corner of each building to comply with the codes. The buildings were filled with content analysts typing away at rows of desks covered with Apple desktop monitors. But if anyone asked, there was a bed in the corner, a closet full of clothes, and some pictures on the wall so it looked like someone's home as well. Some of the neighbors weren't too pleased with the thinly veiled operation, and the LA Department of Building and Safety inspected Snapchat's offices after receiving multiple complaints.

New hires started off working on the Live college campus stories, then moved up to the local team, curating city stories. If they did well on local, they would become content analyst leads and would be in charge of covering big stories like the Grammys or the Super Bowl. Chloe recruited students from nearby colleges like UCLA to offer their perspective on college campus stories, and remote workers overseas helped Snapchat translate Live Stories.

As Snapchat became more and more of a household name, content team members started going to events like the Video Music Awards and Grammys to record content for Live Stories. In addition to user-submitted snaps, analysts back in Venice would look at what Snapchat team members were submitting from the red carpet, backstage, and afterparties.

Snapchat had plenty of eyeballs. But the one thing the company still hadn't figured out yet was how to make money.

CHAPTER TWENTY-TWO

"WE NEED TO MAKE MONEY"

OCTOBER 2014
VENICE, CA

In 2012, Evan and Bobby had experimented with various ways to make users pay for add-ons and extra features in Snapchat. After going back and forth on the tradeoffs between focusing on growth and making money, they ultimately decided to focus on growth above all else. Evan continued to discuss plans to generate revenue as Snapchat turned down Facebook's $3 billion acquisition offer; but once again he decided to focus Snapchat's precious resources on product development, building out Stories, Live, and geofilters.

By 2014, Snapchat was burning over $100 million a year and Evan pushed harder to start monetizing the product. Developing Snapchat into an actual business would put the company on a path toward an initial public offering, a major milestone on the way to achieving Evan's dream of becoming the most important tech company in the world. Revenue would let Snapchat invest more in future product development; but a bad revenue scheme would piss off users and could hurt both growth and engagement, so they had to be careful.

Evan and Bobby, with their board members Mitch Lasky and Michael Lynton, first looked to Asian messaging companies like Line and the Tencent-owned WeChat, which make money from sponsored messaging and in-app purchases for virtual goods like stickers and games. WeChat lets users subscribe to brands that message them; Line lets users buy virtual stickers (little cartoon drawings depicting mini scenes and emotions) to share with friends.

In August 2014, Mitch Lasky sent Michael Lynton a note quoting a hedge fund manager about Asian messaging companies as the two Snapchat board members debated possible monetization strategies for Snapchat:

> It's using "online" (in Asia primarily mobile) to access goods and services "offline"—good example in US would be something like Uber. But in Asia it's way way broader. In China people use WeChat to buy stuff like clothes, order food, book travel, pay for taxis, you name it. My partner Matt* calls it "the mobile phone as the remote control for life."
>
> It's an order of magnitude bigger opportunity than advertising and part of the reason I [Mitch Lasky] was so excited about Snapchat's payment experiments.[†] They could be in a unique position to own time-sensitive/ephemeral offers—unsold inventory that expires like tickets to a concert.

Facebook had been positioning Instagram as an advertising property, aligning its crown jewel acquisition with what it did best. Snapchat could potentially lead the way in online-to-offline in the US. In China, people do everything inside one app, WeChat, so operating systems like iOS and Android have much less power. If Snapchat could become a dominant online-to-offline player, it could have much of the platform power that Apple and Google enjoy.

As attractive as this online-to-offline strategy looked in theory, Evan and Bobby weren't convinced that Snapchat users (primarily in North America and Europe) would behave that similarly to Asian

---

* Matt Cohler, the early Facebook employee who now works with Lasky at Benchmark.
[†] More on this later.

messaging companies' users. Part of the reason Snapchat was able to succeed in the first place is that Western users explicitly don't want to use one app for everything. As they shelved the online-to-offline possibility, Evan and Bobby turned their eyes toward advertising on Snapchat.

Evan and Bobby thought of Snapchat as two businesses: communication and entertainment. Messages and Stories played off each other and drove user engagement, with messaging pulling users in via push notifications and stories providing engaging content that users sought out in moments of boredom. Evan and Bobby decided to monetize the two pillars of the app differently.

Communication comprised all messages between friends—photo, video, text, calling, and video chat. For now, they would test the waters with monetizing communication by letting users pay ninety-nine cents to replay a Snapchat message from a friend. Snapchat Stories and Live Stories made up entertainment and sat in a feed similar to Facebook's and Twitter's—albeit one in which everything disappeared in twenty-four hours—which seemed much more suited for advertising. Evan tasked Emily White and Mike Randall with leading Snapchat's charge into advertising. They had to educate advertisers about Snapchat and entice them to invest time, money, and effort into the platform, all without disrupting the user experience on the app.

Despite the wild changes in media formats over the past century, the amount of money spent on advertising has generally remained constant. Although the past hundred years have seen consumers move from the radio to TV to the internet to smartphone apps, the advertising industry has consistently made up about 1.3 percent of US GDP. In the advertising business, the only way to make money is to steal someone else's share of the pie.

In the first quarter of 2016, a Morgan Stanley analyst estimated that for every new dollar spent on online advertising, 85 cents would go to either Google or Facebook. To compete with those tech giants, Snapchat would have to get into targeted direct marketing, which relied on pay-for-performance ads like cost-per-install ads for apps or cost-per-click ads. But Evan found this kind of targeted advertising "creepy," and besides, Snapchat didn't have nearly enough data on its users and their actions to compete with Facebook and Google. While Facebook and Google built their empires by stealing advertising share from print media,

Snapchat would build its fortune by stealing from television. If Snapchat could successfully woo TV advertisers, the company would not have to compete with Facebook and Google for ad dollars.

White and Randall traveled to New York to convince advertisers of Snapchat's potential. There was a steep learning curve during these initial meetings, as the advertisers and marketers were older than Snapchat's core demographic, so they didn't really use the app with friends and didn't fully understand it. But White and Randall had relationships with advertisers from their days at Facebook, so they taught them how Snapchat worked, how to make accounts for themselves and their clients, and encouraged them to play around with it and see how they could envision advertising working on Snapchat.

The biggest selling point of these early Snapchat sales pitches was engagement. Young people were using Snapchat nonstop, all day, every day. In 2014, seventy-one million people were using the app daily; 40 percent of eighteen- to twenty-four-year-olds in the US with a smartphone used Snapchat.

And in a world in which young people had grown accustomed to advertising on websites and other social networks and ignoring ads on the web and TV (often by looking at their phones), Snapchat had teenagers physically holding their finger down on their phone screens. Every engagement on Snapchat was intentional—a user tapped on what they wanted to see and held their finger down while watching it. Snapchat was able to sell valuable advertising real estate because it had a captive audience of millions of young people who are hard to reach.

Snapchat's early ads were very basic and extremely costly compared to peers' ad offerings—they charged advertisers hundreds of thousands of dollars for a very short spot, typically ten to thirty seconds. This was partially done on purpose to be prohibitively expensive and keep demand low, as Snapchat had a small team and was still building its infrastructure, both technically and organizationally. The early ad products offered advertisers very little in data or analytics.

While other tech companies like Facebook and Google gave advertisers a world of information about how people were interacting with their ads and allowed them to target extremely specific groups of people based on intent (e.g., people who searched for garden hoses in the Philadelphia suburbs) or interests (e.g., people aged twenty-two to twenty-four who like both the NFL and Bruce Springsteen), Snapchat simply told advertisers how many people had seen the advertisement. Snapchat was more focused on advertisements being a good experience for their users than the team was on advertisers being satisfied and getting what they needed out of Snapchat ad products. This made for a tough sell with advertisers and limited the early market mostly to major companies that had big budgets and could afford to experiment with this new, hot social company.

White and Randall emphasized to advertisers how Snapchat was unique compared to other social networks. There was so little branding or advertising on the platform that early advertisers would be able to have highly impactful advertisements.

A few companies, most notably Taco Bell, realized Snapchat's potential for marketing early on. Taco Bell had a brand that fit well with the young, unfiltered app's aesthetic, and they were able to build a significant following for free. Users happily added Taco Bell as a friend manually, alongside their real-life friends, giving the company a valuable free advertising channel. But most companies could not entice users to add them as a friend on Snapchat.

Unlike other social companies like Facebook and Twitter, Snapchat did not encourage brands to develop their own organic followings on the app. Facebook and Twitter had previously courted media organizations and businesses to create accounts and pages so users could "like" and "follow" them. In sharp contrast, Evan told reporters he found it annoying when brands tried to act like people on Snapchat by creating an account.

Snapchat only wanted brands on the app if they were paying for ads. Snapchat didn't ban brands from creating their own organic accounts, but they did nothing to help them grow an organic, free following. In one sense, this was good for companies and brands, as they knew exactly what game they were playing with Snapchat, unlike Facebook, Twitter, and others who spent years telling them to grow their followings only to turn around and charge them to have their posts seen by all of their followers. On the other, the game was quite expensive to play.

White and Randall found a fit for Snapchat in brand advertising; brands succeed by building long-lasting loyalty, so that when you're walking through the supermarket, big names like Gillette and Old Spice are on your mind, and that's what ultimately ends up in your cart. Once consumers pick a brand, they offer strong lifetime value to the company because they keep coming back and buying repeatedly. And, importantly for Snapchat, because brand advertising is about repeated impressions on consumers rather than directly moving them toward a click or a purchase, brand advertisers didn't place as much of an emphasis on data and analytics. Brand advertising is also an enormous business, estimated at $578 billion worldwide in 2016.

Traditionally, brand advertising has found its home on TV, where annual global advertising is a $213 billion business. The Super Bowl is the, um, Super Bowl of advertising. But with streaming services, most of which are ad free and more popular than ever, fewer and fewer young people are watching TV. And when they are, they aren't watching the commercials—they're usually fast-forwarding through them on DVR or looking down at their phones during them, if not the entire time they're actually in front of the television. Snapchat offered advertisers a way to reach those young people and know that they're engaged—they would literally be touching the ad onscreen with their finger.

On October 17, Snapchat put up a post on its website, "Advertising on Snapchat," explaining that the company was putting ads next to Stories content for the first time. "It's going to feel a little weird at first, but we're taking the plunge," the company explained. The post continued:

> We won't put advertisements in your personal communication—things like Snaps or Chats. That would be totally rude. We want to see if we can deliver an experience that's fun and informative, the way ads used to be, before they got creepy and targeted.

The first ad was a twenty-second trailer for a horror movie, *Ouija*. It showed up like a friend's story would, and you only had to watch it if you intentionally clicked on it. And you could immediately swipe out and leave it. Millions of Snapchat users voluntarily clicked on the twenty-second trailer.

Advertisers were happy to fill the newest, hottest medium with experimental advertisements. But Snapchat would quickly need to show its effectiveness to earn long-lasting ad spend. Team Snapchat quickly tested different new ad formats. In November, Snapchat rolled advertising into Our Stories, producing a Samsung-branded story for the American Music Awards. The story flitted from user-generated content from the red carpet and audience to behind-the-scenes shots that featured geofilters with Samsung's name or logo attached. The total revenue figures were small, in the low millions, but encouraging.

Meanwhile, Chloe Drimal and Nick Bell continued driving Live Stories forward, signing partnerships to get better behind-the-scenes access. More eyeballs meant more content to potentially pair ads against; and growing user engagement and daily active users meant the advertisements were not deterring Snapchatters. Snapchat signed deals with sports leagues like the National Football League, Major League Baseball, and the NCAA. They worked with *Vanity Fair* to cover the Oscars and the magazine's exclusive afterparty. Some of the deals involved a split of advertising revenue between Snapchat and a partner, while others just allowed Snapchat better access in exchange for better, free coverage. All of the content was still shot via Snapchat on smartphones, never on professional cameras. Snapchat users loved sending in their submissions to Live Stories, hoping their snap got picked for the show; fans sent in almost sixty hours of content for each NFL game during the 2015 season. Some Live Stories for college football games even featured college players themselves posting to Snapchat from the locker rooms.

Live Stories started regularly racking up 10 to 20 million views each. According to Nielsen ratings, the 2015 Oscars averaged 36.6 million views, while *Breaking Bad*'s famous finale averaged 10.3 million views. Over 40 million people watched Snapchat's Live Story from the Coachella music festival over a weekend in April 2015.

Snapchat continued experimenting with ways to monetize the communication side of the app. In November 2014, they rolled out a feature called Snapcash that let users send and receive money from friends. Users simply type out a dollar sign in Snapchat's chat function, and the send button turns green and they can quickly send money.

One of Lasky's partners at Benchmark, Peter Fenton, a Twitter board member, introduced Evan to Square CEO and Twitter cofounder

Jack Dorsey. In May 2013, Dorsey was testing out a new payments feature called Square Cash; he emailed Evan $25, which Evan could easily transfer to his bank account without any signup.

"Okay this is actually genius," Evan wrote to Dorsey.

Evan later said it was "the most fun and exciting product" he had seen in the last few years. He and Dorsey talked more about collaborating, and Square ended up powering Snapcash, saving Snapchat from building out their own payments infrastructure.

But adoption of Snapcash was slow. For the same reason that people used Snapchat as a fun, lightweight way to escape Facebook and the permanence of the Internet, they did not want to give the company—which also had been hacked several times—their credit card information. But Snapcash's failure did not negatively affect users' experience—it was not a major design overhaul or bet-the-company change. Users simply ignored it. And Snapchat was cleverly designed so that it was easy for users to ignore features they didn't like. Because of this, when Snapchat missed, they missed small. That is, misses didn't cost them users. And when they hit, they hit big, with wild successes like Stories and Live.

CHAPTER TWENTY-THREE

BLANK SPACE

JULY 2014

VENICE, CA

Evan Spiegel loves music. If he hadn't founded Snapchat, he may have created a music-related app. Nonetheless, music continued to play a central role in his life inside and outside of Snapchat—who he took meetings with, what marketing campaigns he dreamed up, and even what features he wanted Snapchat to build.

From his days organizing parties for Red Bull to DJing at Kappa Sigma to blasting music at the Snapchat offices, Evan has always loved music. He loves discovering new music, sharing music with friends, and going to concerts and festivals. Many of the early hires at Snapchat are similarly music buffs themselves. But he thinks most of the current music services are nondifferentiated and offer consumers a bad experience. Digital music isn't social in the same way that music is in real life. Evan had a burning desire to fix that.

Steve Jobs changed the music industry forever in the early 2000s with the iPod and iTunes, but music innovation has stagnated since then. Most new entrants, from Pandora to Spotify, are more business model innovations than changes to the actual way people discover, share, and listen to music, not to mention interact with artists. Evan dreamed of picking up the mantle from his idol and improving an industry that meant so much to him. Snapchat was the best idea Evan had come across when he started working on it, but photo sharing was never his passion. But revolutionizing the way people shared and consumed music? That would be a dream come true.

"Music is really appealing to us right now because it has some of the same attributes that communication had when we were working on Snapchat in the beginning," Evan told an audience of USC students. "Right now on your mobile phone, music is largely nondifferentiated, so you usually search for a song and you can play it. It plays from four or five different places, they roughly cost the same, but it's also high frequency. After communication, [music is] the highest frequency behavior on your phone, and so that, in our view, makes it a really interesting opportunity, and it's something that we are thinking about."

Before Snapchat, communication felt undifferentiated—you texted in iMessage or Facebook Messenger or WhatsApp but used largely the same tools in each one. With Snapchat, pictures became the communication medium and delete became the default, which unlocked new behaviors. Evan hoped to create a music app or feature that similarly unlocked new behaviors. And Snapchat was a cultural tastemaker. Evan understood what real, normal users liked and thought was cool, unlike many Silicon Valley tech companies. As an LA company, they could have a comparable advantage in music.

"When we look at the music industry today, a lot of the conversation about music is really about business model and distribution," Evan said on stage at Recode's Code conference. "The transition from a transaction-based model to a subscription-based model, cloud versus download, those are really what I'm hearing about the industry. And we always try to apply the product perspective: What really do people want from music? What's a great album? What makes a great album? So we're really approaching music from . . . is there some music product that's better than a track listing? There's got to be, and I think that's something that we'd be interested in working on."

Evan runs Snapchat in a very top-down fashion, setting the strategic goals for all of his employees to carry out. He wanted to expand the Snapchat empire beyond communication and social media, so he looked at what people spent their time doing and how he could capture some of that time and value. Luckily, what people spent their time doing, listening to music, lined up perfectly with Evan's passion.

Snapchat board member and Sony Entertainment CEO Michael Lynton used his deep music industry connections to set up influential meetings for Evan all over town with, among others, Grammy winner Meghan Trainor, then-Epic Records president L. A. Reid, and Vevo CEO Rio Caraeff. Rock and Roll Hall of Fame member Lou Adler's sons, Manny and Ike Adler, started working for Snapchat running music partnerships after Lynton introduced them.

Then, Evan wanted to either buy or build a record label to discover and invest in upcoming artists. Snapchat could use its product to promote artists that it signed to its label; Evan wanted Snapchat to have some sort of equity or revenue sharing so that it could participate in the upside of the stars it helped launch. After advisors and Lynton told him that wasn't feasible and would distract from Snapchat's core focus, Evan sensibly shelved the idea.

Evan pushed for relentless experimentation at Snapchat. He much prefers toying around with a prototype to watching a power point, so designers and engineers will build five, ten, twenty versions of a chat app and let Evan play with them all to see what he likes. Team Snapchat was constantly building features and products that were never released. If Evan could succeed with a music product, it would have a massive impact on Snapchat, for both users and revenue.

Evan had a team build a Snapchat music product that combined Snapchat's penchant for communicating through media with Evan's vision for how music should work digitally. However, it was never released, likely because the rights to the music were too complex and expensive.

Employees were happy to work tirelessly on Evan's experiments, music or otherwise. Evan's benevolent dictatorship is not uncommon in tech. Many visionaries like Jobs, Elon Musk, and Jeff Bezos have been described in similar, and even more draconian, ways. But Jobs, Musk, and Bezos have accomplished such spectacular achievements that employees will follow them no matter what. Evan seemed to be following right in their footsteps, but we have only seen him at the helm when

Snapchat is thriving and growing spectacularly well. While he obviously deserves the credit for this, every company goes through periods of intense pain and scrutiny. It is during these periods that Evan will need to prove he is worthy of these lofty comparisons.

"I think our team would say that I'm very decisive but I change my mind a lot. Which is sort of a unique combination," Evan once told Recode's Kara Swisher. "But it really means that we care about making decisions really, really quickly, but we care about the flexibility to change our mind, and we want to make sure that is the key component of our business. So someone on our team would be like, 'Give him six hours.'"

Evan's inclination to changing his mind can frustrate employees. While inexperienced, he can be confident to the point of cocky, and many employees believe he is unwilling to accept their input and advice. He is completely unfiltered, loves cursing, and can be extremely blunt when he thinks something is a bad idea.

Evan constantly experimented with music products at Snapchat, some of which were for marketing, some simply for fun, and some as potential features. Snapchat released advertisements for new features like geofilters and Live Story that put a spotlight on artists like Goldroom, Smallpools, Guards, Vance Joy, and Tiesto. When Snapchat announced Stories, the Team Snapchat account messaged users with a Smallpools music video; after the video finished, users saw an icon that said, "double tap to listen," which sent users to the Smallpools iTunes page.

Popular DJ Zedd made the sounds and ringtone for Snapchat's chat 2.0 update. In February 2015, Madonna premiered the first music video from her new album *Rebel Heart* on Snapchat, letting users watch "Living for Love" for a day on the impermanent app. Later in 2015, Goldroom released his new EP *It's Like You Never Went Away* via Snapchat. Over five days on Snapchat, Goldroom released four music videos, each of a different song, followed by all four combined into a longer continuous story. He shot all four videos vertically, formatted specifically for Snapchat and the vertical orientation of a smartphone, rather than the traditional widescreen format you see on YouTube or on TV that typically requires users to turn their phones sideways to fully see. While these videos fit under the music umbrella, they were also an interesting testing ground for future series of content on Snapchat.

While Evan's passion projects in music haven't cost Snapchat much money or lost them users, they have not added much to the company's bottom line—either in revenue or in user growth. A culture of experimentation is important in a startup, but it's arguably more important to have an intense focus that Evan and Snapchat may be lacking. One of Evan's role models, Steve Jobs, put it this way: "People think focus means saying yes to the thing you've got to focus on. But that's not what it means at all. It means saying no to the hundred other good ideas that there are. You have to pick carefully. I'm actually as proud of the things we haven't done as the things I have done. Innovation is saying no to 1,000 things."

◉

Evan aligned his strategic vision for Snapchat—a blend of technology and art and a culture of constant experiments—with the physical layout of the company's offices. Snapchat's scattered campus of disparate buildings lends itself to a secretive, siloed company structure.

Instead of building a central headquarters like Facebook or Google, Snapchat spent years buying up little offices wherever it could get them, signing leases all over Venice, Santa Monica, and Marina del Rey. Evan moves in between Snapchat's various offices in a black Range Rover accompanied by his security detail. Snapchat's main offices are a cluster of one- and two-story buildings on a one-block stretch of Market Street, barely a block from the beach in Venice.

On Market Street, Snapchat's main office houses the design team, executives' offices, business operations, administrative staffers, and cafeteria. Entering the lobby of the main building, you can look up and see into Evan's glass-walled office on the second floor. Alternatively, he can look down from his office to see anyone entering Snapchat. Two Segways stand near the front desk, complete with nameplates for Evan and Bobby. Eventually, the company grew too big for everyone to fit in the cafeteria, so teams of Snapchat employees started flooding into the local Venice restaurants, grabbing Peruvian takeout from El Huarique or poke bowls from The Poke Shack.

Evan hates the expansive, all-company open-floor plans that many tech giants favor, preferring places where small groups can be in the same room. Each team works in the same room, but only with their team, not the entire division or company.

Evan has arranged for artists who inspire him to decorate Snapchat's offices. Inside, the exposed brick walls are covered in illustrated portraits of Tina Fey, George Clooney, Andy Warhol, Nelson Mandela, Daft Punk, and other celebrities. Every one of the stars is portrayed through a phone screen taking a selfie. In August 2013, a friend of Evan's had been meeting with Paramount Television president Amy Powell and snapped a portrait of Steve Jobs in her office to him. Evan loved it and tracked down the artist, ThankYouX, aka Ryan Wilson. Now, a dozen of Wilson's "Selfie Portraits" hang throughout Snapchat's office, with a thirteenth, a portrait of Steve Jobs that Wilson made for the first time he met Evan, hanging in Evan's office.

Evan gave Wyatt Mills, an artist he knew from Crossroads, a tour of Snapchat one day, and Mills noticed that the exterior walls were blank and boring. Evan told him to pick one and improve it. Mills painted an enormous bright mural on one of the walls above three archways.

Evan very intentionally chose Venice and Los Angeles to escape Silicon Valley. But he may be turning Venice into a second Silicon Valley. Resentment for Snapchat and tech in general is building in Venice and the surrounding area, mirroring long-simmering issues between tech and the community in San Francisco.

A good deal of Snapchat's impact on Venice and the Los Angeles startup scene has been positive. It is attracting high-quality talent and venture capital money to Los Angeles, making it easier for other startups to recruit. Years down the road, if Snapchat has a successful IPO, employees will eventually leave the company to start their own startups and become angel investors. The community will grow and grow as the rising tide lifts all boats.

But Snapchat's success has also led to rising rents and gentrification that has pushed out some longtime residents of Venice. One of the reasons Evan initially liked having Snapchat in Venice was that employees could talk openly about work at a bar without worrying about being overheard by competitors, journalists, or other people in the tech ecosystem. The town that had previously attracted the artists, writers, poets, and beatniks now attracted young professionals looking to strike it rich in the tech world. Snapchat thrived in Venice because no one cared about tech or apps. Now, Snapchat is undeniably changing that.

CHAPTER TWENTY-FOUR

DISCOVER

JULY 2014
VENICE, CA

Snapchat was meant to be the private network, not the social network.

Evan wants users to share frequently with their closest friends, not with thousands of people. Snapchat has fantastic user-generated content in the photo and video compilations people post on their stories. But if users ran out of friends' stories to watch, they would get bored and leave the app, or add more ancillary friends, or even media organizations and personalities who they didn't know in real life. Content is at the heart of every social network, from your friend's lunch on Instagram to the president's tweets to an article your aunt posts on Facebook. And a neverending supply of this content keeps users engaged for as long as possible so these networks can show users advertisements.

On Facebook and Instagram, users saw content from three different groups—close friends, acquaintances, and professional content creators—all in the same feed. Evan wanted nothing to do with content from acquaintances. Snapchat would offer messaging and Snapchat Stories for interacting with your close friends, while Snapchat Live and a new product, Discover, were specifically for watching third-party content.

Every social network eventually gets infiltrated by brands, advertisers, and media companies seeking to meet audiences where they hang out. What would this professional content look like on Snapchat? If they could build a sandbox for media publishers and advertisers early on, offering them their own area of Snapchat, maybe they wouldn't pollute the fun feed of Snapchat Stories.

Evan has long had an intense interest in journalism, dating back to his days taking a journalism class and selling newspaper ads at Crossroads. Like many in the media and in technology, Evan felt that social media had made speed the focus over all else, including accuracy and quality, and that too many feeds were clogged with clickbait headlines dressed up to make users click on low-quality work. He dreamed of a world in which publishers produced higher-quality journalism that attracted a strong, loyal audience that brands could advertise to, all of which would occur in a separate section of Snapchat to keep the Stories feed unpolluted.

So in early 2014, Evan started meeting with the CEOs of media companies and offering them a simple proposition: make content exclusively for Snapchat, host it in our app, and we'll share the ad revenue. He spoke with executives at mainstream media companies like CNN, ESPN, ABC, *Daily Mail*, Comedy Central, *Cosmopolitan*, *National Geographic*, *People*, *Glamour*, *GQ*, and *Wired*; upstarts like BuzzFeed, Vice, Mic, NowThis, Deezer, Right Now, and CSS; music companies like Spotify, Rdio, Soundcloud, Warner Music Group, and Vevo; and even video-on-demand service Hulu.

Snapchat came along at a time of dire need for publishers. The media world had woken up to the reality that readers were increasingly spending their time on mobile and in apps rather than on websites. Even worse, readers were using a small number of apps regularly, and most didn't bother to download publishers' apps. It wasn't just that people weren't picking up the newspaper anymore—they weren't visiting newspapers' websites anymore. Just as the web destroyed print subscriptions, mobile would rock the tenuous equilibrium publishers had reached online. Publishers started to push content across platforms to meet readers where they were spending their time.

The best product available to publishers was Facebook. It had a massive user base both on the web and on mobile and offered extremely relevant advertising that commanded high rates. Publishers had tried to take their old browser-based business model and shove their display and banner ads onto mobile, which wasn't working well. As Evan understood with the camera opening and the speed of delivering snaps, speed is everything on mobile. Every millisecond users waited for content to load, they thought about switching apps.

So Facebook created a new product called Instant Articles, which allowed publishers to create faster-loading, more aesthetically pleasing articles that lived within Facebook's walled garden. Instant Articles launched in May 2015, but, similar to how Snapchat approached the time leading up to the launch of Discover, Facebook employees had been talking with media partners for months prior to the launch. Publishers were apprehensive about handing over their customer relationships to Facebook, especially since the social network had always made it clear that users would come first ahead of publishers. While it would be best for publishers themselves to control their relationships with customers, it would be much better for them to work with two or three technology giants than be at the mercy of one monopolistic power.

In this environment, publishers welcomed Snapchat's creation of a media product. More than merely serving as an alternative to publishing on Facebook, Discover offered media companies their own space on a virtual magazine newsstand inside Snapchat. Publishers could create dynamic daily magazines for millions of Snapchat users. The company was growing so fast that it offered media companies huge upside with little downside.

In April 2014, Snapchat hired Nick Bell away from News Corp. to run the media division. Bell and a new team he assembled, including Josh Stone, an alumnus of both Crossroads and the Kappa Sigma fraternity at Stanford, and Nicole James, the blogger who first wrote about Snapchat back in July 2011. Chloe Drimal continued to run the Live Stories part of content. Evan was involved very early on in Discover, in the initial pitches to publishers; he then handed the project off to Bell, an influential executive in the company who quickly became part of Evan's inner circle.

Content creators from the aforementioned publishing companies were invited down to Venice to pitch Bell, Stone, and the rest of the team on what their Snapchat channel might look like and what kind of content they would put on there. Most of them produced mock editions and were either invited to join the platform or asked to produce more samples to prove themselves. Snapchat was highly secretive about who else they were asking to join Discover, although they liked to show logos of highbrow organizations like *The Wall Street Journal* in sample materials to lend the new platform some credibility.

Initially, Evan had hoped to go live in the summer, but he quickly learned that the timeline was too ambitious to build the feature for users, build a backend publishing tool, and get media companies on board. So he prepared to launch Discover in October 2014. The team was laying the track while the train sped down it, building the product as they signed on content and ad partners and together figured out what Discover would be. Throughout the summer, the Snapchat team was going back and forth with potential publishers, reviewing examples of art boards of what editions might look like and deciding how it all would function and how many stories publishers would post per day. The most controversial decision from Snapchat was that publishers weren't allowed to put links in their stories; unlike Facebook or Twitter posts where they could direct readers to their own websites, everything in Discover would live there, and only there, without users leaving to publishers' kingdoms.

"Discover was created to provide clarity and curation around the most inspiring, informative, and entertaining subjects," the company told publishers in a presentation. Each publisher would produce a daily edition made up of several pieces of content. They were given three principles to follow: keep it simple, mix it up, and make it immersive. Each edition was made up of several stories, each of which featured a top image or short video as a teaser, with more content—longer video, more photos, text articles, etc.—if the user swiped below a story. While they had debated throughout the summer about making Discover something that could be constantly updated like other social media, the Snapchat team ultimately decided to make it static, more like a magazine issue than traditional social media posts. Like a great music album, a great Discover edition would ideally be composed of beautiful individual tracks that came together to tell one powerful, enjoyable story.

Nick Bell, Josh Stone, and Nicole James would meet with publishing partners—always individually, never bringing publishers together—and give them feedback on the sample editions the publishers had been producing. Most of the feedback was their individual editorial commentary and never based on research or focus groups.

The early prototypes of Discover were unnecessarily clunky and complex. Users would have to hold their finger down while watching Discover, meaning publishers would have to make sure users had a place to hold their finger without covering an important part of a story. This kept Discover aligned with how the rest of Snapchat worked (once you lifted your finger, content stopped playing), and Evan loved to talk about how engaged users were—after all, they were literally touching the content on the screen. But did it make sense to force users to hold their fingers down while asking them to watch longer videos from CNN or Vice?

Unlike the nascent Snapchat, which went live looking, well, just downright ugly, the more mature company took time to revise Discover and iron out most of the kinks before releasing it to the world. Over the summer, they dropped the requirement for users to hold down their finger, not just for the secret Discover feature, but for all of Snapchat. A pull-up menu with options for users to share content or tap down to see a longer story or video got simplified to a simple swipe down for longer content and tap-and-hold to share to other users. An inelegant, multitiered graphic overlay system got whittled down to simply adding graphics to videos and pictures.

The Snapchat team was still furiously working to build the platform. In many meetings, Nick Bell or Nicole James would pitch a new feature, like a video uploader, to publishers; but these new features were often just a mockup of what Snapchat was building, and publishers couldn't actually try them out because the engineers didn't have them working yet. The original publisher tools were slow and barely worked; if ESPN uploaded a Discover edition that had an error in it, they couldn't edit anything in the Snapchat system—they had to go back and fix it and then reupload an entirely new version. Between these problems and the changes to the product, development time kept slipping, and Snapchat had to push the October launch date to January 2015.

Eventually, Snapchat built a full-fledged content management system (CMS) for publishers and an app for them to preview how editions would look to users. The team had to teach creators how to take content that had been shot for TV or other widescreen formats and adapt it to Snapchat's vertical video style. Users didn't want to turn their phones sideways to view a video in full screen, so Snapchat offered them full-screen vertical video. Snapchat taught publishers how to cut and reformat existing video to vertical, but really they hoped that publishers would start shooting content in a vertical format specifically for Discover.

Snapchat rebelled against the data-driven, scalability-focused approach that Silicon Valley loved, such as Facebook's algorithmic attention to its News Feed and Trending topics sections, and required that human editors add everything on Discover. "There's a sort of weird obsession with the idea that data can solve anything," Evan once said. "I really haven't seen data deliver the results that I've seen a great editor deliver."

Initially, the team took this ideal too far, though, as they didn't build analytics-reporting tools into the platform until publishers asked for them. These analytics started off as a very rudimentary, engineer's look at activity: a daily Excel spreadsheet showing metrics like how long users had spent in the publisher's edition and how many views each individual story had gotten. Eventually they grew this out into a reporting suite with actionable insights on things like what text placement and colors worked best and what types of stories made users leave in the largest numbers.

As Nick Bell and his team continued negotiating with publishing partners, Snapchat put together a team of its own to publish on Discover. As they were teaching publishers how to create content for the platform, the obvious became unavoidably clear: no one understood Snapchat users better than the people working at Snapchat. So why not create a Discover channel themselves? They could simultaneously show publishers how to win on Discover and create a popular channel for the company to profit from. Once again, Snapchat cast itself within the Hollywood/Netflix crowd rather than the Facebook/Twitter/Silicon Valley crew that favored agnostic platforms that did not create any content.

Snapchat hired Marcus Wiley, a former Fox executive who led the development of comedies like *New Girl*, *Brooklyn Nine-Nine*, *The*

Mindy Project, and *Bob's Burgers*, to run its channel and gave him a large space in Venice to fill with talented creators to film the daily editions. Snap Channel's flagship show was *Literally Can't Even*, written by and starring Sasha Spielberg and Emily Goldwyn (the daughters of Steven Spielberg and John Goldwyn of MGM fame). Emily Goldwyn went to Stanford and graduated the same year as Evan. The scripted series, which consisted of nine 5-minute episodes, featured a comedic version of the duo's escapades around Los Angeles. Just like all other content on Discover, each episode disappeared twenty-four hours after it went live. Music artists also came to Snapchat's Venice offices to shoot videos and songs for the Discover channel.

As the summer rolled into September, advertisers began lining up for the new platform. Snapchat offered to split ad revenue 50/50 with publishers if Snapchat sold the advertisement, and 70/30 in favor of the publisher if the publisher sold the ad on their own. It was a hard bargain, but it was much better than other social media sites like Facebook and Twitter, which shared no advertising revenue with publishers (although they allowed links that drove web traffic). To avoid bombarding users with ads, Snapchat kept advertising spots to a maximum of three per edition, and never within the first three stories in an edition. The company also set the prices and approved every ad, even if publishers sold them. Ads on Snapchat would ideally look as similar to content as possible—full-screen vertical videos with audio that last up to ten seconds.

Snapchat board member and Sony Entertainment CEO Michael Lynton introduced Nick Bell and Josh Stone to other executives at Sony, who promptly signed on to be one of the first advertisers on the platform. Lynton also introduced them to players in the music industry, but they ran into more trouble there.

Vevo, a music video service formed from a joint venture between Sony Music Entertainment and Universal Music Group, dropped out of Snapchat Discover talks when they couldn't agree upon a revenue share. In a note to Nick Bell, Vevo CEO Rio Caraeff said Snapchat's proposed revenue share would be "by far the worst economic deal we have."

In late October, BuzzFeed dropped out of Discover after it couldn't agree with Snapchat on how much creative control Snapchat would have over BuzzFeed's content. But the Discover train kept rolling down the tracks, and in December 2014 publishers started pushing out content on a daily basis despite the fact that Discover hadn't even been formally announced to the public. The publishers produced daily editions exclusively for Snapchat employees to test in the month leading up to the launch. Evan was very involved, watching Discover and giving publishers individual feedback.

It was one of the most complex projects Snapchat had ever undertaken. Engineers had to build products for users and publishers. Nick Bell's media team had to negotiate dozens of deals with potential partners, manage who was let on the platform, deal with companies dropping out, and ensure content was high quality. Emily White, Mike Randall, and the sales team had to convince advertisers to pony up big bucks for a new, unproven product. A new original content team had to come on board and figure out what style and format would work best for a completely new platform. It had been delayed for months, but finally, in 2015, it was ready. On January 27, 2015, Discover launched, with editions from CNN, Comedy Central, *Cosmopolitan*, *Daily Mail*, ESPN, Food Network, *National Geographic*, *People*, Vice, Yahoo News, and Warner Music Group.

Discover felt like a relic of the days before the nonstop news cycle. With static editions and a limited number of channels, it felt like watching TV or using an early 1990s internet portal like Yahoo. Users did not immediately go crazy for Discover, but the user base was so significant that even a small percentage meant publishers were seeing millions of views per day. Publishers could reach a young demographic that was highly engaged, and the content was inexpensive to produce, as the spots were very short.

For Comedy Central, Snapchat quickly became its second most-watched platform, trailing only TV and easily surpassing YouTube, the Comedy Central website, and other social platforms. Comedy Central used its Discover channel to test out comics and shows that they wouldn't normally debut on TV. The network could make a six-episode Snapchat series for a few thousand dollars to showcase a comedian or new talent who couldn't command a budget commitment of millions of dollars to greenlight a new TV show. Comedy Central launched *Quicky with Nicky* on its Discover channel to test out and promote *Not Safe with Nicky Glazer* before the TV show premiered. Michelle Wolf starred in one of Comedy Central's original Snapchat shows and went on to a recurring role on *The Daily Show*.

MTV brought back its 2000s reality TV program *Cribs*, which featured the mansions of celebrities before going off the air in 2011. Its new season was shot vertically specifically for Snapchat Discover. Content producers quickly built out entire teams just for their Snapchat channel. They trained camera operators and producers to think and film vertically so segments could be optimized for Discover.

Unlike Facebook or Twitter, all the channels in Discover stand on equal ground, so whether you are a very established brand like CNN or ESPN or an upstart like Vice, you had an equal shot with viewers. Every young media company on the planet, from Pop Sugar to Refinery29 to Tastemade, started aggressively pitching Snapchat for a spot on Discover. The company that had once been ridiculed by the media as a mere sexting app was now the newest, most important media platform that everyone was dying to be a part of.

While Discover is fascinating, it's also interesting to consider what Snapchat chose not to build. In creating Discover, Snapchat built a mini internet within its walls. The app now had messaging, a social network feed, and a broadcast feed of professional publishers' content. It also had user identity with people's phone numbers, usernames, and friend graphs, and it even had a payments platform in Snapcash (though adoption of Snapcash was slow to nonexistent). These were the building blocks for an app platform, if Snapchat wanted it.

Snapchat could have created a robust API (short for Application Programming Interface, a fancy Silicon Valley term for a clearly defined method for software to interact) and let developers build whatever applications they dreamed up on top of Snapchat. Facebook's identity is woven throughout the internet with its login API—this is the little blue Facebook button that lets you log in to a bunch of other apps using your Facebook information. Apple and Google make boatloads of cash per year on the 30 percent tax they charge paid apps in their app stores. Developers would think of myriad apps on top of Snapchat that the company never even thought of, and the best ones would win out, making

Snapchat a better experience for users, causing them to spend even more time in the app, making Snapchat more money . . . and thus, the virtuous cycle spins.

But Evan didn't want this. He didn't want a *FarmVille* built on top of Snapchat. He wanted to control 100 percent of the experience for Snapchat users, end to end. Open development (letting developers build on top of your platform) versus closed (controlling the entire experience for your users) has been a software debate for decades. Like his idol Jobs with the Macintosh, Evan fell firmly on the closed end of the spectrum. So he built Snapchat closed, which opened the door for the Snapchat Stars.

CHAPTER TWENTY-FIVE

MAJOR 🔑

JANUARY 2016

VENICE, CA

"They don't want me hangin' out with the CEO of Snapchat! That refused three hundred billion! The CEO! Mogul talk! Stay tuned," DJ Khaled shouted into the camera during a January 2016 visit to Snapchat's Venice headquarters. Incorrectly stating that Evan had turned down an offer for Snapchat worth more than the GDP of Denmark, Khaled turned the selfie video to show Evan standing next to him laughing. Khaled captioned the video "The CEO Evan Spiegel major 🔑 !!!!!!!!!!!!!!!" and added a custom geofilter at the bottom featuring Khaled holding a microphone above an adoring crowd with the caption "Fan Luv."

Depending on your age and Snapchat usage, you're probably either thinking, "We finally mentioned DJ Khaled's Snapchat!" or "What the hell did I just read?" Let's step back for a minute.

Khaled Khaled—that's DJ Khaled's real name—is a forty-year-old DJ and producer from Miami; he was a minor figure in the music world best known for his 2010 platinum record, *All I Do Is Win*. In 2015, on a break from touring, a friend told Khaled to give Snapchat a try. He started filming every minute of his day, talking to his lion sculpture, holding his plants and flowers and telling them he loved them, and, most of all, offering followers over-the-top advice about "winning."

His positive vibes had people repeating his catch phrases, from "Major Key" to "We the Best" to "Bless Up." He would talk about how he stocked his bed and tour bus with lots and lots of pillows, which were very important to him, and about defying haters, who he simply called "they," as he would explain how "they don't want you to eat breakfast, so I'ma make sure I eat breakfast." We've grown so used to seeing celebrities' lives be manicured into inauthenticity via reality TV and social media that Khaled's quirkiness, earnest inspirational messages, and comparatively low production quality gave his Snapchat a huge appeal.

The turning point for Khaled came when he took his Jet Ski out on Biscayne Bay, just south of Miami. "The key is to make it," he kept saying as he got lost trying to get home in the dark. He kept taking Snapchat videos with the flash on, telling his followers about how he couldn't find his way home. He took a selfie video commenting, "The key is not to drive your Jet Ski in the dark." The story was hilarious, goofy, and weird; Khaled's Snapchat prowess spread through word of mouth and he quickly amassed six million followers on Snapchat.

Very few people understand Snapchat fully, and even fewer are good at it in a way that's broadly popular. That made DJ Khaled a hot commodity. In 2016 alone, he signed a deal with Cîroc vodka for his Snapchat stories, agreed to host a weekly radio show on Apple Music's Beats 1 station, and made an Apple Music commercial with Ray Liotta. Khaled released his ninth studio album, dubbed *Major Key*, in July 2016, and his tenth, *Grateful*, in June 2017; each album featured collaborations with the biggest names in music, from Jay-Z to Rihanna to Justin Bieber.

It's very hard to find people to follow on Snapchat. Facebook, Twitter, and Instagram are happy to serve up suggestions on which friends and friends of friends and even celebrities and parody accounts you should follow based on who you already follow. After all, the more people you follow and friend, the more potential content there is for you to see, and the more advertisements you can potentially see. But Evan is focused on keeping Snapchat as the antithesis of Facebook and Twitter. Aside from a few celebrities that you love so much

ally became Twitch, a place to watch people play video games; Kan and his partners sold Twitch to Amazon for $970 million in August 2014.

Kan tried out Snapchat in 2013 but didn't really get the appeal at the time. In his own words, "I tried it, mostly for industry research purposes, found the UI confusing, saw I had very few friends active, felt old, and then didn't open it for two years." In 2015, friends were talking about DJ Khaled getting lost on his Jet Ski and laughing and watching the story over and over again. Kan decided to give Snapchat another shot.

He found Snapchat was a much better version of what he had tried with the original Justin.tv. Broadcasting 24/7 was just too much time and involved too many boring moments. With Snapchat, Kan distills an entire day down to two to three minutes of the most interesting ten-second photos and videos. Kan leaves his messages open for his eleven thousand followers and typically gets ten messages an hour.* In May 2016, Kan worked as a partner at the prestigious startup incubator Y Combinator; he let his followers apply to take over his Snapchat account for an hour and pitch their startup for funding from Y Combinator. Eventually, Kan and Y Combinator funded three startups from over four hundred applicants.

Venture capital money isn't just headed to companies pitching on Snapchat. Investors are funding Snapchat-content companies, too. On an unusually windy afternoon in March 2016, I grabbed a coffee from Groundwork Coffee Co. in Venice, a couple blocks down the boardwalk from Snapchat's main headquarters. I hopped in an Uber, and the driver took me north toward Santa Monica, past the scenic Binoculars Building now occupied by Google. As the Santa Monica pier rapidly approached, we pulled onto the 10, zipping past Evan's old stomping grounds, the Crossroads School. Merging onto the 405, we . . . well, we sat in traffic for a while. Heading north, I played with Snapchat on my phone, seeing what geofilters I picked up as we drove through Brentwood, past UCLA, past the Getty Museum, and eventually pulled off

---

* He actually agreed to talk with me for this book when I sent him a message over Snapchat.

onto Mulholland Drive. As we rose into the hills, Los Angeles sprawled out beneath us as we passed Harvard Westlake, a prestigious private school where Snapchat developed an early following, and arrived at the Arsenic House.

I walked in and heard a techno version of Rihanna's "Work" blaring. Half a dozen models were walking around in lingerie getting ready for a photo shoot for *Arsenic*, Snapchat's new *Playboy*. Mimosas and Red Bulls littered the glass desks in the back of the kitchen-office combination as the models rolled dough and baked cakes in the front. An entourage of twentysomethings Snapchatted the photo shoot on iPhones while a couple of guys with professional cameras took pictures. The models and photographers alike danced and sang along to the deafening music.

During the shoot, I chatted with Arsenic's brain trust, Amanda Micallef and Billy Hawkins. Hawkins worked on Wall Street before becoming a Hollywood agent to stars like Will Smith. Micallef produced movies with Jamie Lynn Siegler and Julia Roberts, and started *Arsenic Magazine*—she had originally intended for it to be a print magazine—as a hobby in her spare time. Micallef quickly realized photographers and models were happy to come together and shoot for free if they were given creative freedom and able to showcase their work. As models increasingly used Instagram as a digital resume and leveraged their social media followings to book higher-paying gigs, *Arsenic* grew, primarily on Instagram.

An intern for *Arsenic*, then an undergraduate at USC, suggested they get on Snapchat as well. Micallef and Hawkins knew nothing about Snapchat but told her to run with it and see how it went. It went quite well. *Arsenic* now has over five hundred thousand daily views on its Snapchat story. They've added new Snapchat accounts dedicated to music, art, and behind-the-scenes content to their family of channels. They've done music collaborations with A-listers like Diplo, Skrillex, Jeremih, and Dillon Francis. Katy Evans, a regular *Arsenic* model who has been in *Maxim* and other high-profile magazines, used to only get a few hundred views on her Snapchat stories. Once she started shooting with *Arsenic*, that figure ballooned up to almost fifty thousand, as the models regularly include their Snapchat handles in *Arsenic* shoots, give each other shoutouts on their accounts, and take over other *Arsenic* models' accounts, much like Shonduras and MPlatco did when they were starting out.

So why has *Arsenic* thrived on Snapchat? Is it just porn? That's what I thought at first, but the fact is, anyone with a smartphone is a thumb tap away from all the porn they could possibly want. In fact, *Arsenic* isn't even the porniest thing on Snapchat—there's real porn!

Just as every Vine star and aspiring actor took to Snapchat Stories to promote their work and gain followers, strippers and porn stars also took to Snapchat. Many sent videos and photos of themselves naked for a few dollars; turns out some people did use Snapcash! Others used Snapchat Stories to promote their work elsewhere on the web or just to develop a following. Still others offered to do personalized sex shows, via Snapchat's video messenger, in exchange for cash. Pornography violates Snapchat's community guidelines, and the company has been very aggressive about shutting down porn-related accounts. It still happens on the app—it is the internet, after all—but it's not an epidemic.

So why has a lingerie Snapchat channel thrived? Once again, it comes down to intimacy. No, not that kind. When you watch *Arsenic* TV, you're watching these beautiful women, but they aren't airbrushed or photoshopped to perfection. They're dancing goofily and making silly faces just like your friends. And the low-quality videos are right next to your friends' stories. So there's an intimacy, even though you're one of a million people watching it. The result is that people tell their friends to check out *Arsenic*, and just like DJ Khaled or Shonduras or YesJulz or any of the other stars we've talked about, it spreads through word of mouth.

Alexis Madrigal, then an editor at *The Atlantic*, coined the term "dark social" in 2012 to describe the way we share articles and other links privately via messages and email. He estimated that 70 percent of referrals came not from the Facebooks and Twitters of the world, but from dark social. Snapchat has no links, so the entire rise of these little kingdoms has been through dark social, mimicking the way the app originally spread through high schools and colleges, being whispered about and texted person to person.

As Snapchat grew ever more popular, every brand targeting customers from thirteen to thirty years old knew they needed to be involved with the app in some way, but most didn't really know how. Advertisers and marketers became very comfortable with Twitter and Instagram after cutting their teeth with Facebook in the 2000s. But Snapchat is very different from other social media networks. Comedy brands like Fuck-Jerry and TheFatJewish and parody accounts became very popular on Twitter and Instagram posting funny pictures they'd created or found elsewhere on the internet. Advertisers and marketers could take a page from the most popular accounts' books and try to post funny content that was still relevant to their demographics. But Snapchat is so personal and geared toward an individual person's story that these comedy brands and parody accounts don't work. And neither do brand accounts, for the most part.

A host of digital agencies have sprung up to fill this void between advertisers and Snapchat users. Some, like Naritiv and Delmondo, focus exclusively on bringing together advertisers and Snapchat stars; others, like Niche, offer Snapchat as one of their digital products alongside production for Instagram, Twitter, and other social media sites. These agencies are simultaneously competing and cooperating as they try to standardize key performance indicators and metrics (what counts as a view, what else can we measure in an app with no links, likes, comments, or retweets) for advertisers.

In early 2015, as Discover was just rolling out and Snapchat advertising was still nascent, advertisers were struggling to put engaging content on the platform. Between 60 and 70 percent of viewers closed a Snapchat ad after three seconds of viewing it. Coca-Cola, like most other advertisers, was just repurposing its ads from TV for Snapchat. But the soda giant decided to rethink its strategy after its ads performed poorly during Snapchat's Live Story for the NCAA Final Four.

Coca-Cola turned to a young, rising Snapchat star named Harris Markowitz, known for his sketch comedy and stop-motion stories. Markowitz explained to Coca-Cola that building a following on a Coke Snapchat account would still have value, even though the content disappeared after twenty-four hours, because this shelf life created urgency.

"If Coca-Cola had their own TV station and you guys knew that every single night you guys are guaranteed 30 thousand views, would that be valuable?" Markowitz asked. Of course it would be. "That's Snapchat!" he explained.

For his first Coca-Cola ad, Markowitz made a stop-motion story of picking up a Coca-Cola and handing it to a friend; Coke gained five thousand followers from the promotion. Next, he and a friend fought over a can of Coca-Cola they wanted to give to a girl. Coke gained more followers. Coca-Cola asked him to film an advertisement for Snapchat's fall Back to School Live Story.

Markowitz was given the first advertising slot in the Live Story, which cost Coke hundreds of thousands of dollars. Markowitz studied what other advertisers were putting in Live Stories and noticed they all looked like TV ads awkwardly jammed into Snapchat. He shot a time-lapse video of himself in his apartment trying on different outfits to go back to school, and, of course, grabbing a can of Coke. He shot the entire ad on his iPhone and even lowered the quality of the video to make it look kind of grainy. The ad ran exclusively on the Snapchat live story, and 54 percent of users watched all ten seconds of it, one of the highest performing ads in Snapchat history.

It turned out that the best way to get young Snapchatters to watch an ad was to have one of their own make it.

KEEPING SECRETS

NOVEMBER 2014
CULVER CITY, CA

On a Monday morning in late November 2014, Sony Entertainment CEO and Snapchat board member Michael Lynton was driving to his office at the Sony Pictures' complex in Culver City, just west of Los Angeles. Sony's chief financial officer called Lynton and told him the company had been hacked. The US government would later blame the hack—the most devastating in corporate history—on North Korea, which was angry over Sony's Seth Rogen–James Franco comedy *The Interview* that mocked North Korean leader Kim Jong-Un. By the time Lynton reached the office, Sony's entire system was offline. Lynton had to deal with an onslaught of problems with employees, the press, and the FBI. And he had to call Evan Spiegel.

For Evan, there could hardly be something worse than board-level emails being leaked en masse; besides Snapchat itself being hacked, of course. The media published article after article dredged from the leak, revealing companies Snapchat had quietly acquired and internal maneuverings behind rejecting Facebook's $3 billion offer, among other high-level secrets.

Evan sent a note to the Snapchat team titled "Keeping Secrets." Unlike his bland statements and nonapologies when Snapchat was hacked and users' data was leaked, his message to employees was deeply personal and passionate. He also published the note on Twitter for the press, and the world, to see:

Keeping Secrets

I've been feeling a lot of things since our business plans were made public last night. Definitely angry. Definitely devastated.

I felt like I was going to cry all morning, so I went on a walk and thought through a couple of things. I even ran into one of my high school design teachers. She gave me a huge hug. I really needed it.

And I really need to tell you that I'm so proud of all of you. I want to give you all a huge hug because keeping secrets is exhausting.

Keeping secrets means coming home late, after working all day and night. Curling up with your loved ones, hanging out with your friends, and not being able to share all of the incredible things you're working on. It's painful. It's tiring.

Secrets also bring us together.

We keep secrets because we love surprising people. We keep secrets because it's the best way to keep showing the world that growth is not only possible, it's necessary. We keep secrets because it's the right thing to do, not because it's the easy thing to do.

We keep secrets because we get to do our work free from judgment—until we're ready to share it. We keep secrets because keeping secrets gives you space to change your mind until you're really sure that you're right.

We care about taking the time to get things right. Secrets help us do that.

Secrets keep the space between the community and the

public—space that we need to feel safe in our expression and creativity.

I am so sorry that our work has been violated and exposed.

A couple of people have asked me what we're going to do. First we're going to be really mad and angry and upset. And that's ok.

It's not fair that the people who try to build us up and break us down get a glimpse of who we really are. It's not fair that people get to take away all the hard work we've done to surprise our community, family, and friends.

It's not okay that people steal our secrets and make public that which we desire to remain private.

When we're done being mad and angry and upset we're going to keep doing exactly what we are doing. And then we're going to do it ten times better.

We're going to change the world because this is not the one that we want to live in.

Evan Spiegel

In early 2013, when Reggie filed his lawsuit against Evan, Bobby, and Snapchat, Evan went underground. He was furious at any reporters who covered the lawsuit, despite knowing it was their job. And reporters hammered him for kicking Reggie out of the company and making claims about coming up with the idea with Bobby, conveniently forgetting that it was Reggie's idea. When I reported on the lawsuit for *Tech-Crunch*, where I was a writer at the time, Evan cut off contact with me. After I started covering Reggie's lawsuit, Evan never gave me another interview again.

In the four years since Reggie sued him, Evan has only done a handful of interviews. He rarely makes anyone else at the company, including high-level executives, board members, and investors, available to the media. Speaking with the press can make you feel Evan's wrath, even as a passive investor, advisor, or friend.

When Evan did agree to an interview, it was often alongside a friendly face, like Michael Lynton or *Cosmopolitan* editor in chief Joanna Coles, who later joined Snapchat's board. Evan also occasionally agrees to be interviewed by high school and college students, as he's passionate about helping the next generation of entrepreneurs, artists, and think-ers; but no doubt the questions from students aren't nearly as hard hitting as they would be from professional journalists. One interview with his hometown newspaper, the *Palisadian-Post*, included this disclosure at the bottom: "Full disclosure: Spiegel agreed to be interviewed by the *Palisadian-Post* under the guideline that no controversial questions would be asked. He also would not let this reporter audiotape the interview."

Evan's relationships with many reporters mirror his other relation-ships in life. He tends to treat people in a binary fashion: smart or dumb, useful or useless, yes or no. He's an emotional person and hates putting on a face and smiling and faking his way through anything, whether it's an interview with a reporter or a cocktail event with potential adver-tisers. There are very few—if any—journalists who match Evan, who is still just twenty-seven years old, both in age and career stature. Older, more established journalists have struggled to understand Snapchat, frustrating Evan. Because Snapchat's user base skewed so young, very few reporters covering the company were close in age to its core users.

As a result, media coverage of Snapchat has been fairly harsh. At first, there was the sexting narrative. Then journalists decided that it was just a silly toy. All the while, very few journalists did the work to understand Snapchat, its users, and its impact. Evan has been unwilling to show journalists a significant peek behind the scenes at Snapchat, so the media continues to portray Snapchat as this silly, inconsequential company.

Evan is extremely reluctant to answer very basic questions most CEOs get asked. When a Bloomberg Business reporter writing a cover story on Snapchat asked Evan what his long-term vision for the com-pany is, Evan replied, "These are the kinds of questions I hate, dude." Snapchat investors and advisors, afraid of irritating Evan, have often been unwilling to speak publicly about even basic things like how the company differentiates itself and what its mission is.

Evan is hardly the first tech founder to be secretive. Some of the in-dustry's most revered leaders like Steve Jobs and Jeff Bezos are known for their intense corporate secrecy. As much as Evan has had a rivalry with Mark Zuckerberg, he has also been empowered by Zuckerberg, who blazed the trail for him. Steve Jobs was not the CEO of Apple until his second stint with the company; Google's investors demanded they bring in Eric Schmidt as a more professional CEO than cofounders Larry Page and Sergey Brin. But Zuckerberg's overwhelming success and maturation from immature genius into visionary CEO caused a shift in Silicon Valley to strongly favor founders as CEOs. This profound, rapid shift has given founders of high-growth, breakout-success start-ups the upper hand with the media and investors alike. Zuckerberg's "I'm CEO, Bitch" paved the way for Evan to be anointed Snapchat's sole, unchallengeable leader.

Like Steve Jobs at Apple, Evan keeps all Snapchat acquisitions secret. Jobs believed that every consumer encounter with a brand added either credits or debits to the brand's account with the consumer. And part of the benefit of adding credits is the delight of surprise followed by gratification. Evan wants to announce new features and immediately roll them out to everyone so that users are both surprised and then instantly able to enjoy the new feature or product.

The company's Twitter account retweets a wide range of positive and negative reactions to its product updates. They have slapped their eponymous logo—with no mention of Snapchat or any words at all—on the luggage bins at security at LAX and on massive billboards in Times Square. Many of the billboard panels in Times Square simply were covered in Snapchat yellow. People who know what the logo means are in on the cool secret; those who don't either ask or simply remain ignorant and uncool.

Evan doesn't have a public Snapchat, something that would be unthinkable for Jack Dorsey, Mark Zuckerberg, or Kevin Systrom, all of whom make their profiles on their social networks public. Zuckerberg has a team of eight people curate his Facebook page, posting almost daily to craft a perfectly curated public persona. This is the exact opposite of what Evan wants for Snapchat users—and himself. Evan deleted his Facebook account long ago, and he used to tweet occasionally before he decided to delete all those as well.

◉

Evan's speeches at smaller events, where he is less guarded, are often better than those he gives at bigger venues. At high-profile events, like Recode's conferences, he talks about how Snapchat is entertainment. But in private speeches we see Evan's core philosophy for Snapchat is a vision on how he thinks the world should be. For example, this excerpt from his April 2014 keynote at LA Hacks reveals his philosophy on the distinction between privacy and secrecy:

> Unfortunately, privacy is too often articulated as secrecy, when, as Nissenbaum* points out, privacy is actually focused on an understanding of context. Not what is said—but where it is said and to whom. Privacy allows us to enjoy and learn from the intimacy that is created when we share different things with different people in different contexts.
>
> Kundera† writes, "In private we bad-mouth our friends and use coarse language; that we act different in private than in public is everyone's most conspicuous experience, it is the very ground of the life of the individual; curiously, this obvious fact remains unconscious, unacknowledged, forever obscured by lyrical dreams of the transparent glass house, it is rarely understood to be the value one must defend above all others."
>
> In America, before the internet, the division between our public and private lives was usually tied to our physical location— our work and our home. The context in which we were communicating with our friends and family was clear. At work, we were professionals, and at home we were husbands, wives, sons, or daughters.
>
> On the internet, we organize information by its popularity in an attempt to determine its validity. If a website has been referenced by many other websites, then it is generally determined to be more valuable or accurate. Feelings expressed on social media are quantified, validated, and distributed in a similar fashion. Popular expression becomes the most valuable expression. Social media businesses represent an aggressive expansion of capitalism into our personal relationships. We are

---

* Helen Nissenbaum, a professor of media, culture, and communication and computer science at New York University.
† Milan Kundera is a Czech-born French writer and philosopher, best known for his 1984 novel *The Unbearable Lightness of Being*, which is Evan's favorite book. Evan once wrote a school paper comparing Kundera's book with photographer Josef Koudelka's series of photos of 1968 Prague.

asked to perform for our friends, to create things they like, to work on a "personal brand"—and brands teach us that authenticity is the result of consistency. We must honor our "true self" and represent the same self to all of our friends or risk being discredited.

But humanity cannot be true or false. We are full of contradictions and we change. That is the joy of human life. We are not brands; it is simply not in our nature.

Evan closely cherishes privacy to allow Snapchat to become what he wants it to become away from prying eyes so that the company has room to tinker and grow. Board member Mitch Lasky once noted that Evan is "already super paranoid and I don't want him to go deeper into the bunker." New hires are indoctrinated from day one to not talk about what they work on, even down to telling them not to put a specific role on their LinkedIn pages. They are indoctrinated into the cult that places a huge value on secrecy. Information is shared on a need-to-know basis as employees are separated into their teams. Early employees set the example as they take pride in maintaining the secrecy to the external world.

Spiegel's preferred meetings with employees and investors consist of walking along the two-mile beachfront cement path from Snapchat's Venice office to the Santa Monica pier. He feels these meetings have a hidden-in-plain-sight privacy, as it's difficult to overhear someone's conversation when they're walking in a crowd.

Evan deeply dislikes giving presentations, so he scrapped Snapchat's all-hands meetings, which he used to hold as often as once a week. Before they were discontinued, all-hands meetings, called company gatherings, were used for lighthearted announcements like birthdays and work anniversaries instead of hard-hitting presentations or Q&As on strategy and product. Employees often found out about new Snapchat features via an all-company email on launch day—or by reading about them in the press. At one all-hands meeting an employee asked Evan, "What is the vision for Snapchat as a company?" Evan replied that the goal is just to build fun things. He continued that he doesn't want to have a generic mission statement like Google or Facebook, because he thinks it restricts what the company can do. Evan doesn't want employees to feel like they can't build cool things just because they fall outside the bounds of the company mission statement. Evan has a strong vision of the future and five- and ten-year plans for the company. But he is only willing to share those plans with close confidants and a select few Snapchat employees, notably designers and long-time team members.

This culture can make the transition to Snapchat difficult for employees coming from other tech companies. Many Silicon Valley giants like Facebook, Twitter, and Google are more open and have regular all-hands meetings, Q&As with executives, and generally more of a shared sense of trust in what the company is working on and striving toward. Orientation at Snapchat has a secrecy policy similar to *Fight Club*.

Every Wednesday night, Snapchat employees have Council, where they sit in a circle with nine colleagues and talk about their feelings. Council ranges from deep, introspective talks to community service, like serving meals or furnishing a home for homeless families, to typical team-bonding activities like boxing classes, volleyball, karaoke, painting, and happy hours. When employees join Snapchat, they become part of three core teams: their starting class, their actual work team, and their Council group, which is randomly assigned. Council has three rules (Evan likes the number three). One, speak from the heart. Two, you are obligated to listen. Three, everything that happens in Council stays in Council. Evan believes this privacy creates a space for employees to make themselves vulnerable and share their deepest thoughts and feelings.

Council originated for Evan at Crossroads. The school's founder, Paul Cummins, took the idea from the Ojai Foundation, a nonprofit about 90 miles north of Los Angeles between Oxnard and Santa Barbara that aims to bring connection and wholeness to the world through Council and retreats at its Land Sanctuary. Cummins introduced Council as the core part of a new program he created in the mid-1980s at Crossroads called Mysteries. Students sat in a circle, and only the student with the talking stick could speak. The other students sat in silence or encouraged the speaker with a Native American response, "A-Ho," meaning they agreed with or were moved by something the spaker said. Crossroads seniors took a multiday trip to the Ojai Foundation, where they lived in a yurt, ate vegetarian meals, and bonded with each other. Council had a major impact on Evan at Crossroads, and he took it with him when he started forming Snapchat's culture.

CHAPTER TWENTY-SEVEN

EVAN'S EMPIRE

MARCH 2015
VENICE, CA

In March 2015, Evan gathered the company in the cafeteria for a rare all-hands meeting. He tersely told the assembled staffers that Chief Operating Officer Emily White—Snapchat's putative Sheryl Sandberg—and VP of Business and Marketing Partnerships Mike Randall—effectively the company's revenue chief—had left the company.

White had turned out not to be Snapchat's Sheryl Sandberg, but rather its Owen Van Natta. Van Natta, a former Amazon executive, joined Facebook as COO in 2005, served stints as chief revenue officer and a vice president of operations, and eventually left the company right before Sandberg joined.

White had agreed to join Snapchat instead of starting her own company or taking a CEO role because she believed she would have broad responsibilities and an enormous opportunity to grow with Evan and Snapchat. She and Evan agreed that she would handle business operations, sales, and human resources, while Evan focused on the product. White and Mike Randall were hugely important in getting Snapchat's initial ad products to market. The two worked well together and had long-standing relationships with advertisers and marketers dating back to their days at Facebook.

But Evan came to realize that Snapchat's advertising products, and the way that Snapchat would make money more broadly, would have an enormous impact on users. In short, he came to believe that Snapchat the business and Snapchat the product were inseparable. This left White with little to run.

Thanks to Van Natta's hiring at Facebook not working out, Zuckerberg knew exactly what he needed in a COO by the time he hired Sandberg. Zuckerberg spent over 100 hours with Sandberg before he hired her, making sure they would work well together and outlining her role. Sandberg joined the company in early 2008 when Facebook was four years old. When Emily White joined Snapchat, the company was about two and a half years old. That may not seem like a big difference, but it's an eternity for a company growing as fast as Snapchat was in 2013 (and Facebook in the 2000s). White had cut her teeth at the much larger and more established Google and Facebook; it was difficult for her to translate those experiences to the rapidly changing Snapchat, which had only fifty employees when she arrived.

Once she left Snapchat, White joined the board of directors of Hyperloop Technologies, a startup trying to realize Elon Musk's vision for a high-speed, tube-based transportation system. White also founded Mave, a high-end personal concierge startup in Santa Monica.

White's departure was made worse by the sheer number of high-level executives who left around the same time. Many didn't survive a year at Snapchat. Mike Randall, who had been hired by White and reported to her while at Snapchat, left after seven months. HR head Sara Sperling and VP of Engineering Peter Magnusson were each at the company for just six months. Communications head Jill Hazelbaker lasted a year at the company before departing for Uber.

While Evan is difficult to work with and played a role in these departures, most people around the company don't believe this was the primary reason for the exodus. Snapchat was growing at such an unbelievable rate that it was very difficult to hire people who fit their responsibilities and Snapchat's culture and were able to move and scale at a breakneck pace.

Evan continued to be very aggressive in hiring, spending 40 percent of his time recruiting. (He devoted the rest of his time to product and attending meetings and events, 40 percent and 20 percent, respectively.) He hotly pursued other executives, trying to land former White House press secretary Jay Carney, who ultimately joined Amazon.

Snapchat cheekily tried to poach San Francisco startup employees by adding Snapchat geofilters to their offices. At Uber's headquarters, a geofilter read, "THIS PLACE DRIVING YOU MAD?" along with Ghostface Chillah sadly driving a cab. At Airbnb's office, the ghost lay scared in bed, underneath the caption "NOT SLEEPING WELL?" At Twitter, the shtick was a ghost with a halo and angel wings to the tune, "FLY HIGHER!" And finally, at Pinterest, a ghost lay next to falling bowling pins, asking, "FEELING PINNED DOWN?" All of the filters featured an address for Snapchat's jobs page.

It wasn't always easy to convince talent to leave Silicon Valley for Los Angeles. There are so many great companies to work for in the San Francisco Bay Area, most of which value engineers more highly than Snapchat does. Several of the executives who lasted less than a year still had their families in the Bay Area; while this was not the primary reason that most of them parted ways, it certainly didn't help.

Those who joined Snapchat would work for Evan Spiegel in his kingdom. The company runs through Evan, and his say is final. Ambitious people who buy into the company's mission and fit with the culture tend to stay at Snapchat for a long time. But many leave quite quickly. Arguing with Evan can get you fired. In addition to being CEO, Evan is Snapchat's unofficial head of quality assurance. He will kill features he doesn't like and push for ones he personally loves. He has been known to kill an advertising deal at the eleventh hour. In one instance, an engineering team was ready to launch a new feature, but no one could figure out why it was slowing down Snapchat on Evan's phone specifically. Evan pushed the new feature's launch because it made Snapchat look slow and buggy on his phone, and he didn't want to risk that happening to a single user.

Executives who have succeeded in this environment manage to get along with Evan, handle his quick changes of opinion, scale with the company, and maintain their voice in the company's direction. The short list of power players in the company consists of Chief Strategy Officer

Imran Khan, engineering lead Tim Sehn, content lead Nick Bell, Live head Chloe Drimal, and, of course, cofounder Bobby Murphy.

From day one, Bobby had kept a low public profile at Snapchat, handling engineering in the early days before moving to a research role behind the scenes while Evan handled investors, the media, and partners as the face of the company. While Tim Sehn ran the engineering team day to day, Bobby retained his title as Chief Technical Officer and headed up a small engineering team focused on research and innovation.

Tim Sehn had joined the company from Amazon. Like Evan, he's very set in his ways, and he and Evan often butted heads on work issues. But once a decision was reached, he supported it. Sehn was not personally a big proponent of Snapchat Discover, but once Evan decided to move forward, Sehn got the engineering team on board and working hard on it. He also matches Evan's intensity, often telling engineers that it isn't his main priority to make them feel comfortable but rather to get the best out of them. When Snapchat began hiring rapidly in 2015, Sehn sternly reminded engineers that if their work didn't meet standards they would be fired.

Few employees besides the high-profile executives have left the company voluntarily. Snapchat has also locked employees up by requiring nonlinear stock vesting, where employees get 10 percent of their stock options after their first year, an additional 20 percent after their second, 30 percent after their third, and the final 40 percent after their fourth year.

Evan believed it was essential to Snapchat's success to rebel against what he saw as tech companies touting highfalutin mission statements. While every company in Silicon Valley, even photo-sharing apps, claimed they were on a mission to change the world, Evan wanted Snapchat and its team to focus on having fun and being happy. After all, most of Snapchat's users were there to have fun. Snapchat threw annual parties for seemingly every holiday, from Halloween to a December holiday party to the Fourth of July to New Year's Eve to a September party for Snapchat's anniversary. The parties were open to Snapchat employees and their friends and featured Snapchat signs and yellow decorations everywhere, open bars, food, and bags stuffed with Snapchat-branded swag, from sweatshirts to ghost socks.

Evan tended to spend time with the designers or his aforementioned short list of Snapchat confidantes while at work. On the weekends, if he wasn't working, Evan went out with Bobby and some of Snapchat's earliest hires, like engineers David Kravitz and Daniel Smith. Head of Content Nick Bell was one of the rare few who ran in Evan's close work and social circles.

Chief Strategy Officer Imran Khan joined Snapchat in December 2014, leaving his post as head of internet banking at Credit Suisse. An affable thirty-eight-year-old, Khan was born in Bangladesh and attended the University of Denver's Daniels College of Business, where he majored in finance. He spent six years at JP Morgan Chase analyzing internet stocks. In 2009 Khan was the lead author of a report on mobile advertising and the continued decline of the newspaper industry; funnily enough, Khan's report was skeptical that social networks had significant potential for long-term profits, as he believed advertisers wouldn't want to place their brands alongside "content they can't control."

Khan has been credited with reviving Credit Suisse's reputation with tech companies. During his time there, he strengthened relationships with Asian contacts and advised on behemoth IPOs for Weibo, King, and Groupon. But the biggest fish Khan reeled in was getting Credit Suisse on as an advisor for Alibaba's $25 billion IPO. When he joined Snapchat, it was natural to believe Khan would help with fundraising and, ultimately, the road to an IPO of its own. Spiegel and Khan discussed potential investment and partnership opportunities with Prince Alwaleed bin Talal in Saudi Arabia. And Khan was key to Alibaba investing $200 million in Snapchat, even though Snapchat is blocked in China (more on this later).

"The reason I joined here was Evan," Khan later told *The Wall Street Journal*. "Because it was evident that he was the best product visionary I'd met in my entire life. And with technology companies, if you don't have good product, you die."

While the initial role Evan and Khan had discussed included corporate strategy and advising the CEO, Khan's role dramatically expanded in 2015. He has served as Evan's proxy on all things advertising, relaying feedback from advertisers and marketers back to him. Khan is the only member of Snapchat's inner circle besides Evan who has a significant public presence in the media, another hallmark of Snapchat's secrecy. Khan has stepped into the vacuum left by departed executives and become Evan's right-hand man on business and partnerships. His is a crucial role that helped steer Snapchat's direction for years to come.

Evan and Imran can often be found in the Tree Room, an area in the back of Snapchat's main building, on the first floor below Evan's office, centered around a potted tree. Evan, Imran Khan, Tim Sehn, and other executives sit back there together. Sometimes Evan's then-girlfriend and now wife, supermodel Miranda Kerr, would sit with Evan and the executives in the Tree Room.

Despite significant executive turnover in 2014 and early 2015, Evan settled in with a core group of executives, led by Khan, Sehn, and Bell, to drive Snapchat forward toward an IPO.

CHAPTER TWENTY-EIGHT

THE ROAD TO IPO

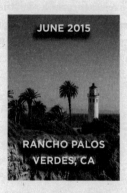

The Code Conference is an annual tech conference held at an exclusive resort in Rancho Palos Verdes, California. The high point of the conference is an interview with tech press legends Kara Swisher and Walt Mossberg. The two have sat in iconic red chairs across from the biggest names in the business, from Steve Jobs to Elon Musk to Bill Gates.

Now, in June 2015, Evan sat in one of those same red chairs as Swisher and Mossberg probed about Snapchat's future.

Initial public offerings are in many ways the finish line for startups. They are liquidity events, giving founders, employees, and investors an actual hard cash return on the years of investment and work they've poured into the company. They supply the company with funds to carry out its grand ambitions for the future. They show the world that public market investors diligently vetted this company and are willing to buy its stock. After an IPO, a company graduates from startup to publicly traded company.

"We need to IPO," Evan told Swisher and Mossberg. "We have a plan to do that. Obviously, I can't give you too much color there. An IPO looks like a lot of things, but most importantly it looks like another dot in the growth of our business. We don't view that as the end, it's just the beginning."

Only a handful of companies in the history of the internet have had as many users as Snapchat had at that moment in 2015. Snapchat sat on a potential goldmine but hadn't yet proven the ability to mine that gold. It was one thing to reject Facebook with the belief that they could probably make the company worth more than the $3 billion offered. It was another to actually earn millions of dollars in revenue without hurting user growth and engagement.

There were two main ways for Evan to increase Snapchat's valuation: user growth at engagement driven by new product offerings and better advertising products to increase Snapchat's revenue per user. Snapchat would need to execute on both fronts.

In the early days of its advertising push, Snapchat was a very difficult company to work with, demanding high prices and customized content and offering advertisements with very few analytics and very little measurement. Team Snapchat understood their power as the new "it" app and gateway to a difficult-to-reach yet valuable demographic. It wasn't uncommon for advertisers to refer to working with Snapchat as "a pain in the ass."

When Martin Sorrell, the CEO of advertising conglomerate WPP, met Evan in 2014, Sorrell told him, "You're the first twenty-five-year-old billionaire I've met." "I'm twenty-four," Evan responded.

The company required a minimum ad spend of $750,000 per day. Snapchat told advertisers that users are nine times more likely to view Snapchat's vertical ads because they don't need to rotate their phones. For advertisers, the higher completion rate was good, but vertical video meant they had to shoot things exclusively for Snapchat rather than re-purposing ads from YouTube and Facebook.

As people increasingly spent time on their mobile phones, vertical video—optimized for holding a smartphone upright—began to make more sense than horizontal—optimized for TVs, laptops, and desktops. Evan didn't see the point in making people turn their phones sideways to see a Snapchat in full screen. So everything on Snapchat was made to be viewed vertically. Advertisers eventually came around to Evan's point of view and shot content specifically for Snapchat despite the extra cost. Now over eight billion vertical videos are viewed every day.

As frustrating as it was for advertisers, Evan was focused on what was best for Snapchat's users. Rather than looking at advertising as a tax on using free products or a necessary evil, he considered it as another product and more content for users. Evan personally rejected ad campaigns that he didn't like or that he thought users wouldn't like; Kevin Systrom had done the same when Instagram launched ads.

When Emily White and Mike Randall left Snapchat in early 2015, Snapchat took a step backward with advertisers. White and Randall had been the face of the company to many advertisers. Then, all of a sudden, neither one was at Snapchat. Some advertisers felt like Snapchat was a black hole for six months as it scrambled to rearrange the sales team.

Imran Khan ran the sales team while Evan searched for someone to run the advertising effort. Khan and Evan were both so busy that some advertisers have likened getting a meeting with them to enjoying an audience with the pope. Like most of Snapchat, the sales team was young and growing fast, with a lot on their plate as they worked to compete with very mature businesses. Evan opened an office in New York City to improve relationships with advertisers and media partners. And Evan and Khan became more receptive to advertisers' feedback.

And Snapchat has come around on prices and measurement. The company has amended their terms of service several times so they can give advertisers more targeted offerings. The result has been a thousand paper cuts into the privacy and antitracking stance Snapchat once held. Snapchat now lets advertisers segment people by location, gender, age, device, operating system, and wireless carrier, although some of these require users to volunteer this information, like their birthday.

Snapchat commissioned Nielsen to do a study of its highly coveted demographics compared to TV networks. The study showed that Snapchat reached 41 percent of all eighteen- to thirty-four-year-olds in the United States, while the top fifteen US TV networks reached only 6 percent of the same group. Snapchat signed another deal with Nielsen to track Snapchat ads using gross ratings point, one of the advertising industry's standard metrics. The brash startup wanted advertisers to compare apples to apples and see for themselves that Snapchat was the new TV.

Evan was constantly looking for ways to improve Snapchat's user experience and increase its revenue. In September 2015, Snapchat purchased a startup called Looksery that could help do both.

Based in Odessa, Ukraine, Looksery had an app that let users select a face filter that altered their appearance. Looksery cofounder Yurii Monastyrshyn liked to open job interviews by asking candidates, "Why did Snapchat become so popular?" Snapchat shut down Looksery's standalone app and integrated the technology into its camera. When users pressed and held down on their face in Snapchat, a menu of lenses (so called to avoid confusion with geofilters) popped up at the bottom of the screen. Depending on which one a user chose, a lens could make them look more attractive, much less attractive, make them vomit rainbows, or make their head explode into a fireball.

Lenses changed daily, drawing users back to check out what new ones appeared and letting Snapchat continuously experiment to see which struck a chord. The popular ones—a flower crown that made you look pretty, a dog's ears and nose, a wide, goofy smile that made your voice sound funny—stayed, while others rotated regularly.

Snapchat had long relied on the selfie as a way of expression and reaction. Looksery took that and made selfies exponentially more expressive. Lenses' integration was a prime example of Snapchat's ability to add features without becoming clunky. If you wanted to use Snapchat like it was 2011, you could still just pull out the app, snap a photo, tap, and send it to a friend. But if you knew what you were doing, you could do so much more—you could hold your finger down on the screen before you took a photo to pull up new lenses; you could swipe after taking a photo or video to add filters and geofilters denoting the time and place of your snap or transforming it into black and white.

Almost immediately after Snapchat launched lenses, it monetized them. In October 2015, Fox Studios bought geofilters and lenses to promote *The Peanuts Movie*, letting users turn themselves into Snoopy or Woodstock. Snapchat briefly offered some lenses as in-app purchases, offering users a daily selection of free lenses and others for $0.99, but it quickly abandoned this effort, shutting down its lens store in January

2016, just two months after it launched. Snapchat users were purchasing tens of thousands of lenses per day, but this revenue did not add up to equal that of even one Snapchat ad, so Snapchat shut down the store to focus on advertising.

Lenses gave Snapchat's sales team another unique creative tool to pitch advertisers. Snapchat's sales team began pitches by emphasizing how the app was about communication and self-expression, and how Snapchat was different from Facebook and Instagram. Then they explained to advertisers that Snapchat could now offer packages mixing and matching ads in Live, ads in Discover, lenses, and geofilters, targeted to specific areas or for the whole world. Snapchat helped marketers pick which ad products would play best based on their brand, and helped with creative creation of ads, lenses, and geofilters. Snapchat did not yet have the scale or data that Facebook or Google offered. But it had a unique media format that was extremely compelling to users and advertisers alike.

Lenses became an increasingly lucrative advertising source as Snapchat worked with brands to create a new interactive advertising format. In December 2015, Imran Khan traveled to Chicago to meet with Gatorade executives. He proposed a Super Bowl lens that dumped a virtual cooler of Gatorade over users, like players do to coaches when they win the Super Bowl. Gatorade shelled out hundreds of thousands of dollars to run the lens for two days over Super Bowl weekend; Snapchat users watched the lens, seeing it in friends' messages and Stories and trying it out themselves, over 160 million times.

Taco Bell's team worked with Snapchat for six weeks to create a sponsored lens for Cinco de Mayo that turned users' heads into a giant taco shell. The lens was viewed 224 million times in a single day. Users played with the lens on average for 24 seconds, adding up to 12.5 years' worth of unique play over the course of the day.

Augmented reality has long been a nerd's utopian dream. It would have been hard to predict even just a few years ago that AR's first big break would be teenagers vomiting rainbows, wearing dog ears, and turning themselves into taco shells with Taco Bell stamped on them. If Evan's biggest bet yet pays off, Snapchat will own the future of AR too.

Advertisers were quickly learning that if they worked with Snapchat, they could create ads that users spent a lot of time interacting with rather than jamming TV commercials into the app. Snapchat geofilters had long been available to advertisers for specific single-day promotions and for chain retailers and restaurants to put at their stores. At McDonald's, users could add a geofilter of a double cheeseburger and french fries to their Snapchats. In February 2016, Snapchat opened up sponsored geofilters to everyone, allowing users to pay for a custom filter for their birthdays, parties, engagements, or whatever else they could come up with. Starting at five dollars, on-demand filters could be as small as an office or as large as multiple city blocks, and could be live for as little as an hour or as long as thirty days (with the price changing based on size, duration, and timing of the filter).

By the fall of 2015, marketers seemed to have figured out how to create ads that aligned with the way users acted on Snapchat. In October 2015, Snapchat let Sony Pictures Entertainment, board member Michael Lynton's studio, buy a twenty-four-hour Discover channel for the new James Bond film *Spectre*. Instead of running ads inside a Discover or Live channel, *Spectre* had its own channel for a day, full of marketing material and clips from the film. The *Spectre* channel, which users viewed over forty million times, was a better-realized version of Snapchat's original ad format, the standalone Live Story advertisement for Universal Pictures' horror movie *Ouija*.

Studios would continue to experiment with ways to use Snapchat to drive people to theaters and their TVs. In May 2016, AMC premiered five minutes of its new series *Preacher* inside Discover. Later that month, 20th Century Fox paid to make every Snapchat lens a different X-Men character for its upcoming *X-Men: Apocalypse* film. If Snapchat users swiped up on one of the several X-Men ads running in Live and Discover, they could buy tickets for the movie without even leaving Snapchat.

CHAPTER TWENTY-NINE

THE NEW TV

OCTOBER 2015

VENICE, CA

Evan was willing to take big swings on developing Snapchat's own content but quick to pull the plug if the team could not produce results.

In October 2015, Evan decided to shut down Snapchat's own channel on Discover. Snapchat's channel had launched with a lot of promise, featuring original shows like Sasha Spielberg and Emily Goldwyn's *Literally Can't Even*. But the short series failed to resonate with viewers and develop a significant following. Marcus Wiley, the former Fox executive leading the team, and many of the fifteen employees working on the channel were laid off.

It came as a major surprise, as Wiley and other Snapchat employees had been pitching shows to major studios and production companies and the channel's programming team had just settled into a twelve-thousand-square-foot studio in Marina del Ray. But it was a stark reminder that Evan was going to try out a lot of wildly different strategies for Snapchat, and not all of them would be successful. In order to best serve users and conserve resources to focus on the things that were working, Evan would be ruthless about cutting things that didn't work.

Earlier in 2015, Evan poached CNN's thirty-three-year-old political reporter Peter Hamby, giving him the newly created role of head of news as Snapchat expanded into more serious content. Hamby had spent a decade at CNN, spending the last eight as a national political reporter.

Like Chloe Drimal, Ellis Hamburger, Nathan Jurgenson, and others, Hamby had original and often provocative opinions about the the coarsening impact of the digital era on politics. In 2013, Hamby wrote a ninety-five-page report criticizing campaign coverage in the digital era. Drawing on his experiences from the 2012 campaign trail, Hamby wrote that social media forced both the media and campaigns "to adapt to a treacherous media obstacle course that incentivized speed, smallness and conflict, leaving little room for good will or great journalism—but plenty of tweets."

At first glance it may seem deeply ironic that Hamby would choose to join Snapchat two years after writing that. But Evan shares Hamby's qualms with the media's focus on speed and smallness. It's one of the main reasons he created Discover as a walled garden with no retweets or hourly updates. Spiegel offered Hamby a chance to use Snapchat's power as a camera and broadcasting device in millions of people's pockets to produce high-quality journalism.

Hamby hired CNBC producer Katy Byron to be his managing editor at Snapchat. They next hired half a dozen more colleagues from CBS, ABC, and cable networks to staff their new Snapchat Discover show. Hamby's clout and access immediately paid dividends, as he interviewed New Orleans mayor Mitch Landrieu during a Snapchat Live Story covering the Hurricane Katrina commemoration.

But the main stage for Hamby and Snapchat's news team was reporting on the 2016 US presidential election.

"I'm Peter. I'm a reporter. I've been covering politics for a really long time. I've crushed beers with Hillary Clinton, flipped burgers with Mitt Romney and argued with very important people on television," Hamby said in January 2016 to kick off the inaugural episode of Snapchat's election show *Good Luck America* from the campaign trail in Iowa.

"We're now in the middle of the weirdest election I've ever seen. Let me show you the people and places that really matter."

Good Luck America aired whenever there was interesting political content to cover, from caucuses to primary races to debates. It didn't have a schedule or announcements, it simply popped up in Snapchat's Live section when there was an episode. Every episode Snapchat produced was viewed by at least a million people, and twenty-two million people watched a portion of the twelve-episode debut season of *Good Luck America*.

Hamby mixed live reporting with user-recorded footage, reporting the news and explaining a bit of the political process to Snapchat's young audience. "Think of the primaries like *The Hunger Games*—but with much less attractive people," Hamby explained in the pilot episode. The result was an interesting hybrid of the professionally produced Discover and the user-generated Live Stories.

Users were soon submitting photos and videos taken behind the scenes, often at events closed to the press. Hamby interviewed a cast of characters, from a canvasser for Bernie Sanders to Republican presidential candidate Chris Christie to an Iowa high schooler who registered "Deez Nuts" as a candidate.

The format had its drawbacks. Hamby's segments were shot on high-resolution cameras and allowed to run longer than ten seconds, the limit Snapchat traditionally imposed. But user-submitted snaps were shot on smartphones and subject to the normal limitations of the app, so it was often difficult to hear exactly what a candidate was saying. And many candidates' speeches or remarks at debates were difficult to fit into a ten-second Snapchat.

To mitigate this, Snapchat adapted geofilters to add a layer of context. While they had initially been used solely to denote where a user was, geofilters now could include quotes from a candidate's speech, an explanation of what had happened, and live-updating results from primary races.

Soon the candidates started using Snapchat's geofilters as well, paying to have custom filters at debate halls and rallies. In January 2016, Ted Cruz mocked Donald Trump's absence at the final Republican debate with a filter asking, "Where is Ducking Donald?" accompanied by a yellow duck sporting a Trump haircut. Bernie Sanders's campaign ran a different geofilter every day for nine straight days leading up to the Iowa caucus. Most urged voters to "Feel the Bern" and get out to vote on caucus night. In May 2016, Hillary Clinton's campaign placed a geofilter at the Anaheim Convention Center, the site of a Trump rally. The filter showed Trump's own words from 2006 against a yellow background: "I sort of hope [a housing crash] happens because then people like me would go in and buy."

In October 2016, the month before Election Day, Democratic candidate Hillary Clinton appeared on Hamby's *Good Luck America* Snapchat show for an interview. A week before Election Day, 4.4 million Snapchat viewers watched *Good Luck America* as Hamby spoke with President Barack Obama about the importance of voting. Republican nominee Donald Trump declined an interview request from Snapchat. Trump would only join Snapchat after he defeated Clinton. He would use it to snap special events like his inauguration.

In December 2015, a shooting in San Bernadino, California killed fourteen people and injured seventeen more. As the tragedy unfolded, Snapchat created a live story open to everyone in the United States. The story brought viewers photos and videos from the scene as well as narrative developments and statements from authorities. It brought users citizen journalism, aggregated and narrated by professionals.

Internally, Snapchat calls everything it produces "content," and Hamby's crew follows suit, but the intentions of his team are clear: to use the platform to mix high-quality professional journalism with citizen-journalist-produced documentation of breaking news stories. Snapchat has the potential to broadcast stories curated from users on the ground at the core of the action. But it remains to be seen if users want hard-hitting news in the same app that they employ to send videos of themselves vomiting rainbows to each other.

Media companies that haven't been granted a sacred spot on Snapchat Discover have been trying to use the Stories feature to build an independent audience. If users don't want to get their political coverage from Hamby's *Good Luck America*, maybe they would from *The Washington Post*'s Snapchat story. Snapchat still wants Stories to be intimate, so discovery of news organizations is still very difficult, hampering their growth. Most of them are still experimenting and both trying to develop a following and figuring out how to use the platform. Monetization plans are far off, if they even exist. When viewers click on a Snapchat Story, they have no idea what they're about to watch—there's no headline or teaser to urge them to click. So the only real lever media companies have to make users come back every day is to consistently make good content.

As it does for users with messaging, Snapchat also offers publishers unparalleled intimacy. Mic.com, a millennial-focused media company, posted a Snapchat story on mental health awareness and left its messages open to its thousands of followers. Readers' reactions came flooding in. Unlike comments and replies on most social media, each one of these replies was a one-on-one dialogue between Mic and a reader. Some wrote that they were severely depressed and didn't know what to do. Editors at Mic connected them with counseling resources and kept tabs on them, messaging them regularly to check in on them. The letter to the editor became an email, then a Facebook comment or tweet, and now it was a Snapchat.

Snapchat's first in-house content began with Live Stories at the Electric Daisy Carnival in Las Vegas. It progressed to capturing interviews with candidates vying to be the leader of the free world. Snapchat was growing up.

CHAPTER THIRTY

DISCOVER FALTERS

JUNE 2016

VENICE, CA

Despite its highly anticipated launch, it was clear just months later that Snapchat Discover was not working. Evan had high hopes as publishers signed on for the next big thing in journalism, and indeed, the lineup was impressive, featuring some of the biggest names in media, like CNN, Comedy Central, *Cosmopolitan*, and ESPN. In spite of the lineup, user traffic to Discover had dropped off 30 to 50 percent since the January 2015 launch.

In July 2015, Snapchat redesigned Discover. Some believed that users were ignoring Discover because it wasn't given a prominent location. To solve this problem, Snapchat added little icons for Discover to the top of the Stories page, which users visited daily.

The design change gave Discover channels more visibility in Snapchat and boosted publishers' traffic significantly. But Snapchat was far from done with changes. In late July, six months to the day since Discover launched, Snapchat killed Warner Music Group (WMG) and Yahoo's Discover channels. Yahoo's Discover editions opened with Katie Couric sitting behind an anchor's desk, reading into the camera like a classic news broadcast. Snapchat and Yahoo, which worked out of the same building in New York, met several times to work on the latter's ratings. But Snapchat offered Yahoo very little data, simply telling them they were in the bottom rung of Discover channels by viewership.

Evan had hoped Warner Music Group could make music videos cool again on Snapchat by asking, "Is there a way here to re-create MTV's *Total Request Live*?" WMG's Discover channel was neither able to capture the nostalgic feelings Evan had for MTV nor draw in Snapchat viewers. Few Snapchat users even knew what WMG was, forcing the company to add "Warner Music" to the stylized W icon it had used since the 1970s.

When Snapchat kicked WMG and Yahoo off Discover after six months and killed the in-house-created but underperforming Snap Channel a few months later, the message was loud and clear to publishers: Snapchat would not waste valuable space on underperforming channels. In spite of this Darwinian approach to the platform, media companies continued to push hard to get a spot on Discover's limited real estate. Snapchat soon announced replacements for Yahoo and WMG: iHeartRadio would take the music spot, while BuzzFeed would take Yahoo's spot. Snapchat and BuzzFeed managed to work out the issues that had caused BuzzFeed to drop out right before Discover's launch.

In November 2015, Snapchat hoped to boost traffic by letting publishers share links that took readers directly to their Discover content. On mobile, these links either led a reader to the publisher's Discover page in Snapchat or to a page to download Snapchat. On a desktop, the links led users to a QR code that they could scan on their phone to open the content.

Despite shutting down its Snap Channel, Snapchat still made original content opportunistically. Stephen Colbert starred in a five-day miniseries on Snapchat before his debut on *The Late Show*. Nick Bell's content team produced a Year in Music review at the end of 2015, dedicating each day to recapping the year's big stories for a different music genre. Spotify signed on to sponsor the entire series.

Snapchat also kept signing up new partners for Discover, from established newspapers like *The Wall Street Journal* to upstarts like the women's lifestyle publication Refinery29 and the mobile-focused food

media startup Tastemade. Evan initially agonized about adding channels, because the jump from twelve to fifteen channels added another
row that didn't fit neatly onto one phone screen. But the extra content
for users was ultimately worth the aesthetic sacrifice. Snapchat brought
on do-it-yourself startup Brit & Co. to produce special holiday Discover
editions for Mother's Day, Father's Day, the Fourth of July, Halloween,
Thanksgiving, and Christmas.

Earning a spot on Discover could be transformational for startup
media companies. Tastemade raised $40 million in venture capital and
brought on twenty new employees after it was added to Discover. The
company has studios in Santa Monica where cameras are propped at
ninety-degree angles to shoot footage specifically for Snapchat. One of
the company's sets is a 1950s-style kitchen with the furniture arranged
to fit as much as possible into the camera's narrow vertical frame. Tastemade shoots videos for other platforms as well but marks the TV monitors in its studios with black tape to show Snapchat's frame. The startup
tries to film as much as possible in the middle third of the frame so that
it can be easily ported over to Snapchat. At Refinery29, a female-focused
media startup, a team of ten puts fourteen pieces of content on Discover
every day.

But too much of this content, not just from Tastemade and Refin-
ery29 but from all Discover publishers, was fluffy clickbait. Snapchat
had designed Discover to be the antithesis of clickbaity nonsense. But
Discover partners felt the heat as Snapchat demanded performance, and
they catered their content to what they believed the young teenage audience wanted. BuzzFeed, the most digitally savvy of the publishers on
Discover, should have one of the better channels; yet it features none of
its viral content or serious reporting. Instead, BuzzFeed Discover articles
run the gamut from "19 Delightful Dog Pictures for Anyone Who Is
Stressed Out" to "What Does Your Vagina Look Like?"

Given the structure of Discover, which catered to bored, multitasking young people, long form, investigative journalism and breaking news
updates don't really work. And given the teenage audience, many publishers unimaginatively started publishing fluffy pieces. Ideally, they
would be producing stories that felt more like Snapchat Stories and Live
Stories—a more raw, on-the-ground, unfiltered look at interesting
events. But that aesthetic is very tough to nail—especially from a media

office in New York—and very few reporters, even young social media editors and community managers at these companies, truly understand Snapchat and its users.

From the beginning, it was clear that without headlines and links, Discover publishers couldn't rely on gimmicks to drive traffic. They would have to consistently produce good content to develop a loyal audience. This was supposed to be a good thing—freed of the incessant stream of Facebook and Twitter, journalists could get back to making pure, great content that users loved. The problem, of course, was that the content was actually crap. But we can't pin all the blame on publishers. Snapchat spent years building a distinctive brand that made it difficult for Facebook to copy; but this same youthful, fun aesthetic made it difficult for Discover, Snapcash, and other serious endeavors to work. Teenagers didn't want to use the same app to send dumb drunk photos to friends and get serious world news. And as much as Snapchat thought they might be starting a revolution, they didn't believe their own hypothesis enough. Discover still placed too much emphasis on the publishers' brands. But users didn't care if the CNN logo was popping up in Discover. They cared about individual stories.

Discover wasn't necessarily a failure outright. Some channels continue to do very well on it. *Cosmopolitan* does the best with over four million daily unique views, and the *Daily Mail* isn't too far behind. Other publishers run their Discover channel at a net loss but feel that they have to be there to remain relevant to younger readers. But overall, Discover has not had nearly the same outsized positive impact on the company's growth and potential that Live Stories, geofilters, and lenses have had.

In June 2016, Snapchat unveiled a second redesign of Discover, trying to address some of these issues. The new Discover scrapped the old design, which simply showed each publisher's logo, and replaced it with a new tiled layout that let publishers include an image and headline for the day's edition, along with their logo. Users could also subscribe to publishers' Discover channels, which would place new editions from that channel below friends' updates on the Stories page. But by far the most significant part of the redesign is that it combined Discover and Live Stories in one place. Previously Discover channels had small icons at the top of the combined friends' Stories and Live Stories page, and a gallery of all Discover channels appeared on the next page over. Now, small Discover and Live tiles shared the very top spot, followed by friends' new stories, followed by a much larger section of Live Stories tiles, followed by friends' old stories (ones that had been posted within the past twenty-four hours but that a user had already viewed). Swiping right, one could see large rectangular panes showing both Discover and Live Stories content where the Discover gallery used to be.

Discover and Live were converging into a broader content section. Live was simply better content, as it took advantage of Snapchat's unique value proposition of having a camera in over a hundred million people's hands, and it was far more popular with users than Discover. Discover looked like lists and goofy articles had been taken from the web and slapped into Snapchat. Live looked like nothing else on the internet. And Snapchat worked hard to keep it that way, exerting more editorial control over the stories and convincing celebrities to use the social media app all their cool young fans were using.

Snapchat's coverage of the Rio Summer Olympics in August 2016 featured exclusive footage from partner NBC mixed with on-the-ground photo and video snaps from fans and athletes themselves. NBC decided to air the games on a tape delay, and aggressively pursued other social networks to take down footage from the games that fans or media outlets posted, making Snapchat one of the best ways to follow the Olympics. Live Stories from Rio ranged from event-specific footage of a swimming race to crowd reactions to a compilation of US swimmer Ryan Lochte in his room in the Olympic village goofily trying out Snapchat lenses to make his face look different.

Snapchat's Live Story for the Opening Ceremony started with a video from NBC of President Barack Obama and First Lady Michelle Obama wishing the US athletes luck. Then viewers saw golfer Rickie Fowler walking through the Olympic village. Team USA basketball star Kyrie Irving filmed a selfie video of himself and teammate Kevin Durant. Tennis superstar Serena Williams posted four Snapchats from her point of view in the Olympic Village and hanging out with basketball star Carmelo Anthony. Snapchat mixed in footage of the Olympic torch traveling through Brazil with flashbacks of the 2008 and 2012 opening ceremonies. Athletes from a wide range of countries posted to the story, from the Italian water polo team to the Nigerian basketball team.

Brazilian model Gisele Bündchen blew the camera a kiss and thanked them for making a Snapchat geofilter just for her.

Around fifty million people, one-third of Snapchat's daily active users, watched at least one of the Olympics Live Stories. Snapchat partnered with seven broadcasters, including NBC in the United States and the BBC in the UK, to show footage. NBC gave BuzzFeed staffers full editorial control over its daily Rio Olympics story, which ranged in content from highlights and recaps to BuzzFeedy stories like "Can You Guess the Sport by the Athlete's Butt?" NBCUniversal invested $200 million in BuzzFeed in 2015, which probably helped the two companies work together; the stories were NBC branded, with no BuzzFeed logos.

Advertisers don't think about Live and Discover very differently, as they just look to align their advertising with the right audience. Live offers advertisers more opportunities to plan ahead, as Snapchat sends advertisers a calendar of Live Stories months in advance. Planned stories range from sports games to music festivals to holidays to "Study Abroad" to spotlights on cities from Reykjavik, Iceland, to Lagos, Nigeria. Most are focused on one geographic location (a stadium, city, etc.) while others, like "College Graduation" and "Prom," are not.

Increasingly, Snapchat is going directly to the source for content it wants on Live Stories. *People*, a Discover partner, pitched a Live Story collaboration for the Oscars, but Snapchat simply worked with the Academy and event organizers to produce their own Live Story. In 2016, Snapchat struck a deal with the NFL to create Live Stories for each of the 256 regular-season games, every playoff game, the Super Bowl, and other league events like the NFL Draft. In 2015, the NFL and Snapchat collaborated on fifty-eight Live Stories covering games and the draft; seventy million people worldwide tuned in to watch.

Twenty-one million people tuned in to watch the Video Music Awards on a Snapchat Live Story in 2016. These people—up from twelve million who watched the same Live Story for the 2015 show—watched 30.5 million total video views. On linear television, only 6.5 million people watched the VMAs, down 34 percent from 2015, despite the awards show being broadcast on eleven networks (MTV, MTV2, MTV Classic, VH1, Comedy Central, Spike, TV Land, BET, CMT, Centric, and Logo). Live shows like the VMAs and Oscars and sports are cable's last big appeal, and thus huge for Snapchat. If you want to watch this content but not badly enough to pay for cable or watch at a bar, Snapchat's Live Stories are good enough. Snapchat isn't just becoming a replacement for Facebook—it's becoming a replacement for TV.

NBCUniversal signed a multiyear deal with Snapchat in August 2016 to create new content for Discover. NBC won't simply be repurposing TV content, like it does on Facebook and YouTube, but will be shooting content specifically for Snapchat's vertical video format. First up, *The Voice* came to Snapchat, with users submitting performances and celebrity coaches like Miley Cyrus and Blake Shelton judging them, all via Snapchat. NBC will also showcase comedic talent from *Saturday Night Live* and *The Tonight Show Starring Jimmy Fallon* to create short series on Snapchat. Snapchat spoke with content creators about making original shows for Snapchat like Peter Hamby's *Good Luck America*.

As it made room for new shows, Snapchat continued to cut what wasn't working. The company killed off its local stories, the city stories in New York and Los Angeles that let anyone in the city contribute to a daily story that only those in the city could watch. Local just wasn't as popular as the larger, event-based Live Stories—although college Campus Stories were still very popular and were not cut. Fifteen curators worked on Local Stories. Nick Bell called them all into a security room at Snapchat, which typically would have been filled by the company's security guards. Bell abruptly told the group that this would be their last day at Snapchat as the company shuttered Local Stories.

What was once envisioned as a daily digital magazine had blossomed into much more. But the growth and success have not come from the Discover publishers, leaving them in a strange purgatory. Like the rest of Snapchat, Discover has been fertile ground for experimentation. Snapchat hasn't been shy about redesigning Discover or moving on from underperforming publishers. If users continue gravitating toward stories focused around specific events and topics rather than the publisher-branded digital magazines, Snapchat will invest more in Stories and less in Discover. It's possible they may even kill Discover outright at some point.

On the other hand, does Snapchat really want to build a new-age Conde Nast or Hearst publishing within its walls? Live Stories is already an enormous undertaking; users sent in over eight hundred hours of video to the Coachella Live Story, which content analysts had to sift through to pull out the very best to go on the story. In the future, machine learning and image-recognition software can help with this load, but Evan will likely still want to rely on human editors at least to some extent. Rather than producing all of this content itself, Snapchat may partner with publishers around specific stories, like it has for the Rio Olympics, rather than giving publishers free reign to post publisher-branded stories every day. Publishers could still share revenue with Snapchat and have their branding somewhere on the Live Stories they produce.

Snapchat will keep experimenting, pivoting, and evolving as it figures out an ideal content strategy. But Snapchat is not the only tech company trying to convince media outlets that it is the future of publishing. Snapchat has competition from Facebook on every front.

FEAR AND LOATHING IN MENLO PARK

MARCH 2016
MENLO PARK, CA

Just before Facebook went public in 2012, Mark Zuckerberg had a bound red book titled *Facebook Was Not Originally Created to Be a Company* placed on every employee's desk. The book's penultimate page offered a grave rallying cry:

> If we don't create the thing that kills Facebook, someone else will.
>
> "Embracing change" isn't enough. It has to be so hardwired into who we are that even talking about it seems redundant. The Internet is not a friendly place. Things that don't stay relevant don't even get the luxury of leaving ruins. They disappear.

Like any good religion, the cult-like startup world has a holy scripture: *The Innovator's Dilemma*, a 1997 book by Harvard Business School professor Clayton Christensen. Christensen wrote the book before "disruptive innovation" was a punchline on the HBO comedy *Silicon Valley*, and it has managed to maintain its revered status for two decades.

We can see the core concept of *The Innovator's Dilemma* at work in Snapchat's story: a new entrant makes a product that is so far beneath what an incumbent does that it seems silly—why would we waste our time down there? Who cares about a sexting app? But the entrant fills a need, as teenagers prefer using an impermanent messaging app. Then the entrant gets better (adding more features like video sharing and geofilters) and moves upmarket (adding Snapchat Stories and moving into the social network space), attracting a bigger share of the market (passing Twitter in daily active users) and better customers (older, more affluent users, and celebrities and media companies signing on as publishers).

Mark Zuckerberg is hyper aware of this potentially lethal threat from startups; he builds separate teams at Facebook to create new apps and snatches up the best new companies by making aggressive offers for hot startups like Instagram, WhatsApp, and Oculus Rift. But Evan wouldn't sell, so Snapchat became the one that got away. And Snapchat keeps moving up and up, attracting more users and stealing more photos and videos that users formerly posted to Facebook or Instagram.

It's tempting to think that whoever has the better team and better technology will win. But that's simply not true in social media. In fact, the pure technology probably matters least. What matters most is culture and customs—what you value and how that plays out in your actions. If you compare Facebook and Snapchat right now, you *can* do the same things on Facebook and Instagram that you do on Snapchat: post photos, message friends, send money, read articles, watch celebrities' videos, etc. But you don't do the same things because the different apps were built in different orders for different audiences. They have different aesthetics and different customs.

Snapchat's ethos was so directly antithetical to that of Facebook that anyone who chose to work at the latter would struggle to understand the former. It wasn't merely arrogance that promoted this misunderstanding, though that was the case in the beginning. Rather, if you believed in the mission of connecting the world through a permanent online social network, believed so strongly that you chose to spend your time working on that network, how could you ever fully appreciate the long-term potential of an app where everything disappeared every twenty-four hours? It became an ideological holy war. You were part of the Facebook-Instagram religion, based on permanence and data, or you were part of the Snapchat religion, focused on ephemerality and a small group of people's decisions without data. You couldn't believe in both.

In the summer of 2016, Mark Zuckerberg told Facebook employees at an all-hands meeting they shouldn't let their pride get in the way of doing what's best for users, even if that meant copying rival companies. Zuckerberg's message became an informal slogan at Facebook: "Don't be too proud to copy." And it certainly wasn't.

Snapchat had proven there was an enormous market for its ephemeral approach. Thus, undaunted by his failed attempts to buy and copy Snapchat, Zuckerberg set out to attack Facebook's biggest threat on multiple fronts.

In early 2016, Facebook made a big push to get media companies and celebrities to use its live video broadcasting tool, Facebook Live. Facebook had seen from its Onavo data how people were watching live video on a startup named Meerkat and Twitter's Periscope app; the company could also see how many snaps per day Snapchat users were sending, many of which were videos. Facebook had to drastically increase its video offerings. Facebook Live let Facebook users watch live video or video replays after the broadcast had ended. Broadcasts ranged from celebrity interviews to reporters covering events to regular people talking to their friends.

With Facebook's unparalleled scale, even—or perhaps especially—the inane could go viral. In April 2016, BuzzFeed produced a Facebook Live video of two employees adding rubber bands to a watermelon until the watermelon exploded. The video lasted forty-five minutes, with 807,000 people tuning in simultaneously at its peak; millions more replayed the video on Facebook. A month later, Candace Payne bought herself a *Star Wars* Chewbacca mask that roared when she opened her mouth. Payne filmed herself on Facebook Live trying it on and laughing hysterically. Her video has been viewed almost 160 million times.

Live video was great for celebrities and interesting events, but, as we saw with Justin Kan's Justin.tv experiment, most people rarely have interesting enough lives to broadcast live video. Neither Facebook nor Snapchat had fully figured out their content strategy yet. Both tried to win over media companies and experimented with producing original content.

Facebook COO Sheryl Sandberg personally visited talent agencies in Los Angeles to pitch them on Facebook Live. Facebook signed deals with 140 media companies and celebrities, paying them more than $50 million total to post Facebook Live videos for a year. Like those who signed with Discover, the list of media companies ran from well-established outfits like CNN and *The New York Times* to smaller upstarts, and the two companies shared many of the same publishers. Tastemade will earn around $1 million from Facebook to produce over one hundred Facebook Live shows every month for a year. While Facebook had never paid content creators before, it now handed out seventeen contracts worth over $1 million; the highest bounty went to BuzzFeed for a little over $3 million for a year. Even celebrities like Kevin Hart, Gordon Ramsay, and Russell Wilson took checks from Facebook.

As Snapchat grew ever more popular with media companies and celebrities, many took to making their profile pictures on Facebook and Twitter a Snapcode—a Snapchat-generated QR code that allows one user to add a second user on Snapchat if the first user takes a snap of the second's QR code. Facebook and Twitter didn't like these influencers using their sites to grow their Snapchat followings. Facebook suggested to one media company that if they didn't stop using a Snapcode as their profile picture, it could affect their posts' rankings in the all-important Facebook News Feed. Facebook then updated its policies, informing media companies and celebrities that they could only share sponsored content if their profile pictures and cover photos didn't feature third-party brands or sponsors. Twitter asked the *Huffington Post* to change their profile picture from a Snapcode to something else. Instagram warned users not to use "links asking you to add someone on another service."

This behavior attempted to slow Snapchat's growth and served to continue the pissing contest Snapchat and Facebook had been having for years; early on after Snapchat released geofilters, they had placed a geofilter over Facebook's campus featuring the Snapchat ghost pointing and laughing. As for Twitter, Snapchat didn't even bother fighting back, as Snapchat passed Twitter in daily active users (150 million to 140 million) in June 2016.

In August 2016, Instagram released Instagram Stories, a new feature essentially copying Snapchat Stories that let users post photo and video slideshows that disappeared after twenty-four hours. Like Snapchat Stories—and unlike normal Instagram—Stories had no likes, no comments, and no sharing tools, so there was no anxiety about posting. Instagram put users' stories in little bubbles at the top of its feed, both to drive adoption of the new feature and to leave Instagram's normal feed alone. With this setup, users didn't have to feel anxiety about clogging the feed and could post as many impermanent photos and videos as they wanted.

A few days after Instagram launched Stories, Facebook began testing face filters that were extremely similar to Snapchat's lenses. In Brazil and Canada, users who opened their Facebook app would see an open camera window—similar, again, to Snapchat opening directly to the camera—that let them apply Brazilian- or Canadian-themed face paint to cheer on their country in the Olympics. They could also add geofilter lookalikes on top of their photos that said "Team Canada" and "Team Brazil." Facebook copied Snapchat throughout 2016, testing the Stories features wherever it could—in its Facebook, Messenger, WhatsApp, and Instagram apps—and adding impermanent messaging options to Instagram and Messenger.

Snapchat had always strived to have the best camera to lock up the best, most creative content and the coolest users—the hip, young crowd and creative influencers. Facebook and Instagram had learned that they couldn't simply copy Snapchat's app to beat it. But by adopting all of Snapchat's features in different parts of their empire, the combined giant could certainly slow Snapchat's growth. Hundreds of millions of people use Facebook and Instagram but don't use Snapchat. If they started enjoying silly Facebook lenses or recognized the appeal of impermanent Instagram Stories, they might never bother downloading Snapchat.

Instagram founder Kevin Systrom was very open about copying Snapchat in an interview with *TechCrunch*'s Josh Constine:

> Instagram deserves all the credit for bringing filters to the fore-
> front. This isn't about who invented something. This is about a

format, and how you take it to a network and put your own spin on it.

Facebook invented feed, LinkedIn took on feed, Twitter took on feed, Instagram took on feed, and they all feel very different now and they serve very different purposes. But no one looks down at someone for adopting something that is so obviously great for presenting a certain type of information.

Innovation happens in the Valley, and people invent formats, and that's great. And then what you see is those formats proliferate. So @ usernames were invented on Twitter. Hashtags were invented on Twitter. Instagram has those. Filtered photos were not invented on Instagram.

And I think what you see is that every company looks around and adopts the best of the best formats or state-of-the-art technology. Snapchat adopted face filters that existed elsewhere first, right? And slideshows existed in other places too. Flipagram was doing it for a while. So I think that's the interesting part of the Valley. You can't just recreate another product. But you can say "what's really awesome about a format? And does it apply to our network?"

Don't you think that Snapchat's done a really awesome job? And Facebook's done a great job. And Instagram's done a great job. I think all of these companies have done a great job. Some people invent stuff. We've invented things.

Gmail was not the first email client. Google Maps was certainly not the first map. The iPhone was definitely not the first phone. The question is what do you do with that format? What do you do with that idea? Do you build on it? Do you add new things? Are you trying to bring it in a new direction?

I don't believe these [Instagram and Snapchat] are substitutes, and that's okay.

Facebook had finally realized after failing with Poke and Slingshot that just slapping ephemerality onto its services was not working. But Instagram made more sense. Instagram was still cool among younger users.

Instagram Stories became a massive success. Just two months after its launch, it had 100 million daily active users, a number that doubled to 200 million by April 2017 and 250 million by June 2017, figures that dwarfed Snapchat's 166 million daily active users.

Throughout the end of 2016 and early 2017, I remember friends commenting on how many more views they got on their Instagram Stories than on their Snapchat Stories. Instagram had over 700 million daily active users (on the whole app, not just Stories), compared to just 166 million for Snapchat, and most users had more friends and followers on Instagram than they did on Snapchat. The thrill of seeing how many people were watching your story that Snapchat had tapped into was now getting taken over by Instagram's larger user base.

Snapchat was never meant to be a place where you had thousands of followers and strove for the most possible views of your story. After all, is chasing story views that different from chasing likes and retweets? But the way Evan envisioned Snapchat wasn't conducive to growth. Instagram is far more tailored for it, as the app suggests friends to follow and makes it much easier to find and follow accounts you might like.

Instagram Stories hurt Snapchat's engagement and growth at a critical time for Snapchat, as it prepared for its initial public offering. But Instagram may also be merely recreating the early 2010s Facebook that led to Snapchat's popularity in the first place. High story views and follower counts are a sugar rush now, but they lead to bloated feeds and a deep lack of intimacy.

ESPN reporter Kate Fagan wrote about this lack of intimacy in her 2017 book, *What Made Maddy Run: The Secret Struggles and Tragic Death of an All-American Teen*, which covered the life of nineteen-year-old Maddy Holleran. In her book, Fagan discusses how the way we communicate with each other is highly filtered:

> Perhaps the most important distinguishing feature of a social account is its public nature, the understanding each user has, from the moment of launch, is that everything is for public consumption. But perhaps we are overstating the effect of this distinction. If in private, most of us allow ourselves to say or write certain truths we otherwise wouldn't, then perhaps the reverse holds true. Perhaps we share things in public that we couldn't offer in private. If we've accepted that we are different

in private, is this not also true for how we reveal ourselves in public? And which version of ourselves is more real?

As young people, we are trying to find our voice. Trying out who we are, again and again, until something feels more accurate than the previous thing . . . We believe what we see. And we can't be what we can't see. We are so credulous when we assume that everyone else must be the version of themselves they portray in public, even if we are hardly the people we present ourselves as.

We put time into our social media because we believe it affords us the unique opportunity to fashion our own identity. We care about the images we post and the lines we write underneath those images, because it's all part of reflecting who we are and constructing who we want to become. Would you put more time, or less, into a post if you knew it was your last? Would you want the image and words to be perfect, an ideal, lasting representation of you? Or would you quickly recognize the futility of the pursuit, that the whole thing was a mirage merely reflecting distorted images of the real world? And would you instead, spend your time absorbing the world itself?

Ultimately, absorbing the world itself is what Snapchat wants to empower its users to do. But this is often at odds with users' short term desires, and Snapchat's goals for growth and profit. The more intimate an area is, the harder it is to place advertiesements there. So while Snapchat messaging may be more raw and unfiltered than glamorous Instagram shots, Snapchat Stories posts are growing more and more staged and similar to other social media feeds.

Some young people in Snapchat's core demographic have addressed this by creating second Instagram accounts to share more authentic, personal photos and videos with their closest friends. Dubbed "Finstagrams," short for Fake Instagrams, they restrict their following to a few dozen of their closest friends, or perhaps even less, and abandon the typical social norms of Instagram; they post multiple pictures per day, mundane photos, screenshots of text conversations, and silly selfies.

Nonetheless, it's telling that these users decided to create second

Instagram accounts to foster this sense of intimacy versus using Snapchat more. And while Evan may not want to make Snapchat a social network focused on the number of views your posts get, those high numbers attract more advertising dollars.

Facebook tried to copy Snapchat a million times. But the failures didn't matter—only the success would.

SNAP INC.

VENICE, CA

When Snapchat released its S-1, an SEC filing that companies
looking to go public must make, in early 2017, it shed light on
Snapchat's strategy of placing many bets and failing fast:

> Our strategy is to invest in product innovation and take risks
> to improve our camera platform. We do this in an effort to drive
> user engagement, which we can then monetize through adver-
> tising. We use the revenue we generate to fund future product
> innovation to grow our business.
>
> In a world where anyone can distribute products instantly
> and provide them for free, the best way to compete is by inno-
> vating to create the most engaging products. That's because it's
> difficult to use distribution or cost as a competitive advantage—
> new software is available to users immediately, and for free. We
> believe this means that our industry favors companies that
> innovate, because people will use their products.

As Zuckerberg set out to copy any feature that Snapchat found success with, Evan focused on experimenting at a rapid pace.

He doubled down on what had made Snapchat a hit in the first place with messaging, releasing a Chat 2.0 that let users record and send ten-second (or shorter) Audio or Video Notes. These notes played like little messages in chat, with the Video Notes playing in a gif-like loop. Users could also now use Snapchat to call or video chat with each other even if the person they were contacting wasn't already in the chat; previously, Evan had said he didn't want Snapchat to be like a phone that rang, preferring instead to focus on having people in chat at the same time. But, as with many issues, he changed his mind and became convinced calling would be useful to users.

In July 2016, Snapchat released Memories, a way for users to save their photos, videos, and stories in the app and, more importantly, a way for users to upload old photos from Snapchat or even their camera roll to send to friends or post to their story. For the first five years of the company, you couldn't upload anything—every photo or video had to be shot in Snapchat and immediately shared, focusing everything on the here and now.

Memories's permanence was antithetical to Snapchat's core ethos, but it was released late enough that users' behaviors and norms were already well established. Had Snapchat released Memories in 2012, it may have been a disaster that cut into Snapchat's real-time, fleeting nature. But because Snapchat already had hundreds of millions of users snapping for years before it released Memories, it was able to add to the product without changing core behaviors. Memories makes Snapchat's camera even more useful, as it lets users store photos, videos, their own Snapchat stories in their entirety—indeed, their memories—all on Snapchat's servers rather than taking up space on their phone. It is another step toward making Snapchat people's default camera.

By the time it added Memories, Snapchat had essentially built Facebook in reverse. It started with impermanent picture messaging, added a social feed that stuck around for twenty-four hours rather than ten seconds, then changed the immediate nature of posts.

Returning to Snapchat's S-1, we can see Evan's strategy driving product development:

> We invest heavily in future product innovation and take risks to try to improve our camera platform and drive long-term user engagement. Sometimes this means sacrificing short-term engagement to introduce products, like Stories, that might change the way people use Snapchat. Additionally, our products often use new technologies and require people to change their behavior, such as using a camera to talk with their friends. This means that our products take a lot of time and money to develop, and might have slow adoption rates. While not all of our investments will pay off in the long run, we are willing to take these risks in an attempt to create the best and most differentiated products in the market.

In March 2016, Snapchat acquired Bitstrips, one of the most intriguing new social products. The company was founded in Toronto in 2007 to help teachers create teachable comics using templates. Teachers could create little cartoons, add in speech bubbles, and put characters in costumes. In 2014, the company hit it big with the idea of simplifying the cartoon strips to single-panel sketches of people with their friends. Using some pretty impressive custom image rendering software behind the scenes, Bitstrips managed to make cartoon avatars—emojis that they called Bitmojis—that looked exactly like users. Users could then use their little cartoon avatar in a variety of situations and expressions to message friends and post on social media.

Evan loved the company because it blended technology and art in a beautiful way. The rock stars of the company were not the developers but rather the artists. The founders came from animation and media backgrounds. The walls of the office were covered in personalized cartoons, giving it the feel of an art studio rather than a tech startup.

Later that year, in July, Snapchat announced the deal in a Bitstrips cartoon panel on its website. In a reversal of how they handled previous acquisitions, Snapchat maintained Bitstrips' flagship Bitmoji as a standalone app, the first step into Snapchat growing beyond its singular identity. The company urged users to download Bitmoji and link it to their Snapchat accounts, where they could use "Friendmoji" cartoons featuring users and their Snapchat friends' likenesses together. Snapchat's employee badges quickly displayed their cartoon Bitmoji self in lieu of an actual photograph of them.

A few days after rolling out the Bitmoji integration, Evan proposed to his girlfriend Miranda Kerr. Kerr said yes and posted a photo on Instagram of her engagement ring with a Bitmoji cartoon laid on top of Evan proposing to her, with big letters below the two of them saying, "Marry Me!"

The Bitstrips acquisition opened up the possibility of Snapchat as a platform—potentially a very lucrative one. Snapchat could already sell marketers on a wide range of products within its app: Discover ads, Live Stories ads, geofilters, lenses, and e-commerce opportunities like ticketing. Now, the company could begin making money off other apps, whether they were apps like Bitstrips that Snapchat owned or apps the company integrated with from a wider developer community.

Again returning to the S-1, we can see Snapchat's strategy behind using its creative products to drive advertising:

> To create effective advertising products that our community might enjoy, we often base our advertising products on existing consumer products and behavior. The same team that designs our consumer products also helps design our advertising products. This means that these formats are engaging and familiar to our users. For example, Taco Bell's Sponsored Lens campaign that let people turn their head into a taco increased overall engagement on our platform because it provided a fun Creative Tool that people wanted to use and share with their friends.

In 2015, Snapchat invested in a mobile shopping app called Spring. *The Wall Street Journal* has been vocal about its desire to sell newspaper subscriptions through Snapchat. Soon after *Cosmopolitan* editor in chief Joanna Coles joined Snapchat's board of directors, she told Recode's Kara Swisher that Snapchat would move into e-commerce soon.

"Sweet is a channel on Snapchat that Hearst and Snapchat have done together, and the tagline is 'Love something new every day,'" Coles said. "But at some point that will morph into an e-commerce platform so you will be able to buy from it."

Snapchat has also been experimenting with new types of advertising that take advantage of Snapchat's QR code-scanning technology. Remember the earliest promotion on Snapchat? Frozen yogurt chain 16 Handles messaged its followers a coupon they had to use in the store before the ten-second photo disappeared. Snapchat's new ads could do that at scale, letting users scan a QR code that unlocks a special time-sensitive deal on an advertiser's product.

Once again, Snapchat could look to Asian messaging giant Line, which they had previously studied when exploring early revenue models for Snapchat, and its success with stickers to see a model for Bitstrips. Line made over $200 million in sticker sales in 2015, almost $100 million of which is from third-party sellers who create and sell sticker packs on Line; the company made even more—over $300 million—from sponsored stickers (which are free to users, with Line raking in revenue from advertisers). You could easily claim that sponsored geofilters are already Snapchat's sponsored stickers. When Snapchat rolled out geofilters, it included cultural icons like Soul Cycle and Disneyland. While those geofilters were not paid advertisements, it's not hard to imagine sponsored stickers on Snapchat featuring users' and their friends' likenesses working out at Soul Cycle, eating at In-N-Out, or sharing Coca-Cola bottles.

Memories expanded Snapchat's world of content. Because most Snapchat users let the app know where they are (to unlock features like geofilters), you could be at a restaurant in Madrid you haven't been to in two years, and a special "Throwback Thursday" option could pop up with your photos and videos from the last time you were there, provided you'd saved them to Snapchat Memories. The company has been fond of making old technologies like QR codes and top friend lists cool again, and could easily resurrect something like Foursquare's mayor badges (whoever checked in the most at the local burger joint became the mayor of it). Snapchat could award special filters and lenses to the mayor of a given location. There are obvious opportunities for sponsorship and revenue with this location approach as well.

◉

In January 2007, Steve Jobs revealed the iPhone to the world and took a step to reflect the growing ambitions of his company. Apple Computer

Inc. would shorten its name to Apple Inc., becoming more than just a computer company. By the fall of 2016, Evan set his sights on growing Snapchat beyond its eponymous app, changing the company name to Snap Inc. and announcing his first attempt to broaden the company: Snapchat Spectacles.

Vergence Labs, the secretive hardware startup Snapchat purchased in March 2014, had been working for years on a pair of sunglasses that could record video for Snapchat. Evan tested a prototype in early 2015 while hiking with his fiancée Miranda Kerr.

"It was our first vacation, and we went to Big Sur for a day or two," Evan later recalled. "We were walking through the woods, stepping over logs, looking up at the beautiful trees. And when I got the footage back and watched it, I could see my own memory, through my own eyes—it was unbelievable. It's one thing to see images of an experience you had, but it's another thing to have an experience of the experience. It was the closest I'd ever come to feeling like I was there again."

With Spectacles, users can tap a button on the left corner of the sunglasses to start recording a ten-second Snapchat video. The glasses then transfer the video to your phone via Bluetooth or WiFi. Spectacles records video in a 115-degree circular format that is meant to more closely mimic how the human eye sees things.

One of the biggest problems with Snapchat the app is that it takes you out of the moment. You and your friends are having a silly dance party, or just hiked to a beautiful view, or are surrounded by costumed people running through the streets. So you stop to pull your phone out to Snapchat it, and in doing so you lose the magic. What's more, because all your friends are snapping too, the awesome moment is now ugly, with half of your friends also recording during your shot. If you and your friends have Spectacles, none of that happens. You can instantly record something, then add filters and effects and send it later. Although this isn't happening in real time, that's okay—the cultural norm around Snapchat that its content is curated yet close to live is so ubiquitous that people will continue to post close to real-time content.

In September 2016, Snapchat teased the Spectacles launch with billboards on Wall Street and elsewhere of Ghostface Chillah, his eyes stylized to appear like the lenses of the sunglasses. The product debuted in the glossy *WSJ Magazine*, and Evan was photographed wearing

Spectacles, along with his classic white v-neck, by fashion icon Karl Lagerfeld.

Quick to distance the product from the nerdy and invasive Google Glass and to avoid overhyped expectations, Evan characterized Spectacles in interviews as a fun toy. Years before, Evan had noted that Snapchat would not build an app for Google Glass because he found the product "invasive," like "a gun pointed at you." To relieve people of the feeling that Spectacles were a social media gun aimed at them, and to address privacy concerns, little lights on the front of the sunglasses illuminate when the user is taking a picture or recording video.

Growing up, Evan wished he had been part of the PC revolution. He was fortunate enough to be a major part of the mobile revolution. And he has grand aspirations to be an even bigger part of what comes next.

Dominant tech companies are disrupted when new technologies emerge and platforms shift—from mainframes to PC and PC to mobile. Smart emerging players can ride these platform shifts from a nondominant position to a dominant one; it's much easier to do this if you play a role in causing that shift. While Spectacles has been positioned as just a toy, it has enormous potential. If Spectacles truly succeeds, it will replace the iPhone as people's primary camera and most personal device. This would be Evan's greatest accomplishment, to replace the legendary device that was created by his hero. The same device that gave his company a chance.

CHAPTER THIRTY-THREE

SPECTACLES

DECEMBER 31, 2016
NEW YORK, NY

I sat on the train from Philly to New York, absentmindedly Snapchatting. I watched a Snapchat from my friend Chelsea, who was celebrating the New Year with her high school friends in Mammoth Mountain out in California. We had a five-day streak going, which means nothing except that Snapchat puts a fire emoji and the number of days in a row you've Snapchatted each other next to your names. High schoolers have dozens of these "streaks" going with friends, many of which are hundreds, if not thousands, of days long.

I had told myself I would get some writing done on the train, but found myself constantly checking my phone, looking at friends' snap stories and football highlights on ESPN's Discover channel. Arriving at Penn Station, I ducked and weaved through the throng of people and onto the subway, popping up at Fifth Avenue.

As I approached the picturesque glass box of the flagship Apple Store, I saw the Spectacles logo, a black circle inside a white circle with a black border on a yellow background, looming like a big eye behind it. The Spectacles pop-up store was a plain, small storefront with a sign that simply read SPECTACLES.

Internally at Snap, many felt Spectacles's rollout was almost more important than the product itself. After announcing Spectacles in late September, Snapchat made it quite difficult to actually buy the sunglasses. The company used a vending machine, called a Snapbot, to sell the first runs of Spectacles. The Snapbot started in Venice and would announce its location twenty-four hours before it touched down. The Snapbot moved around California a lot, in Santa Monica, Pasadena, Brentwood, and Big Sur, but it also appeared in seemingly random places, like Route 66 in Catoosa, Oklahoma, the Grand Canyon, and Florida State University's campus. Some people waited for hours in line for Spectacles—usually Snapchatting, tweeting, and Instagramming the experience. The artificial scarcity let Snapchat portray Spectacles as a toy, avoid harsh scrutiny about sales numbers, and run one of the most unique marketing campaigns in recent memory.

The Snapbot avoided Silicon Valley and, for a while, New York. In November, I visited the new Snapchat pop-up shop that had opened in Manhattan, right behind the Apple Store on Fifth Avenue. It was cold, maybe forty degrees, but for New York in December, I'd take it. I had heard of lines as long as hundreds of people and customers receiving wristbands to come back, and I expected a long wait. So I was pleasantly surprised that there was almost no line.

Inside, TVs lined the walls rotating in a circle to show off Spectacles's circular recording style. There were three Snapbots in the back of the store; I walked up to one and used the screen to see what each color—black, teal, and coral—would look like on me. I settled on black, swiped my card, and the Snapbot spit out a pair of Spectacles.

I headed over to meet up with friends in the West Village, eager to show them the somewhat ridiculous purchase I'd just made. We'd be going out to a party and then a bar—a fun night but nothing that would hold a candle to Snapchat's New Year's Eve parties of years past. It felt like a lifetime had gone by since we rang in 2013 with Evan and Bobby at their baby blue beachfront house in Venice. It seemed impossible that it had been just four short years.

Back then, Snapchat had just added video messaging, which was very exciting. Now, there were stories and geofilters and lenses and Live Stories and Discover. Thirty employees had become fifteen hundred. Snapchat had become Snap Inc. In a few short months, Evan and Bobby would ring the bell at the New York Stock Exchange and Snap would be a publicly traded company.

In just a few weeks, Snap would begin its roadshow for its March IPO. Michael Lynton stepped down from his Sony role to focus on helping Evan with strategy full time, and he was named chairman of Snap's board in late 2016. Bankers for Snap's IPO would portray Evan, still just twenty-seven years old, as one of Snap's primary assets and a visionary comparable to Steve Jobs and Mark Zuckerberg.

It seemed like a fairy-tale ending. But for Snap, the IPO is far from an ending. It's the beginning of a very difficult new chapter for the company.

"Five years ago, we came to the realization that the camera can be used for more than capturing memories," Evan said when Spectacles launched. "We showed it can be used for talking. The dream for us is expanding the camera and what it can do for your life. It has capabilities beyond making memories."

Snapchat explores this possibility in its S-1 filing: "In the way that the flashing cursor became the starting point for most products on desktop computers, we believe that the camera screen will be the starting point for most products on smartphones. This is because images created by smartphone cameras contain more context and richer information than other forms of input like text entered on a keyboard. This means that we are willing to take risks in an attempt to create innovative and different camera products that are better able to reflect and improve our life experiences."

Evan is working to make Snapchat the starting place for an entire generation of internet users, akin to previous generations' homepages and portals. As billions of people come online in the coming years, their first and primary way of connecting to the internet will be a phone. Everyone will have internet-connected cameras in their hands—although it's not clear if they will all be able to have Snapchat, as the app is currently blocked in China, for example.

We should look at Snapchat through the lens of three acts: (1) luck,

(2) recording the world, (3) controlling the world. In act one, Snapchat was a simple picture and video sharer that came out at the perfect time and exploded in popularity. In act two, Evan and Bobby brilliantly made Snapchat the must-have app, packed with fun filters and lenses and engaging content with Stories and Live. If they can successfully pull off act three, Snapchat will take another leap, larger than the twenty-fold valuation jump from $800 million to $16 billion that Snapchat took from act one to act two.

In act three, Snapchat goes from being a recorder capable of capturing and broadcasting the world around you to a remote control capable of affecting the world around you. The best remote control app we have right now is Uber, which allows you to pull your phone out, tap a button, and be whisked away to wherever you'd like to go. Snapchat could fulfill the original goal of Scan, the QR code-scanning app it acquired, and bridge the digital and physical world.

Snapchat has been investing deeply in machine learning and image recognition, and it has trained users to constantly record the world around them. The company has worked on an image search, which would understand images in users' photographs and provide information about them, like a Google search or a visual Shazam. Or they could take a photograph—of a barcode or QR code to start, but of a product itself in the future—of something they want to buy in a store, and be offered options to purchase it through Snapchat.

Alexa and Siri can hear. Soon, Snapchat and other cameras will be able to see.

On every front, Snapchat will continue to battle Facebook. But if by this point you're only thinking about whether Snapchat will beat Facebook, then we haven't looked at the bigger picture enough. Evan's ambitions are much grander than that. He doesn't merely want Snapchat to be a great technology startup. Nor will being a great technology company satisfy his appetite. He simply wants to be great. Period. Take a moment and appreciate the full scale of this ambition. There are very few people, or companies, who can be placed in a category of noncategorical greatness. Snapchat and Evan are obviously not there yet. But that is where he wants to go.

Famed business consultant and writer Jim Collins, the author of manager-bibles *Built to Last* and *Good to Great*, has written about three things that make a company truly spectacular: (1) superior financial results; (2) making a distinctive impact, where if you didn't exist, you wouldn't easily be replaced; and (3) lasting endurance beyond multiple cycles of technology, marketing, and people. Very, very few companies satisfy all three criteria.

Obviously Snapchat will need superior financial results to live up to its lofty market cap.

You could argue that the company has already made a distinctive impact. But can this distinctive impact last and deepen? Can Snapchat be cool in perpetuity? And if it can't, how will it survive? Facebook made the awkward transition to middle age by acquiring cool companies and becoming a very useful utility. Facebook also made this transition because it is an exceptionally well-run company; Snapchat will need to hire and scale in an outstanding fashion if it is to match Facebook rather than fall into the organizational chaos of Twitter. Evan is so central to Snapchat that it is difficult to imagine the company without him, but, by Collins's definition, Snapchat will have to one day be great beyond Evan and the current team if it is to be a truly spectacular company.

Snapchat has challenged most of our assumptions. Have we learned from it?

Mobile is a bigger and better market than desktop. Can we expect a mobile-only Amazon, et al., to be bigger and better than their predecessors? While tech's giant companies, from Facebook to Google to Amazon to Apple, seek more and more data about us, Snapchat deletes everything and knows comparatively little about its users. Do we want everything, or even most things, on the internet to be permanent?

Fundamentally, Snapchat marked a rebellion against the social network status quo of the early 2010s, when the things that had made Facebook and Instagram so appealing—the ability to put forward an idealized version of our lives and get instant approval for it—began to feel less a novelty than a burden. It allowed young people to express themselves in a more genuine way without as much fear that presenting an imperfect and more real version of themselves would come back to haunt them.

Somewhere, perhaps in a Donner dorm room, or a continent away, the next Evan Spiegel is dreaming up a new way to interact on the internet. And it will arrive out of the blue, like a snap popping up on your phone.

We know it will not look or feel like Snapchat, or Instagram, or Facebook. It may well feel silly or self-indulgent. It will probably look like a toy. At least at first.

ACKNOWLEDGMENTS

This book has been incredibly fun and intellectually stimulating to write. I am deeply grateful to everyone who spoke to me for this book, particularly those who risked professional and personal relationships.

In May 2012, I had just accepted an internship with *TechCrunch* for the upcoming summer and was talking with my new boss, Kim-Mai Cutler, about writing a couple of stories profiling two startups that were hot on Stanford's campus at the time: Clinkle and Snapchat. That turned out to be a pretty good idea. I covered Snapchat for *TechCrunch* for two years and learned an incredible amount from the company.

Fast-forward a few years, and I had graduated from both Stanford and *TechCrunch*. I was having lunch with Philip Taubman, a *New York Times* and *Stanford Daily* alum, who had taught and mentored me at Stanford. Phil urged me to continue covering Snapchat by writing a book about the company's fascinating rise. Philip introduced me to his fantastic agent, Binky Urban, who in turn introduced me to my wonderful agents Amelia Atlas and Richard Pike. I particularly owe a major thanks to Amelia, who stuck with me through a wretched first proposal and many, many rejections. Thank you to my tireless editor, Tim Bartlett, and the wonderful staff at St. Martin's Press, particularly Alice Pfeifer, Donna Cherry, and Ryan Masteller, who copyedited the manuscript. Thank you to Jamie Joseph and the entire team at Virgin Books UK.

One of the most enjoyable aspects of writing this book has been talking to other authors about their experiences. I truly appreciate all the authors who generously gave me their time and advice, notably Alex Banayan, Nick Bilton, Matthew Berry, Blake Harris, Kevin Roose, and Ashlee Vance. A special thank-you to Larry Langton and Langton Media for inspiring me to think about this book and these characters in a new light.

Thank you to Mary Ritti and the Snapchat PR team for their help with fact-checking.

I am very grateful to all of the teachers, students, and alumni of The Haverford School, where I learned to read and write and, most important, how to appreciate both. In particular I must thank Richard Duffany for teaching me the mechanics of writing at a young age.

Thank you to my classmates and professors at Stanford University for constantly challenging me while making me feel at home. I am particularly grateful to everyone at *The Stanford Daily*, especially Kate Abbott, Kathleen Chaykowski, Marwa Farag, Brendan O'Byrne, Margaret Rawson, Stephanie Weber, and Zach Zimmerman. Thank you for teaching me to chase important stories.

I owe so much to my fellow writers and editors at *TechCrunch*, particularly John Biggs, Alexia Bonatsos, Mike Butcher, Matt Burns, Josh Constine, Jordan Crook, Kim Mai-Cutler, Ned Desmond, Eric Eldon, Anthony Ha, Leslie Hitchcock, Susan Hobbs, Ryan Lawler, Ingrid Lunden, Matthew Panzarino, Jon Shieber, Colleen Taylor, and Alex Wilhelm. Thank you for teaching me how to cover startups and ask the right questions, and for allowing me to make mistakes.

Thank you to my coworkers at Khosla Ventures, Vinod Khosla, Samir Kaul, Keith Rabois, David Weiden, Ben Ling, Kathy Chan, Nick Moryl, and Hari Arul. Thank you for giving me my first job and teaching me to see the potential in nascent ideas.

Thank you to all my friends and classmates at the Stanford GSB for your nonstop support as I wrote and edited this book during the past year. In particular, I want to thank Mannie Ajayi, Dhruv Amin, Ashley Brasier, Jake Bullock, Patrick Chase, Pam Chirathivat, David Demeres, Caroline Duffy, Calen Engert, Savannah English, Claire Fisher, Dana Gingrich, Jill Greenberg, Zach Horat, Devin Kelsey, Sam Krieg, Tim Latimer, Jeff Lyon, Alex Maceda, Lauren Martinez, Kelsey Mason, Mihir Mehta, Alex Menke, Robbie Mitchnik, Taylor Ray, Annie Robertson, Bobby Samuels, Steph Scott, Whitt Virgin-Downey, Frances Wehrwein, and Megan Welch.

I'm very grateful to share my life with great friends. Thank you to Chris Baldock, Sam Barsh, Lauren Birks, Gigi Constable, Chase Disher, Skylar Dorosin, Tim Dougherty, Bob Greco, Joey Grubb, Cam Hutton, Hunter Kodama, Cam Lindsay, Chelsea Lewis, Nick Mahowald, Eric Malumed, Tyler Marks, Bonnie McLindon, Peggy Moriarty, Sean O'Brien, Danny Organ, Philip Origlio, Caitlin Pura, Nolan Pura, Will Rockafellow, John Romer, David Roos, Louie Schley, Robby Schwenke, Jake Silverman, Lauren Taylor, Stuart Upfill-Brown, Michelle Valentine, Roberto Vargas, Dru Warden, and Jack Werner.

Most importantly, my family. I am blessed to have an incredible family that is extremely supportive. Thank you to Eileen McAneny Gallagher, Nick Gallagher, Dennis Gallagher, Paul and Lisa Badame, Tim O'Brien, Carol O'Brien and Ken O'Brien, Kim O'Brien Langton and Larry Langton, Ross DiBono and Lucille DiBono, Ross DiBono II, Cynthia DiBono Weaver, Reverend Jack McNamee, Ro Seavey, and Jay Weiner. To my dad, Mike, I wish we could have spent more time together. Rest in peace.

Sadly, too many names have been omitted from these acknowledgments. There are countless people who helped me in this process in small ways they may not even realize. Thank you.

And finally, thank you to you, the reader. I hope you've enjoyed it.

WORKS CITED

Prologue: Initial Public Offering

Bilton, Nick. "Why I Use Snapchat: It's Fast, Ugly and Ephemeral." *New York Times*, January 27, 2014. https://bits.blogs.nytimes.com/2014/01/27/why-i-use-snapchat-its-fast-ugly-and-ephemeral/

Dave, Paresh. "Exclusive Interview: How Snapchat Founder Evan Spiegel Feels after the Historic IPO." *Los Angeles Times*, March 2, 2017. http://www.latimes.com/business/technology/la-fi-tn-evan-spiegel-bobby-murphy-20170302-story.html

Farrell, Maureen, Corrie Driebusch, and Sarah Krouse. "Snapchat Shares Surge 44% in Market Debut." *Wall Street Journal*, March 2, 2017. https://www.wsj.com/articles/snapchat-parent-snap-opens-higher-in-market-debut-1488471695

Johnson, Hollis, Alex Heath, and Portia Crowe. "'Right Now We're Just Celebrating': Inside Snap's Crazy $33 Billion IPO." *Business Insider*, March 2, 2017. http://www.businessinsider.com/inside-snapchats-crazy-33-billion-ipo-2017-3?op=1/#a-giant-snap-inc-banner-adorned-the-the-new-york-stock-exchange-on-thursday-signaling-the-companys-hotly-anticipated-ipo-1

Mahler, Jonathan. "Campaign Coverage via Snapchat Could Shake Up the 2016 Elections." *New York Times*, May 3, 2015. https://www.nytimes.com/2015/05/04/business/media/campaign-coverage-via-snapchat-could-shake-up-the-2016-elections.html

New Yorker cartoon. "Looks like another case of someone over forty trying to understand Snapchat." *New Yorker*, April 22, 2016. http://www.newyorker.com/cartoon/a19868

Spiegel, Evan. "What Is Snapchat?" YouTube video, June 16, 2015. https://www.youtube.com/watch?v=ykGXIQAHLnA

Chapter One: Rush

Auletta, Ken. "Get Rich U." *New Yorker*, April 30, 2012. http://www.newyorker.com /magazine/2012/04/30/get-rich-u

Bowles, Nellie. "Three LA Boys: Snapchat's Evan Spiegel, Tinder's Sean Rad and Whisper's Michael Heyward." Recode, June 11, 2014. https://www.recode.net/2014/6/11/11627844 /three-la-boys-evan-spiegel-sean-rad-and-michael-heyward

Colao, J. J. "The Inside Story of Snapchat: The World's Hottest App or a $3 Billion Disappearing Act?" *Forbes*, January 6, 2014. https://www.forbes.com/sites/jjcolao/2014/01/06 /the-inside-story-of-snapchat-the-worlds-hottest-app-or-a-3-billion-disappearing-act /#3961325c67d2

DiGiacomo, Frank. "School for Cool." *Vanity Fair*, March 2005. https://www.vanityfair.com /news/2005/03/crossroads-school200503

Spiegel, Evan. Keynote speech at "Design Yourself" Conference, Stanford Women in Business, April 7, 2013. https://download.docslide.net/documents/design-yourself-conference -opening-keynote-by-evan-spiegel-ceo-of-snapchat.html

Van Grove, Jennifer. "Snapchat's Evan Spiegel: Saying No to $3B, and Feeling Lucky." *CNET*, November 26, 2013. https://www.cnet.com/news/snapchats-evan-spiegel-saying-no-to-3b -and-feeling-lucky/

Chapter Two: Future Freshman

Colao, J. J. "The Inside Story of Snapchat: The World's Hottest App or a $3 Billion Disappearing Act?" *Forbes*, January 6, 2014. https://www.forbes.com/sites/jjcolao/2014/01/06 /the-inside-story-of-snapchat-the-worlds-hottest-app-or-a-3-billion-disappearing-act /#3961325c67d2

Nguyen, An Le. "University Explains Kappa Sigma Decision." *Stanford Daily*, March 28, 2011. http://www.stanforddaily.com/2011/03/28/university-explains-kappa-sigma-decision/

Spiegel, Evan, and Nikesh Arora. Interview, YouTube, October 12, 2015. https://www.youtube .com/watch?v=R-UAjGVPFIE

Chapter Three: Million-Dollar Idea

Colao, J. J. "The Inside Story of Snapchat: The World's Hottest App or a $3 Billion Disappearing Act?" *Forbes*, January 6, 2014. https://www.forbes.com/sites/jjcolao/2014/01/06 /the-inside-story-of-snapchat-the-worlds-hottest-app-or-a-3-billion-disappearing-act /#3961325c67d2

Gallagher, Billy. "The Snapchat Lawsuit, Or How to Lose Your Best Friend over $70 Million." *TechCrunch*, March 7, 2013. https://techcrunch.com/2013/03/07/snapchat-lawsui/

Shontell, Alyson. "These Leaked Videos Could Lead to a Huge Payday for Ousted Snapchat Co-Founder." *Business Insider*, November 20, 2013. http://www.businessinsider.com /snapchat-lawsuit-video-depositions-2013-11

———. "SNAPCHAT LAWSUIT VIDEOS: After a 37-Second Pause, Snapchat's CEO Describes Regrets about the Friend He Ousted." *Business Insider*, November 25, 2013. http://www. businessinsider.com/snapchat-lawsuit-videos-2013-11

Spiegel, Evan. Keynote speech at "Design Yourself" Conference, Stanford Women in Business, April 7, 2013. https://download.docslide.net/documents/design-yourself-conference -opening-keynote-by-evan-spiegel-ceo-of-snapchat.html

Chapter Four: The Other Startup

Alden, William, and David Gelles. "In WhatsApp Deal, Sequoia Capital May Make 50 Times Its Money." *New York Times*,Auletta, Ken. "Get Rich U." *New Yorker*, April 30, 2012. http://www.newyorker.com/magazine/2012/04/30/get-rich-u

Constine, Josh. "Flaming Wreckage of Clinkle Rebuilds as a Referral Service." *TechCrunch*,

December 29, 2015. https://techcrunch.com/2015/12/29/i-know-you-thought-it-was-dead-but/

————. "Clinkle Implodes as Employees Quit in Protest of CEO." *TechCrunch*, May 15, 2015. https://techcrunch.com/2015/05/15/clunk/

Del Rey, Jason. "Clinkle's Still a Hot Mess as Its Big Shot COO Departs (Updated)." Re-code, March 13, 2014. http://www.recode.net/2014/3/13/11624542/clinkles-still-a-hot-mess-as-its-big-shot-coo-departs

————. "Why Longtime Netflix CFO Barry McCarthy Just Agreed to Work for Clinkle's 22-Year-Old CEO." AllThingsD, October 22, 2013. http://allthingsd.com/20131022/why-longtime-netflix-cfo-barry-mccarthy-just-agreed-to-work-for-a-22-year-old-ceo/

Efrati, Amir. "Startup's Deep Roots: Stanford." *Wall Street Journal*, April 3, 2013. http://www.wsj.com/article_email/SB10001424127887324020504578396912443242512-lMyQjAxMTAzMDAwMzEwNDMyWj.html

Fitchard, Kevin. "Clinkle Becomes a Tech Celebrity Magnet, Landing Richard Branson as an Investor." GigaOm, September 26, 2013. https://gigaom.com/2013/09/26/clinkle-becomes-a-tech-celebrity-magnet-landing-richard-branson-as-an-investor/

Gallagher, Billy. "Stanford University Is Going to Invest in Student Startups Like a VC Firm." *TechCrunch*, September 4, 2013. http://techcrunch.com/2013/09/04/stanford-university-is-going-to-invest-in-student-startups-like-a-vc-firm/

————. "Clinkle Raises Celebrity-Filled $25M Round as It Gears Up to Eliminate the Physical Wallet." *TechCrunch*, June 27, 2013. http://techcrunch.com/2013/06/27/clinkle-raises-celebrity-filled-25m-round-as-it-gears-up-to-eliminate-the-physical-wallet/

Mac, Ryan. "Clinkle up in Smoke as Investors Want Their Money Back." *Forbes*, January 22, 2016. http://www.forbes.com/sites/ryanmac/2016/01/22/clinkle-up-in-smoke-as-investors-want-their-money-back/#5dced7db35b6

Rowley, Jason D. "The Startup Funding Graduation Rate Is Surprisingly Low." Mattermark, September 28, 2016. https://mattermark.com/startup-graduation-rate-surprisingly-low/

Shontell, Alyson. "A SILICON VALLEY DISASTER: A 21-Year-Old Stanford Kid Got $30 Million, Then Everything Blew Up." *Business Insider*, April 14, 2014. http://www.businessinsider.com/inside-story-of-clinkle-2014-4?op=1

Thompson, Nicholas. "Stanford and Its Startups." *New Yorker*, September 11, 2013. http://www.newyorker.com/business/currency/stanford-and-its-start-ups

————. "The Trouble with Stanford." *New Yorker*, April 12, 2013. http://www.newyorker.com/tech/elements/the-trouble-with-stanford

————. "The End of Stanford?" *New Yorker*, April 8, 2013. http://www.newyorker.com/tech/elements/the-end-of-stanford

Tiku, Nitasha. "Clinkle Is Bribing College Students with a Vending Machine Full of Cash." Valleywag, November 25, 2014. http://valleywag.gawker.com/clinkle-is-bribing-college-students-with-a-vending-mach-1663325836

Chapter Five: Lawsuit Possible

Colao, J. J. "The Inside Story of Snapchat: The World's Hottest App or a $3 Billion Disappearing Act?" *Forbes*, January 6, 2014. https://www.forbes.com/sites/jjcolao/2014/01/06/the-inside-story-of-snapchat-the-worlds-hottest-app-or-a-3-billion-disappearing-act/#3961325c67d2

Driver, Carol. "CANNES LIONS: Entrepreneur Evan Spiegel Reveals He Drew Ghost Logo for Snapchat on His Computer in His Dorm Bedroom." *Daily Mail*, June 22, 2015. http://www.dailymail.co.uk/tvshowbiz/article-3134555/CANNES-LIONS-Billionaire-Evan-Spiegel-reveals-drew-ghost-logo-Snapchat-computer-dorm-bedroom.html

Gallagher, Billy. "The Snapchat Lawsuit, Or How to Lose Your Best Friend over $70 Million." *TechCrunch*, March 7, 2013. https://techcrunch.com/2013/03/07/snapchat-lawsui/

Wenerd, Brando. July 31, 2014 tweet, Twitter. https://twitter.com/brandonwenerd/status/494895839467147265/photo/1

Chapter Six: The Fight

Gallagher, Billy. "The Snapchat Lawsuit, Or How to Lose Your Best Friend over $70 Million." *TechCrunch*, March 7, 2013. https://techcrunch.com/2013/03/07/snapchat-lawsui/

Chapter Seven: Snapchat

"Now That's a Historical Selfie! A Teen Grand Duchess Anastasia Is Seen Capturing Her Own Reflection in 1913 Russia." *Daily Mail*, November 26, 2013. http://www.dailymail.co.uk/femail/article-2514069/Russian-Grand-Duchess-Anastasia-seen-capturing-reflection-1913-Russia.html

"TigerText." Crunchbase, n.d. https://www.crunchbase.com/organization/tigertext#/entity

Auletta, Ken. "Get Rich U." *New Yorker*, April 30, 2012. http://www.newyorker.com/magazine/2012/04/30/get-rich-u

———. "Get Rich U." *New Yorker*,Bonanos, Christopher. "The Man Who Inspired Jobs." *New York Times*, October 7, 2011. http://www.nytimes.com/2011/10/07/opinion/the-man-who-inspired-jobs.html

Colao, J. J. "The Inside Story of Snapchat: The World's Hottest App or a $3 Billion Disappearing Act?" *Forbes*, January 6, 2014. https://www.forbes.com/sites/jjcolao/2014/01/06/the-inside-story-of-snapchat-the-worlds-hottest-app-or-a-3-billion-disappearing-act/#3961325c67d2

Cornelius, Robert. "Robert Cornelius, Self-Portrait; Believed to Be the Earliest Extant American Portrait Photo," c. 1839. Library of Congress. http://www.loc.gov/pictures/item/2004664436/

Eggers, Barry. "Lightspeed's Snap Story." *Medium*, March 2, 2017. https://medium.com/lightspeed-venture-partners/lightspeeds-snap-story-5d3723e97667

Gallagher, Billy. "No, Snapchat Isn't about Sexting, Says Co-Founder Evan Spiegel." *TechCrunch*, May 12, 2012. https://techcrunch.com/2012/05/12/snapchat-not-sexting/

Kahney, Leander. "John Sculley on Steve Jobs, the Full Interview Transcript." Cult of Mac, October 14, 2010. https://www.cultofmac.com/63295/john-sculley-on-steve-jobs-the-full-interview-transcript/63295/

Kaplan, Dan. "Real Engines of Growth Have Nothing to Do with Growth." *TechCrunch*, March 22, 2014. https://techcrunch.com/2014/03/22/the-real-engines-of-growth-on-the-internet/

Pace, Eric. "Edwin H. Land Is Dead at 81; Inventor of Polaroid Camera." *New York Times*, March 2, 1991. http://www.nytimes.com/1991/03/02/obituaries/edwin-h-land-is-dead-at-81-inventor-of-polaroid-camera.html?pagewanted=all

Sharaf, Shirin. "All the Cool Kids Are Doing It." *Stanford Daily*, March 5, 2004. http://stanforddailyarchive.com/cgi-bin/stanford?a=d&d=stanford20040305-01.2.13#

Spiegel, Evan, and Nikesh Arora. Interview, YouTube, October 12, 2015. https://www.youtube.com/watch?v=R-UAjGVPFIE

Swisher, Kara. "Full Transcript: Venture Capitalist Jeremy Liew on Recode Decode." Recode, March 5, 2017. https://www.recode.net/2017/3/5/14809104/transcript-venture-capitalist-jeremy-liew-innovation-silicon-valley-recode-decode

Wortham, Jenna. "A Growing App Lets You See It, Then You Don't." *New York Times*, February 8, 2013. http://www.nytimes.com/2013/02/09/technology/snapchat-a-growing-app-lets-you-see-it-then-you-dont.html

Chapter Eight: Sexting

"Study Reveals Majority of Adults Share Intimate Details via Unsecured Digital Devices." McAfee, February 4, 2014. https://www.mcafee.com/us/about/news/2014/q1/20140204 -01.aspx?culture=en-us&affid=0&cid=140622&pir=1

"What They're Saying about Sexting." *New York Times*, March 26, 2011. http://www.ny-times.com/2011/03/27/us/27sextingqanda.html

Bilton, Nick. "Disruptions: Indiscreet Photos, Glimpsed then Gone." *New York Times*, May 6, 2012. https://bits.blogs.nytimes.com/2012/05/06/disruptions-indiscreet-photos -glimpsed-then-gone/

Bonanos, Christopher. "Before Sexting, There Was Polaroid." *The Atlantic*, October 1, 2012. https://www.theatlantic.com/technology/archive/2012/10/before-sexting-there-was -polaroid/263082/

boyd, danah. "Let Kids Run Wild Online." *Time*, March 13, 2014. http://time.com/23031 /danah-boyd-let-kids-run-wild-online/

———. "Teen Sexting and Its Impact on the Tech Industry." Read Write Web 2WAY Conference 2011, June 13, 2011. http://www.danah.org/papers/talks/2011/RWW2011.html

Colbert, Stephen. "Evan Spiegel and Bobby Murphy." *The Colbert Report*, April 30, 2013. http://www.cc.com/video-clips/z5q514/the-colbert-report-evan-spiegel—-bobby -murphy

Drouin, Michelle, and Carly Landgraff. "Texting, Sexting, and Attachment in College Students' Romantic Relationships." Computers in Human Behavior (via Science Direct), March 2012. http://www.sciencedirect.com/science/article/pii/S0747563211002329 ?via%3Dihub

Gallagher, Billy. "The Snapchat Lawsuit, Or How to Lose Your Best Friend over $70 Million." March 7, 2013. *TechCrunch*, https://techcrunch.com/2013/03/07/snapchat-lawsui/

———. "No, Snapchat Isn't about Sexting, Says Co-Founder Evan Spiegel." *TechCrunch*, May 12, 2012. http://techcrunch.com/2012/05/12/snapchat-not-sexting/

Hill, Kashmir. "Snapchat Tells Teen Users: No Nudes!" Splinter, February 20, 2015. http:// fusion.kinja.com/snapchat-tells-teen-users-no-nudes-1793845467

Honan, Mat. "Your Dick Pics Are about to Be All Over the Internet." *Wired*, February 17, 2015. https://www.wired.com/2015/02/dick-pics/

Lacy, Sarah. "Calling Snapchat 'the Sexting App' Misses a Huge Shift in Mobile, Photos, and Communication." Pando, December 16, 2012. https://pando.com/2012/12/16/calling -snapchat-the-sexting-app-misses-a-huge-shift-in-mobile-photos-and-communication/

Namuo, Clynton. "UNH Study Finds 'Sexting' Not so Prevalent." *New Hampshire Union Leader*, December 4, 2011. http://www.unionleader.com/article/20111205/NEWS04 /712059957

Vogels, Josey. "Textual Gratification: Quill or Keypad, It's All about Sex." *Globe and Mail*, May 3, 2004. https://www.theglobeandmail.com/technology/textual-gratification-quill -or-keypad-its-all-about-sex/article1136823/?page=all

Chapter Nine: Betrayal

Ballhaus, Rebecca, Peter Nicholas, and Alexandra Berzon. "Two Top Sony Movie Executives Are Longtime Obama Supporters." *Wall Street Journal*, December 19, 2014. https:// www.wsj.com/articles/two-top-sony-movie-executives-are-longtime-obama-supporters -1419033876

Bertet, Elsa. "Michael Lynton Timeline." *Variety*, September 6, 2007. http://variety.com/2007 /film/news/michael-lynton-timeline-1117971490/

Colao, J. J. "Snapchat: The Biggest No-Revenue Mobile App since Instagram." *Forbes*, November 27, 2012. https://www.forbes.com/sites/jjcolao/2012/11/27/snapchat-the-biggest -no-revenue-mobile-app-since-instagram/#57abce9d7200

Flynn, Kerry M. "Michael M. Lynton." *Harvard Crimson*, May 23, 2012. http://www.thecrimson.com/article/2012/5/23/Lynton-CEO-Sony/

Hempel, Jessi, and Adam Lashinsky. "Countdown to the Snapchat Revolution." *Fortune*, December 18, 2013. http://fortune.com/2013/12/18/countdown-to-the-snapchat-revolution/

Isaac, Mike. "Snapchat Closes $60 Million Round Led by IVP, Now at 200 Million Daily Snaps." AllThingsD, June 24, 2013. http://allthingsd.com/20130624/snapchat-closes-60-million-round-led-by-ivp-now-at-200-million-daily-snaps/

Spiegel, Evan. "Evan Spiegel USC Commencement Speech | USC Marshall School of Business Commencement 2015." YouTube video, May 15, 2015. https://www.youtube.com/watch?v=-Ng0fXIITt0

———. "How Did David Kravitz and Daniel Smith Get Recruited to Snapchat?" Quora, April 17, 2013. https://www.quora.com/How-did-David-Kravitz-and-Quora-User-get-recruited-to-Snapchat

———. Keynote speech at "Design Yourself" Conference, Stanford Women in Business, April 7, 2013. https://download.docslide.net/documents/design-yourself-conference-opening-keynote-by-evan-spiegel-ceo-of-snapchat.html

Stevenson, Seth. "Snapchat Releases First Hardware Product, Spectacles." *Wall Street Journal*, September 24, 2016. https://www.wsj.com/articles/snapchat-releases-first-hardware-product-spectacles-1474682719

Vega, Sebastian. "CEO of Snapchat Discusses New Media." *Daily Trojan*, February 19, 2015. http://dailytrojan.com/2015/02/19/ceo-of-snapchat-discusses-new-media/

Wagner, Kurt. "Inside Evan Spiegel's Very Private Snapchat Story." Recode, May 9, 2016. https://www.recode.net/2016/5/9/11594144/evan-spiegel-snapchat

Wallenstein, Andrew. "Sony's Michael Lynton Poised to Hit Jackpot with Snapchat Investment (Exclusive)." *Variety*, December 12, 2013. http://variety.com/2013/biz/news/sonys-michael-lynton-poised-to-hit-jackpot-with-snapchat-investment-exclusive-1200947334/

Chapter Ten: A Not-So-Innocent Toy

"Mitch Lasky." Crunchbase. https://www.crunchbase.com/person/mitch-lasky#/entity

Carlson, Nicholas. "Zuckerberg's Huge Win: Instagram Proves to Be a Bargain at $1 Billion." *Business Insider*, September 11, 2012. http://www.businessinsider.com/facebook-instagram-zuckerberg-growth-9-2012

Colao, J. J. "The Inside Story of Snapchat: The World's Hottest App or a $3 Billion Disappearing Act?" *Forbes*, January 6, 2014. https://www.forbes.com/sites/jjcolao/2014/01/06/the-inside-story-of-snapchat-the-worlds-hottest-app-or-a-3-billion-disappearing-act/#3961325c67d2

Eldon, Eric. "Sources: Snapchat Raising 'North of $10M' at around $70M Valuation, Led by Benchmark's Mitch Lasky." *TechCrunch*, December 12, 2012. https://techcrunch.com/2012/12/12/sources-snapchat-raising-north-of-10m-at-around-70m-valuation-led-by-benchmarks-mitch-lasky/

Gallagher, Billy. "Facebook and Snapchat Go Toe to Toe: Why It's Good for Both Companies." *TechCrunch*, December 17, 2012. http://techcrunch.com/2012/12/17/facebook-and-snapchat/

———. "Snapchat Releases Video Sharing, Is Prototyping Monetization Features (Oh, and It's Still Not for Sexting)." *TechCrunch*, December 14, 2012. http://techcrunch.com/2012/12/14/snapchat-does-video/

———. "You Know What's Cool? A Billion Snapchats: App Sees over 20 Million Photos Shared per Day, Releases on Android." *TechCrunch*, October 29, 2012. http://techcrunch.com/2012/10/29/billion-snapchats/

McLaughlin, Kelly. "The ORIGINAL Venice Canals in LA That Have Vanished Forever beneath a Sea of Concrete." *Daily Mail*, June 8, 2015. http://www.dailymail.co.uk/news/article -3114848/Venice-America-s-history-shows-canals-hidden-pavement.html

Takahashi, Dean. "Benchmark's Mitch Lasky: Game Publishers Will Evolve or Die (Interview)." VentureBeat, July 17, 2012. https://venturebeat.com/2012/07/17/mitch-lasky -game-publishers-will-evolve-or-die-interview/view-all/

Tzu, Sun. *The Art of War*. date unknown. https://www.amazon.com/Art-War-Sun-Tzu/dp /1599869772/ref=sr_1_1?s=books&ie=UTF8&qid=1501497433&sr=1-1&keywords =the+art+of+war

Chapter Eleven: Poked

Carlson, Nicholas. "Zuckerberg's Huge Win: Instagram Proves to Be a Bargain at $1 Billion." *Business Insider*, September 11, 2012. http://www.businessinsider.com/facebook -instagram-zuckerberg-growth-9-2012

Colao, J. J. "The Inside Story of Snapchat: The World's Hottest App or a $3 Billion Disappearing Act?" *Forbes*, January 6, 2014. https://www.forbes.com/sites/jjcolao/2014/01/06 /the-inside-story-of-snapchat-the-worlds-hottest-app-or-a-3-billion-disappearing-act /#3961325c67d2

Constine, Josh. "Facebook Launches Snapchat Competitor 'Poke,' an iOS App for Sending Expiring Text, Photos, and Videos." TechCrunch, December 21, 2012. https://techcrunch. com/2012/12/21/facebook-poke-app/

———. "Mark Zuckerberg Is the Voice Behind the 'Poke' Notification Sound and Wrote Code for the App." *TechCrunch*, December 21, 2012. https://techcrunch.com/2012/12 /21/mark-zuckerberg-voice-of-poke/

Gallagher, Billy. "Snapchat Co-Founder Evan Spiegel Responds to Poke: 'Welcome, Facebook. Seriously.'" *TechCrunch*, December 21, 2102. http://techcrunch.com/2012/12/21 /snapchat-co-founder-evan-spiegel-responds-to-poke-welcome-facebook-seriously/

———. "Facebook and Snapchat Go Toe to Toe: Why It's Good for Both Companies." *TechCrunch*, December 17, 2012. http://techcrunch.com/2012/12/17/facebook-and-snapchat/

———. "Snapchat Releases Video Sharing, Is Prototyping Monetization Features (Oh, and It's Still Not for Sexting)." December 14, 2012. *TechCrunch*, http://techcrunch.com/2012 /12/14/snapchat-does-video/

Malik, Om. "Snapchat Rises: Why Poke's Decline Shows Facebook's Inability to Invent." GigaOm, December 26, 2012. https://gigaom.com/2012/12/26/snapchat-rises-why-pokes -decline-shows-facebooks-inability-to-invent/

Panzarino, Matthew. "Facebook's Poke: A Snapchat-like App That Lets You Send Messages That Expire after 1, 3, 5 or 10 Seconds." Next Web, December 21, 2012. https://thenextweb .com/facebook/2012/12/21/facebook-announces-poke-a-snapchat-like-app-that-lets -people-send-private-messages-that-expire-after-1-3-5-or-10-seconds/#.tnw_0pq4RGGG

Rusli, Evelyn M. "In Rejecting Facebook, Snapchat Still Extracts Value." *Wall Street Journal*, November 15, 2013. https://blogs.wsj.com/digits/2013/11/15/in-rejecting-facebook -snapchat-still-extracts-value/

Siegler, M. G. Untitled. Paris Lemon, December 21, 2012. http://parislemon.com/post /38489227402/facebook-poke-for-mobile

Taylor, Colleen. "Data Shows Online Buzz about Snapchat Is Skyrocketing after the Launch of Facebook Poke." *TechCrunch*, December 28, 2012. https://techcrunch.com/2012/12 /28/data-shows-online-buzz-about-snapchat-is-skyrocketing-after-the-launch-of -facebook-poke/

Wingfield, Nick, and Mike Isaac. "Mark Zuckerberg, in Suit, Testifies in Oculus Intellectual Property Trial." *New York Times*, January 17, 2017. https://www.nytimes.com/2017 /01/17/technology/mark-zuckerberg-oculus-trial-virtual-reality-facebook.html?_r=0

Chapter Twelve: Reggie's Return

Gallagher, Billy. "Snapchat Founders Face New Twist in Legal Battle as Alleged Co-Founder Files to Disqualify Their Lawyers." *TechCrunch*, July 1, 2013. http://techcrunch.com /2013/07/01/ephemeral-representation/

————. "Snapchat's Spiegel Admits Brown 'Came up with the Idea for Disappearing Picture Messages' in New Court Documents." *TechCrunch*, July 1, 2013. http://techcrunch. com/2013/07/01/new-snapchat-docs/

Mac, Ryan. "Want to Sue a Startup? Hire This Man." *Forbes*, April 14, 2015. https://www. forbes.com/sites/ryanmac/2015/04/14/cofounder-lawsuits-luan-tran-snapchat-yik-yak /#79c96b6f3398

Shontell, Alyson. "SNAPCHAT LAWSUIT VIDEOS: After a 37-Second Pause, Snapchat's CEO Describes Regrets about the Friend He Ousted." *Business Insider*, November 25, 2013. http://www.businessinsider.com/snapchat-lawsuit-videos-2013-11

————. "These Leaked Videos Could Lead to a Huge Payday for Ousted Snapchat Co-Founder." *Business Insider*, November 20, 2013. http://www.businessinsider.com /snapchat-lawsuit-video-depositions-2013-11

Chapter Thirteen: The Phenomenon

Benner, Katie. "Snap's Chief Taps into the 'Right Now.'" *New York Times*, February 1, 2017. https://www.nytimes.com/2017/02/01/technology/snapchat-snap-ceo-evan-spiegel.html ?rref=collection%2Fsectioncollection%2Ftechnology&action=click&contentCollection =technology&region=stream&module=stream_unit&version =latest&contentPlacement=1&pgtype=sectionfront

Bezos, Jeffrey P. Letter to shareholders, US Security and Exchange Commission, April 2016. https://www.sec.gov/Archives/edgar/data/1018724/000119312516530910/d168744dex991 .htm

Colao, J. J. "In Less Than Two Years, Snapchat Is an $860 Million Company." *Forbes*, June 24, 2013. https://www.forbes.com/sites/jjcolao/2013/06/24/snapchat-raises-60 -million-from-ivp-at-800-million-valuation/#506ba341677d

————. "In Less Than Two Years, Snapchat Is an $860 Million Company." *Forbes*, June 24, 2013. https://www.forbes.com/sites/jjcolao/2013/06/24/snapchat-raises-60-million-from -ivp-at-800-million-valuation/#506ba341677d

Drimal, Chloe. "DRIMAL: Newest Diet: Facebook Cleanse." *Yale Daily News*, March 27, 2013. http://yaledailynews.com/blog/2013/03/27/drimal-newest-diet-facebook-cleanse/

————. "DRIMAL: Snapchat: The Phenomenon." *Yale Daily News*, December 7, 2012. http:// yaledailynews.com/blog/2012/12/07/drimal-snapchat-the-phenomenon/

————. "DRIMAL: Profile of a SWUG." *Yale Daily News*, September 24, 2012. http:// yaledailynews.com/blog/2012/09/24/drimal-profile-of-a-swug/

Elman, Josh. "'How Will They Make Money?' Is the Wrong Question." Medium, June 11, 2013. https://medium.com/i-m-h-o/how-will-they-make-money-is-the-wrong-question -a5890c2c2cc0

Gallagher, Billy. "Taco Bell Asks Twitter Followers to Add Them on Snapchat, Users May Soon See Snaps from Brands." *TechCrunch*, May 1, 2013. http://techcrunch.com/2013 /05/01/taco-bell-joins-snapchat/

Herrman, John. "Meet the Man Who Got inside Snapchat's Head." BuzzFeed, January 27, 2014. https://www.buzzfeed.com/jwherrman/meet-the-unlikely-academic-behind -snapchats-new-pitch?utm_term=.njpqz3oO87#.suoBzJA67M

Jurgenson, Nathan. "Pics and It Didn't Happen." New Inquiry, February 7, 2013. https:// thenewinquiry.com/pics-and-it-didnt-happen/

————. "Digital Dualism versus Augmented Reality." Cyborgology, February 24, 2011. https:// thesocietypages.org/cyborgology/2011/02/24/digital-dualism-versus-augmented-reality/

Levy, Steven. "Snapchat's Non-Vanishing Message: You Can Trust Us." Backchannel, April 2, 2015. https://medium.com/backchannel/snapchat-s-non-vanishing-message-you-can -trust-us-6606e6774b8b

Morris, Betsy and Seetharaman, Deepa. "The New Copycats: How Facebook Squashes Competition From Startups" *Wall Street Journal*, August 9, 2017. https://www.wsj .com/articles/the-new-copycats-how-facebook-squashes-competition-from-startups -1502293444

McDermott, John. "Brands Experiment with Photo-Messaging Service Snapchat, Facebook Poke." *Advertising Age*, January 4, 2013. http://adage.com/article/digital/brands -experiment-photo-messaging-service-snapchat-facebook-poke/238979/

Primack, Dan. "What Is Behind Snapchat's Massive Valuation?" *Fortune*, June 24, 2013. http://fortune.com/2013/06/24/what-is-behind-snapchats-massive-valuation/

Silverman, Justin Rocket. "Meet the SWUGs of Yale: Women 'Washed Up' at 21." The Cut, April 10, 2013. https://www.thecut.com/2013/04/meet-the-swugs-of-yale-women-washed -up-at-21.html

Stevenson, Seth. "Snapchat Releases First Hardware Product, Spectacles." *Wall Street Journal*, September 24, 2016. https://www.wsj.com/articles/snapchat-releases-first-hardware -product-spectacles-1474682719

Tiku, Nitasha. "Source: Snapchat Cofounders Unloaded Personal Stock for $20 M." Valleywag, June 25, 2013. http://valleywag.gawker.com/source-snapchat-cofounders -unloaded-personal-stock-for-574730704

Wasserman, Todd. "Is Snapchat the Next Frontier for Marketers?" Mashable, January 3, 2013. http://mashable.com/2013/01/02/snapchat-marketers/#wgdSNMg2aEq3

Wortham, Jenna. "A Growing App Lets You See It, Then You Don't." *New York Times*, February 8, 2013. http://www.nytimes.com/2013/02/09/technology/snapchat-a-growing -app-lets-you-see-it-then-you-dont.html

Chapter Fourteen: Stories

Anderson, Tom. "Technology Advancing Art: Photo Apps Are the Folk Art of Our Generation." *TechCrunch*, September 30, 2011. https://techcrunch.com/2011/09/30/technology -advancing-art-photo-apps/

Constine, Josh. "Facebook Admits Some Decrease of Usage amongst Young Teens for the First Time." *TechCrunch*, October 30, 2013. https://techcrunch.com/2013/10/30 /facebook-teens-drop/

Crook, Jordan. "With an Eye on Revenue, Snapchat 'Experiments' with a Click-to-Buy Button." October 3, 2013. *TechCrunch*, https://techcrunch.com/2013/10/03/with-an-eye-on -revenue-snapchat-experiments-with-a-click-to-buy-button/

Gallagher, Billy. "A Tale of Two Patents: Why Facebook Can't Clone Snapchat." *TechCrunch*, June 22, 2014. http://techcrunch.com/2014/06/22/facebook-slingshot-snapchat-patents/

———. "Snapchat Now Sees 350M Photos Shared Daily, Up from 200M in June." *TechCrunch*, September 9, 2013. https://techcrunch.com/2013/09/09/snapchat-now-sees-350m -photos-shared-daily-up-from-200m-in-june/

———. "What's Ahead for Snapchat? CEO Evan Spiegel Drops Clues in Disrupt Talk." *TechCrunch*, September 9, 2013. http://techcrunch.com/2013/09/09/snapchat-future -disrupt-hints/

Hamburger, Ellis. "Snapchat's Next Big Thing: 'Stories' That Don't Just Disappear." *Verge*, October 3, 2013. https://www.theverge.com/2013/10/3/4791934/snapchats-next-big-thing -stories-that-dont-just-disappear

Kan, Justin. "Why I Love Snapchat." Medium, November 13, 2016. https://justinkan.com /why-i-love-snapchat-23d31ea87d3c

Swisher, Kara. "Instagram Business Lead Emily White to Be Named COO of Snapchat."

AllThingsD, December 3, 2013. http://allthingsd.com/20131203/exclusive-instagram
-business-lead-emily-white-to-be-named-coo-of-snapchat/

Vega, Sebastian. "CEO of Snapchat Discusses New Media." *Daily Trojan*, February 19, 2015.
http://dailytrojan.com/2015/02/19/ceo-of-snapchat-discusses-new-media/

Chapter Fifteen: How to Turn Down Three Billion Dollars

"Makers of Snapchat Turn Down $3 Billion." *Good Morning America*, November 15, 2013.
https://gma.yahoo.com/video/makers-snapchat-turn-down-3-232317879.html

Blodget, Henry. "EXCLUSIVE: How Snapchat Plans to Make Money." *Business Insider*,
November 20, 2013. http://www.businessinsider.com/how-snapchat-will-make-money
-2013-11

Colao, J. J. "The Inside Story of Snapchat: The World's Hottest App or a $3 Billion Disap-
pearing Act?" *Forbes*, January 6, 2014. https://www.forbes.com/sites/jjcolao/2014/01/06
/the-inside-story-of-snapchat-the-worlds-hottest-app-or-a-3-billion-disappearing-act
/#3961325c67d2

Constine, Josh. "Snapchat Snags Facebook's Mike Randall as Monetization VP." *Tech-
Crunch*, June 24, 2014. https://techcrunch.com/2014/06/24/facebook-steals-features
-snapchat-steals-talent/

Hempel, Jessi. "Snapchat Doesn't Think It Needs an Adult Like Facebook Did." *Wired*,
March 18, 2015. https://www.wired.com/2015/03/snapchat-doesnt-think-needs-adult
-like-facebook/

MacMillan, Douglas. "Snapchat Poaches Google Veteran in Engineering Push," *Wall Street
Journal*, February 18, 2014. https://blogs.wsj.com/digits/2014/02/18/snapchat-poaches
-google-veteran-in-engineering-push/

Primack, Dan. "Ex-Snapchat COO Emily White Has a New Startup." *Fortune*, March 2,
2016. http://fortune.com/2016/03/02/ex-snapchat-coo-emily-white-new-startup/

Rusli, Evelyn M. "In Rejecting Facebook, Snapchat Still Extracts Value." *Wall Street Journal*, November 15, 2013. https://blogs.wsj.com/digits/2013/11/15/in-rejecting-facebook
-snapchat-still-extracts-value/

———, and Douglas MacMillan. "Snapchat Spurned $3 Billion Acquisition Offer from Face-
book." *Wall Street Journal*, November 13, 2013. https://blogs.wsj.com/digits/2013/11
/13/snapchat-spurned-3-billion-acquisition-offer-from-facebook/

Slutsky, Irina. "Meet the Ex-Googlers Running Facebook." *Advertising Age*, June 1, 2011.
http://adage.com/article/digital/meet-googlers-running-facebook/227833/

Spiegel, Evan. "Evan Spiegel USC Commencement Speech | USC Marshall School of Busi-
ness Commencement 2015," YouTube, May 15, 2015. https://www.youtube.com/watch
?v=-Ng0fXIITt0

———, and Nikesh Arora. Interview, YouTube, October 12, 2015. https://www.youtube.com
/watch?v=R-UAjGVPFIE

Thompson, Ben. "The Facebook Epoch." Stratechery, September 30, 2015. https://stratechery.
com/2015/the-facebook-epoch/

———. "Old Fashioned Snapchat." February 24, 2015. Stratechery, https://stratechery.com
/2015/old-fashioned-snapchat/

Tsotsis, Alexia. "Monetization TBD . . . Instagram Hires Facebook's Emily White as Director of Business Operations." *TechCrunch*, April 2, 2013. https://techcrunch.com/2013
/04/02/instagram-hires-facebooks-emily-white-as-director-of-business-operations/

Wagner, Kurt. "Inside Evan Spiegel's Very Private Snapchat Story." Recode, May 9, 2016.
https://www.recode.net/2016/5/9/11594144/evan-spiegel-snapchat

Wortham, Jenna. "Rejecting Billions, Snapchat Expects a Better Offer." *New York Times*,
November 13, 2013. http://www.nytimes.com/2013/11/14/technology/rejecting-billions
-snapchat-expects-a-better-offer.html

Chapter Sixteen: Happy New Year!

Swann, Elaine. "What's the Etiquette of 'Selfies' at Funerals?" CNN, December 12, 2013. http://edition.cnn.com/2013/12/11/opinion/swann-selfie-funeral-etiquette/

Wallop, Harry. "Oscars 2014: The Most Famous 'Selfie' in the World (Sorry Liza)." *The Telegraph*, March 3, 2014. http://www.telegraph.co.uk/culture/film/oscars/10674655/Oscars-2014-The-most-famous-selfie-in-the-world-sorry-Liza.html

Chapter Seventeen: Hangover

"Finding Friends with Phone Numbers." Snapchat, December 27, 2013. https://www.snap.com/en-US/news/post/finding-friends-with-phone-numbers/

Blue, Violet. "Researchers Publish Snapchat Code Allowing Phone Number Matching after Exploit Disclosures Ignored." ZDNet, December 25, 2013. http://www.zdnet.com/article/researchers-publish-snapchat-code-allowing-phone-number-matching-after-exploit-disclosures-ignored/

Kastrenakes, Jacob. "Snapchat Dismisses Concerns over Exploit That May Compromise User Phone Numbers." *Verge*, December 27, 2013. https://www.theverge.com/2013/12/27/5249304/snapchat-dismisses-concerns-over-phone-number-finder-exploit

Lane, Randall. "Snapchat's Evan Spiegel and the Antics of a 23-Year-Old Novice." *Forbes*, January 6, 2014. https://www.forbes.com/sites/randalllane/2014/01/06/snapchats-evan-spiegel-and-the-antics-of-a-23-year-old-novice/#34abcb031a51

McCormick, Rich. "4.6 Million Snapchat Phone Numbers and Usernames Leaked." *Verge*, January 1, 2014. https://www.theverge.com/2014/1/1/5262740/4-6-million-snapchat-phone-numbers-and-usernames-leaked

Panzarino, Matthew. "Snapchat Says It's Improving Its App, Service to Prevent Future User Data Leaks." *TechCrunch*, January 2, 2014. https://techcrunch.com/2014/01/02/snapchat-says-its-improving-its-app-service-to-prevent-future-leaks/

Primack, Dan. "Does Snapchat's CEO Need to Go?" *Fortune*, January 3, 2014. http://fortune.com/2014/01/03/does-snapchats-ceo-need-to-go/

Roberts, Jeff. "Feds Issue Final Order over Snapchat Privacy Incidents, but No Fine." GigaOm, December 31, 2014. https://gigaom.com/2014/12/31/feds-issue-final-order-over-snapchat-privacy-breach-but-no-fine/

Stump, Scott. "Snapchat CEO: 'We Thought We Had Done Enough' to Prevent Hack." *Today*, January 3, 2014. https://www.today.com/money/snapchat-ceo-we-thought-we-had-done-enough-prevent-hack-2D11848259

Wortham, Jenna. "Off the Record in a Chat App? Don't Be Sure." *New York Times*, May 8, 2014. https://www.nytimes.com/2014/05/09/technology/snapchat-reaches-settlement-with-federal-trade-commission.html

Ziegler, Chris. "Alleged Snapchat Hackers Explain How and Why They Leaked Data on 4.6 Million Accounts." *Verge*, January 1, 2014. https://www.theverge.com/2014/1/1/5263156/alleged-snapchat-hackers-explain-how-and-why-they-leaked-data-on-accounts

Chapter Eighteen: The More Personal Computer

"Snap Inc." Crunchbase. https://www.crunchbase.com/organization/snapchat#/entity

"Uber." Crunchbase. https://www.crunchbase.com/organization/uber#/entity

Biddle, Sam. "Snapchat Lost a Ton of Money Last Year." Gawker, August 19, 2015. http://gawker.com/snapchat-lost-a-ton-of-money-last-year-1706957414

Gallagher, Billy. "Facebook's WhatsApp Acquisition Leaves Snapchat Hanging." *TechCrunch*, February 19, 2014. http://techcrunch.com/2014/02/19/facebooks-whatsapp-acquisition-snapchat/

Kawamoto, Dawn. "Amazon.com IPO Skyrockets." *CNET*, May 15, 1997. http://www.cnet.com/news/amazon-com-ipo-skyrockets/

Morris, Betsy and Seetharaman, Deepa. "Facebook's Onavo Gives Social-Media Firm Inside Peek at Rivals' Users" *Wall Street Journal*, August 13, 2017. https://www.wsj.com/articles /facebooks-onavo-gives-social-media-firm-inside-peek-at-rivals-users-1502622003

Morris, Betsy and Seetharaman, Deepa. "The New Copycats: How Facebook Squashes Competition From Startups" *Wall Street Journal*, August 9, 2017. https://www.wsj.com /articles/the-new-copycats-how-facebook-squashes-competition-from-startups -1502293444

Rowan, David. "WhatsApp: The Inside Story." *Wired*, February 19, 2014. http://www.wired .co.uk/article/whatsapp-exclusive

Spiegel, Evan. "2014 AXS Partner Summit Keynote." Scribd, January 25, 2014. https://www .scribd.com/doc/202195145/2014-AXS-Partner-Summit-Keynote

Stevenson, Seth. "Snapchat Releases First Hardware Product, Spectacles." *Wall Street Journal*, September 24, 2016. https://www.wsj.com/articles/snapchat-releases-first-hardware -product-spectacles-1474682719

Swisher, Kara, and Walt Mossberg. "Snapchat CEO Evan Spiegel on Diversity, Features for the Olds and More at Code Conference 2015." Recode, June 8, 2015. https://www.recode .net/2015/6/8/11563322/snapchat-ceo-evan-spiegel-on-diversity-features-for-the-olds -and-more

Webb, Cynthia L. "Google's IPO: Grate Expectations." *Washington Post*, August 19, 2004. http://www.washingtonpost.com/wp-dyn/articles/A14939-2004Aug19.html

Winkler, Rolfe, and Matt Jarzemsky. "Silicon Valley: Feel the Froth." *Wall Street Journal*, October 27, 2013. https://www.wsj.com/articles/tech-valuations-stir-memories-of-the -dotcom-bust-1382916515

Chapter Nineteen: Snapchat Everywhere

Constine, Josh. "Snapchat Plans Music Feature, Acquired QR Scan.me for $50M and Vergence Eyeglass Cam for $15M." *TechCrunch*, December 16, 2014. https://techcrunch. com/2014/12/16/snapchat-emails-not-so-ephemeral/

Dave, Paresh. "Snapchat Has Changed through Acquisitions, and It's Hunting for More People and Tech to Buy." *Los Angeles Times*, May 10, 2017. http://www.latimes.com /business/technology/la-fi-tn-snapchat-acquisitions-20170510-htmlstory.html

Gallagher, Billy. "What's Ahead for Snapchat? CEO Evan Spiegel Drops Clues in Disrupt Talk." *TechCrunch*, September 9, 2013. http://techcrunch.com/2013/09/09/snapchat -future-disrupt-hints/

Hamburger, Ellis. "Real Talk: The New Snapchat Brilliantly Mixes Video and Texting." *Verge*, May 1, 2014. https://www.theverge.com/2014/5/1/5670260/real-talk-the-new -snapchat-makes-texting-fun-again-video-calls

Heath, Alex. "How Snapchat Secretly Bought a Struggling Startup, Then Bet the Future on It." *Business Insider*, November 23, 2016. http://www.businessinsider.com/untold-story -vergence-labs-snapchat-acquired-spectacles-2016-11?op=1

Hollister, Sean. "SnapGlass? HoloChat? Snapchat Is Secretly Hiring Wearable Technology Experts." *CNET*, March 11, 2016. https://www.cnet.com/news/snapchat-glasses -vergence-snap-labs-hints-wearable/

Krishnan, Sriram. "Building Something No One Else Can Measure." Sriram Krishnan, April 23, 2017. http://sriramk.com/building-unmeasurable-things

Panzarino, Matthew. "How a Startup Accidentally 'Hacked' Shark Tank with a QR Code." *TechCrunch*, February 4, 2014. https://techcrunch.com/2014/02/04/how-a-startup -accidentally-hacked-shark-tank-with-a-qr-code/

Wadhwa, Vivek. "Wearable Tech and the Futurists' Conundrum." *Washington Post*, April 23, 2013. https://www.washingtonpost.com/news/innovations/wp/2013/04/23/wearable-tech -and-the-futurists-conundrum/?utm_term=.1326d8c366e7

Wagner, Kurt. "Inside Evan Spiegel's Very Private Snapchat Story." Recode, May 9, 2016. https://www.recode.net/2016/5/9/11594144/evan-spiegel-snapchat

Walker, Alissa. "Google's Marissa Mayer Assaults Designers with Data." Fast Company, October 13, 2009. https://www.fastcompany.com/1403230/googles-marissa-mayer-assaults-designers-data

Yarow, Jay, Alyson Shontell, and James Cook. "It Looks Like Snapchat Paid $15 Million to Buy a Google Glass-Like Startup." *Business Insider*, December 17, 2014. https://www.businessinsider.com.au/snapchat-acquires-vergence-labs-2014-12

Chapter Twenty: Goodbye Reggie

Biddle, Sam. " 'Fuck Bitches Get Leid,' the Sleazy Frat Emails of Snapchat's CEO." Valleywag, May 28, 2014. http://valleywag.gawker.com/fuck-bitches-get-leid-the-sleazy-frat-emails-of-snap-1582604137

Casti, Taylor. "You Must Read Stanford's Response to the Snapchat CEO's 'Demeaning' Emails." *Huffington Post*, May 30, 2014. http://www.huffingtonpost.com/2014/05/30/stanford-snapchat-email-response_n_5419628.html

Chang, Andrea. "Snapchat CEO 'Mortified' by Leaked Stanford Frat E-Mails." *Los Angeles Times*, March 28, 2014. http://www.latimes.com/business/technology/la-fi-tn-snapchat-evan-spiegel-20140528-story.html

Crook, Jordan. "Confirmed: Snapchat's Evan Spiegel Is Kind Of an Ass." *TechCrunch*, May 28, 2014. https://techcrunch.com/2014/05/28/confirmed-snapchats-evan-spiegel-is-kind-of-an-ass/

Frier, Sarah. "Snapchat CEO Apologizes for His Frat Boy E-mails." *SF Gate*, May 29, 2014. http://www.sfgate.com/technology/article/Snapchat-CEO-apologizes-for-his-frat-boy-e-mails-5514514.php

Maheshwari, Sapna. "Snapchat Concedes in Settlement: Ousted Co-Founder Came Up with App Idea." BuzzFeed, September 9, 2014. https://www.buzzfeed.com/sapna/snapchat-concedes-in-settlement-ousted-co-founder-came-up-wi?utm_term=.roWblYWXQL#.asqRgMv2d7

McGregor, Jena. "Snapchat, Sexism and the Reason Women Don't Stay in Tech." *Washington Post*, May 30, 2014. https://www.washingtonpost.com/news/on-leadership/wp/2014/05/30/snapchat-sexism-and-the-reason-women-dont-stay-in-tech/?utm_term=.caad6d740c9d

Chapter Twenty-One: Snapchat Live!

Carr, Austin. "Inside Snapchat CEO Evan Spiegel's Entertainment Empire." Fast Company, October 19, 2015. https://www.fastcompany.com/3051612/media-tech-and-advertising-to-snapchat-i-aint-afraid-of-no-ghost

Constine, Josh. "Snapchat's 'Our Story' Is a Genius, Collaborative Reinvention of the Livestream." *TechCrunch*, June 21, 2014. https://techcrunch.com/2014/06/21/snapchat-our-story/

Crook, Jordan. "Snapchat Launches Collaborative Timelines Based on Events." *TechCrunch*, June 17, 2014. https://techcrunch.com/2014/06/17/snapchat-launches-collaborative-timelines-based-on-events/

Dave, Paresh. "How Illusionist David Blaine Helped Inspire Snapchat's Live Stories." *Los Angeles Times*, September 16, 2015. http://www.latimes.com/business/technology/la-fi-tn-snapchat-nick-bell-20150916-story.html

———. "Snapchat Turns Geofilter Digital Stickers into Revenue Source." *Los Angeles Times*, June 15, 2015. http://www.latimes.com/business/la-fi-0613-snapchat-geofilters-20150616-story.html

Etherington, Darrell. "Snapchat Adds Geofilters for Quick Image Location Tags, and a New

Revenue Possibility." *TechCrunch*, July 15, 2014. https://techcrunch.com/2014/07/15/snapchat-adds-geofilters-for-quick-image-location-tags-and-a-new-revenue-possibility/

Gallagher, Billy. "A Tale of Two Patents: Why Facebook Can't Clone Snapchat." *TechCrunch*, June 22, 2014. http://techcrunch.com/2014/06/22/facebook-slingshot-snapchat-patents/

Kircher, Madison Malone. "The Real Story behind That Viral College Snapchat Love Story." *New York Magazine*, May 3, 2016. http://nymag.com/selectall/2016/05/the-real-story-behind-that-viral-college-snapchat-love-story.html

Steel, Emily. "Snapchat Plans a Global View of New Year's Festivities." *New York Times*, December 31, 2014. https://www.nytimes.com/2014/12/31/business/media/Snapchat-Plans-a-Global-View-of-New-Years-Festivities.html

Webster, Andrew. "Snapchat's Geofilters Are Now Open to Everyone." *Verge*, December 2, 2014. https://www.theverge.com/2014/12/2/7319317/snapchat-geofilters-community

Chapter Twenty-Two: "We Need to Make Money"

"Advertising on Snapchat." Snapchat, October 17, 2014. https://www.snap.com/en-US/news/post/advertising-on-snapchat/.

Carr, Austin. "Inside Snapchat CEO Evan Spiegel's Entertainment Empire." Fast Company, October 19, 2015. https://www.fastcompany.com/3051612/media-tech-and-advertising-to-snapchat-i-aint-afraid-of-no-ghost

Chemi, Eric. "Advertising's Century of Flat-Line Growth." Bloomberg, March 3, 2014. http://www.bloomberg.com/news/articles/2014-03-03/advertisings-century-of-flat-line-growth

Colao, J. J. "In Less Than Two Years, Snapchat Is an $860 Million Company." *Forbes*, June 24, 2013. https://www.forbes.com/sites/jjcolao/2013/06/24/snapchat-raises-60-million-from-ivp-at-800-million-valuation/#506ba341677d

Constine, Josh. "Snapchat's Newest Money Maker Is a Sponsored Our Story for Samsung and the AMAs." *TechCrunch*, November 23, 2014. https://techcrunch.com/2014/11/23/snapchat-sponsored-our-story/

DeAmicis, Carmel. "Snapchat's 'Our Stories' Are Generating Tens of Millions of Views." GigaOm, February 24, 2015. https://gigaom.com/2015/02/24/snapchats-our-stories-are-generating-tens-of-millions-of-views/

Donnelly, Matt. "Snapchat, Conde Nast Team for Live Events Including Vanity Fair Oscar and GQ Grammy Parties." The Wrap, October 2, 2015. http://www.thewrap.com/snapchat-lands-vanity-fair-oscar-party-invite-conde-nast-and-social-platform-team-for-live-events/

Marshall, Jack. "Snapchat Will Feature Weekly Content from MLB and Baseball Fans." *Wall Street Journal*, May 13, 2015. https://blogs.wsj.com/cmo/2015/05/13/snapchat-will-feature-weekly-content-from-mlb-and-baseball-fans/

McDermott, John. "Coming to Snapchat: Live Sports Broadcasting." DigiDay, March 11, 2015. https://digiday.com/media/madness-snapchat-moves-closer-becoming-sports-broadcaster/

Thompson, Ben. "The Facebook Epoch." Stratechery, September 30, 2015. https://stratechery.com/2015/the-facebook-epoch/

Wagner, Kurt. "Snapchat Inks NFL Deal to Bring Football into Its Live Stories." Recode, September 17, 2015. https://www.recode.net/2015/9/17/11618660/snapchat-inks-nfl-deal-to-bring-football-into-its-live-stories

———. "Snapchat to Let You Send Money to Friends, Thanks to Square." Recode, November 17, 2014. https://www.recode.net/2014/11/17/11632930/snapchat-to-let-you-send-money-to-friends-thanks-to-square

Wortham, Jenna. "Rejecting Billions, Snapchat Expects a Better Offer." *New York Times*,

November 13, 2013. http://www.nytimes.com/2013/11/14/technology/rejecting-billions
-snapchat-expects-a-better-offer.html

Zeitlin, Matthew, and Matthew Lynley. "This Is What Snapchat's First Ad Looks Like."
BuzzFeed, October 19, 2014. https://www.buzzfeed.com/matthewzeitlin/this-is-what
-snapchats-first-ad-looks-like?utm_term=.nhjA7ZDWKa#.ufr1qavmN6

Chapter Twenty-Three: Blank Space

Buerger, Megan. "Exclusive: Madonna to Premiere Music Video from 'Rebel Heart' on Snapchat Discover Today." *Billboard*, February 5, 2015. http://www.billboard.com/biz
/articles/news/digital-and-mobile/6465179/exclusive-madonna-to-premiere-rebel-heart
-music-video

Carr, Austin. "Inside Snapchat CEO Evan Spiegel's Entertainment Empire." Fast Company,
October 19, 2015. https://www.fastcompany.com/3051612/media-tech-and-advertising
-to-snapchat-i-aint-afraid-of-no-ghost

Carson, Biz. "Snapchat to Lease Part of Santa Monica Airport, Including 8 Hangars." *Business Insider*, May 16, 2016. http://www.businessinsider.com/snapchat-to-lease-part-of
-santa-monica-airport-including-eight-airport-hangars-2016-5

Connolly, Kevin. "Snapshot Affair: The Enduring Power of the Polaroid." BBC, June 22,
2010. http://www.bbc.com/news/10355526

Constine, Josh. "Snapchat Plans Music Feature, Acquired QR Scan.me for $50M and Ver-
gence Eyeglass Cam For $15M." *TechCrunch*, December 16, 2014. https://techcrunch.
com/2014/12/16/snapchat-emails-not-so-ephemeral/

Crook, Jordan. "With an Eye on Revenue, Snapchat 'Experiments' with a Click-to-Buy Button." *TechCrunch*, October 3, 2013. https://techcrunch.com/2013/10/03/with-an-eye-on
-revenue-snapchat-experiments-with-a-click-to-buy-button/

Dave, Paresh. "Is Snapchat's Rapid Growth Changing Venice's Funky Vibe?" *Los Angeles
Times*, March 31, 2015. http://www.latimes.com/business/la-fi-snapchat-real-estate
-20150331-story.html

Flanagan, Andrew. "Sony Hack Reveals Snapchat Wanted a Record Label, Too Much Money
from Vevo." *Billboard*, December 17, 2014. http://www.billboard.com/articles/business
/6406613/sony-leaks-snapchat-record-label-vevo

Gallo, Carmine. "Steve Jobs: Get Rid Of The Crappy Stuff." *Forbes*, May 16, 2011. https://
www.forbes.com/sites/carminegallo/2011/05/16/steve-jobs-get-rid-of-the-crappy-stuff
/#76edac507145

McIntyre, Hugh. "This Musician Is Releasing His New Album on Snapchat, a First for
the Platform." *Forbes*, May 19, 2015. https://www.forbes.com/sites/hughmcintyre/2015
/05/19/this-artist-is-releasing-his-new-ep-on-snapchat-a-first-for-the-platform
/#3e529dc26010

Stone, Brad, and Sarah Frier. "Evan Spiegel Reveals Plan to Turn Snapchat into a Real Business." Bloomberg, May 26, 2015. https://www.bloomberg.com/news/features/2015-05-26
/evan-spiegel-reveals-plan-to-turn-snapchat-into-a-real-business

Stone, Madeline. "Meet the Street Artist Whose 'Selfie Portraits' Line the Walls of Snapchat HQ." *Business Insider*, June 4, 2015. http://www.businessinsider.com/thankyoux
-art-at-snapchat-offices-2015-6

Swisher, Kara, and Walt Mossberg. "Snapchat CEO Evan Spiegel on Diversity, Features for
the Olds and More at Code Conference 2015." Recode, June 8, 2015. https://www.recode
.net/2015/6/8/11563322/snapchat-ceo-evan-spiegel-on-diversity-features-for-the-olds
-and-more

———. "Snapchat CEO Evan Spiegel on Diversity, Features for the Olds and More at Code
Conference 2015." Recode, June 8, 2015. https://www.recode.net/2015/6/8/11563322
/snapchat-ceo-evan-spiegel-on-diversity-features-for-the-olds-and-more

Vega, Sebastian. "CEO of Snapchat Discusses New Media." *Daily Trojan*, February 19, 2015. http://dailytrojan.com/2015/02/19/ceo-of-snapchat-discusses-new-media/

Chapter Twenty-Four: Discover

Carr, David. "Facebook Offers Life Raft, but Publishers Are Wary." *New York Times*, October 26, 2014. https://www.nytimes.com/2014/10/27/business/media/facebook-offers
-life-raft-but-publishers-are-wary.html?mtrref=www.google.com&gwh=D0442AB860
621BD4CEEC3808C3FF0CE3&gwt=pay&assetType=nyt_now

Constine, Josh, and Jordan Crook. "Hands-On with Snapchat Discover: Fun Content for Short Attention Spans." *TechCrunch*, January 27, 2015. https://techcrunch.com/2015/01
/27/hands-on-with-snapchat-discover-fun-content-for-short-attention-spans/

Jarvey, Natalie. "Sasha Spielberg, Emily Goldwyn to Star in Snapchat Web Series." *Hollywood Reporter*, January 30, 2015. http://www.hollywoodreporter.com/news/sasha
-spielberg-emily-goldwyn-star-768501

McDermott, John. "Inside Snapchat's Original Media Ambitions." DigiDay, January 22, 2015. https://digiday.com/media/snapchat-start-producing-original-media/

Perlberg, Steven. "Why the BuzzFeed-Snapchat Discover Deal Fell Through." *Wall Street Journal*, February 4, 2015. https://blogs.wsj.com/cmo/2015/02/04/buzzfeed-snapchat
-discovery/

Roose, Kevin. "Snapchat Discover Could Be the Biggest Thing in News since Twitter." Splinter, February 11, 2015. http://splinternews.com/snapchat-discover-could-be-the-biggest
-thing-in-news-si-1793845256

Stone, Brad, and Sarah Frier. "Evan Spiegel Reveals Plan to Turn Snapchat into a Real Business." Bloomberg, May 26, 2015. https://www.bloomberg.com/news/features/2015-05-26
/evan-spiegel-reveals-plan-to-turn-snapchat-into-a-real-business

Vega, Sebastian. "CEO of Snapchat Discusses New Media." *Daily Trojan*, February 19, 2015. http://dailytrojan.com/2015/02/19/ceo-of-snapchat-discusses-new-media/

Chapter Twenty-Five: Major ☝

Berlinger, Max. "Meet YesJulz, Snapchat Royalty." *New York Times*, June 28, 2016. https://
www.nytimes.com/2016/06/30/fashion/-yesjulz-snapchat-celebrity-julieanna-goddard
.html

Bilton, Nick. "Strippers Go Undercover on Snapchat." *New York Times*, February 25, 2015.
https://www.nytimes.com/2015/02/26/style/strippers-go-undercover-on-snapchat.html
?mtrref=www.google.com&gwh=B4C830408DAF3958B3EE60A444F09B0E&gwt
=pay

Chafkin, Max, and Sarah Frier. "How Snapchat Built a Business by Confusing Olds." Bloomberg, March 3, 2016. https://www.bloomberg.com/features/2016-how-snapchat-built-a
-business/

Kan, Justin. "Why I Love Snapchat." Medium, November 13, 2016. https://justinkan.com
/why-i-love-snapchat-23d31ea87d3c

Madrigal, Alexis C. "Dark Social: We Have the Whole History of the Web Wrong." *Atlantic*, October 12, 2012. http://www.theatlantic.com/technology/archive/2012/10/dark
-social-we-have-the-whole-history-of-the-web-wrong/263523/

Yapalater, Lauren. "This Guy Is the Van Gogh of Snapchat." BuzzFeed, January 16, 2014.
https://www.buzzfeed.com/lyapalater/this-guy-is-the-van-gogh-of-snapchat?utm_term
=.wlXBXPRomL#.ooNao96AYx

Chapter Twenty-Six: Keeping Secrets

Biddle, Sam. "Snapchat Founder Requires Controversy-Free Interview." Valleywag, Octo-

ber 7, 2013. http://valleywag.gawker.com/snapchat-founder-requires-controversy-free
-interview-1442160637

Colao, J. J. "The Inside Story of Snapchat: The World's Hottest App or a $3 Billion Disap-
pearing Act?" *Forbes*, January 6, 2014. https://www.forbes.com/sites/jjcolao/2014/01/06
/the-inside-story-of-snapchat-the-worlds-hottest-app-or-a-3-billion-disappearing-act
/#3961325c67d2

Constine, Josh. "Snapchat Is Paying Ex-Apple Exec Scott Forstall 0.11% to Be an Advisor."
April 16, 2015. *TechCrunch*, https://techcrunch.com/2015/04/16/scottchat/

DiGiacomo, Frank. "School for Cool." *Vanity Fair*, March 2005. https://www.vanityfair.com
/news/2005/03/crossroads-school200503

Driver, Carol. "CANNES LIONS: Entrepreneur Evan Spiegel Reveals He Drew Ghost Logo for
Snapchat on His Computer in His Dorm Bedroom." *Daily Mail*, June 22, 2015. http://
www.dailymail.co.uk/tvshowbiz/article-3134555/CANNES-LIONS-Billionaire-Evan
-Spiegel-reveals-drew-ghost-logo-Snapchat-computer-dorm-bedroom.html

Flynn, Kerry. "How Snapchat CEO Evan Spiegel Speaks Millennial—Not Just by Using the
Popular Mobile App." *International Business Times*, May 1, 2016. http://www.ibtimes
.com/how-snapchat-ceo-evan-spiegel-speaks-millennial-not-just-using-popular-mobile
-app-2362380

Holmes, David. "Snapchat's Evan Spiegel: Our Secrets Are Sacred, but Yours Aren't." Pando
Daily, December 17, 2014. https://pando.com/2014/12/17/snapchats-evan-spiegel-our
-secrets-are-sacred-but-yours-arent/

Ignatius, Adi. "'They Burned the House Down': An Interview with Michael Lynton." *Harvard Business Review*, July–August 2015. https://hbr.org/2015/07/they-burned-the-house
-down

Spiegel, Evan. "2014 LA Hacks Keynote." Scribd, April 11, 2014. https://www.scribd.com
/doc/217768898/2014-LA-Hacks-Keynote

Stone, Brad, and Sarah Frier. "Evan Spiegel Reveals Plan to Turn Snapchat into a Real Business." Bloomberg, May 26, 2015. https://www.bloomberg.com/news/features/2015-05-26
/evan-spiegel-reveals-plan-to-turn-snapchat-into-a-real-business

Swisher, Kara, and Walt Mossberg. "Snapchat CEO Evan Spiegel on Diversity, Features for
the Olds and More at Code Conference 2015." Recode, June 8, 2015. https://www.recode
.net/2015/6/8/11563322/snapchat-ceo-evan-spiegel-on-diversity-features-for-the-olds
-and-more

Wagner, Kurt. "Inside Evan Spiegel's Very Private Snapchat Story." Recode, May 9, 2016.
https://www.recode.net/2016/5/9/11594144/evan-spiegel-snapchat

Chapter Twenty-Seven: Evan's Empire

Carr, Austin. "What Snapchat's High-Profile Exec Departures Really Tell Us about CEO Evan
Spiegel." Fast Company, October 20, 2015. https://www.fastcompany.com/3052436/what
-snapchats-high-profile-exec-departures-really-tell-us-about-ceo-evan-spiegel

Chaykowski, Kathleen, and Ryan Mac. "Snapchat Sneakily Uses Its Own App to Poach
Uber, Airbnb Engineers." *Forbes*, April 15, 2015. https://www.forbes.com/sites/kathleen
chaykowski/2015/04/15/snapchat-sneakily-uses-its-own-app-to-poach-uber-engineers
/#1e45881673ec

Dotan, Tom. "Snapchat's Adult in the Room." The Information, September 29, 2015. https://
www.theinformation.com/snapchats-adult-in-the-room.

Hempel, Jessi. "Take It from Snapchat—Messaging Is the Medium." *Wired*, April 21, 2015.
https://www.wired.com/2015/04/imran-khan/

———. "Snapchat Doesn't Think It Needs an Adult Like Facebook Did." *Wired*, March 18,
2015. https://www.wired.com/2015/03/snapchat-doesnt-think-needs-adult-like-facebook/

MacMillan, Douglas. "Snapchat Poaches Star Tech Banker Imran Khan from Credit Suisse."

Wall Street Journal, December 8, 2014. https://blogs.wsj.com/digits/2014/12/08/snapchat
-poaches-star-tech-banker-imran-khan-from-credit-suisse/

Perez, Sarah. "Snapchat VP of Engineering Peter Magnusson Departs Startup after Just 6
Months." *TechCrunch*, July 31, 2014. https://techcrunch.com/2014/07/31/snapchat-vp
-of-engineering-peter-magnusson-departs-startup-after-just-6-months/

Primack, Dan. "Ex-Snapchat COO Emily White Has a New Startup." *Fortune*, March 2,
2016. http://fortune.com/2016/03/02/ex-snapchat-coo-emily-white-new-startup/

Shao, Heng. "Snapchat CSO Imran Khan Was Key to $200 Million Investment by Alibaba."
Forbes, March 12, 2015. https://www.forbes.com/sites/hengshao/2015/03/12/alibaba
-invests-200-mil-in-snapchat-cso-imran-khan-is-key-to-the-deal/#4a9e502dfcfc

Slutsky, Irina. "Meet the Ex-Googlers Running Facebook." Advertising Age, June 1, 2011.
http://adage.com/article/digital/meet-googlers-running-facebook/227833/

Spiegel, Evan, and Nikesh Arora. Interview, YouTube, October 12, 2015. https://www.youtube
.com/watch?v=R-UAjGVPFIE

Stevenson, Seth. "Snapchat Releases First Hardware Product, Spectacles." *Wall Street Journal*, September 24, 2016. https://www.wsj.com/articles/snapchat-releases-first-hardware
-product-spectacles-1474682719

Swisher, Kara, and Kurt Wagner. "Exclusive: Snapchat COO Emily White to Depart Ephemeral Messaging Phenom." Recode, March 13, 2015. https://www.recode.net/2015/3/13
/11560196/exclusive-snapchat-coo-emily-white-to-depart-ephemeral-messaging

Wagner, Kurt. "Inside Evan Spiegel's Very Private Snapchat Story." Recode, May 9, 2016.
https://www.recode.net/2016/5/9/11594144/evan-spiegel-snapchat

———. "Snapchat Revenue Boss Mike Randall Departs after Seven Months." Recode, January 20, 2015. https://www.recode.net/2015/1/20/11557912/snapchat-revenue-boss-mike
-randall-departs-after-seven-months

Chapter Twenty-Eight: The Road to IPO

Bonanos, Christopher. "The Man Who Inspired Jobs." *New York Times*, October 7, 2011.
http://www.nytimes.com/2011/10/07/opinion/the-man-who-inspired-jobs.html

Bowles, Nellie. "Three LA Boys: Snapchat's Evan Spiegel, Tinder's Sean Rad and Whisper's
Michael Heyward." Recode, June 11, 2014. https://www.recode.net/2014/6/11/11627844
/three-la-boys-evan-spiegel-sean-rad-and-michael-heyward

Carr, Austin. "Inside Snapchat CEO Evan Spiegel's Entertainment Empire." Fast Company,
October 19, 2015. https://www.fastcompany.com/3051612/media-tech-and-advertising
-to-snapchat-i-aint-afraid-of-no-ghost

———. "Inside Snapchat CEO Evan Spiegel's Entertainment Empire." Fast Company, October 19, 2015. https://www.fastcompany.com/3051612/media-tech-and-advertising-to
-snapchat-i-aint-afraid-of-no-ghost

Carson, Biz. "Snapchat Users Now Spend 25 to 30 Minutes Every Day on the App, and It's
Trying to Attract the TV Money because of It." *Business Insider*, March 25, 2016. http://
www.businessinsider.com/how-much-time-people-spend-on-snapchat-2016-3

Chafkin, Max, and Sarah Frier. "How Snapchat Built a Business by Confusing Olds." Bloomberg, March 3, 2016. https://www.bloomberg.com/features/2016-how-snapchat-built-a
-business/

Chemi, Eric. "Advertising's Century of Flat-Line Growth." Bloomberg, March 3, 2014. http://
www.bloomberg.com/news/articles/2014-03-03/advertisings-century-of-flat-line
-growth

Constine, Josh. "Snapchat Paves Way to IPO with Ads API and Inserts between Stories."
TechCrunch, June 13, 2016. https://techcrunch.com/2016/06/13/snapchat-ads/

Heine, Christopher. "Snapchat Launches a Colossal Expansion of Its Advertising, Ushering in a New Era for the App." Ad Week, June 13, 2016. http://www.adweek.com/digital/snapchat-launches-colossal-expansion-its-advertising-ushering-new-era-app-171924/

Herrman, John. "Media Websites Battle Faltering Ad Revenue and Traffic." *New York Times*, April 17, 2016. https://www.nytimes.com/2016/04/18/business/media-websites-battle-falteringad-revenue-and-traffic.html

Kahney, Leander. "John Sculley on Steve Jobs, the Full Interview Transcript." Cult of Mac, October 14, 2010. https://www.cultofmac.com/63295/john-sculley-on-steve-jobs-the-full-interview-transcript/63295/

O'Reilly, Lara. "Here's What People Are Saying about What It's Like to Work with Snapchat Right Now." *Business Insider*, July 26, 2015. http://www.businessinsider.com/what-snapchat-is-like-as-an-ad-sales-organization-2015-7

Perlberg, Steven. "Viacom to Sell Snapchat Ads in Multiyear Deal." *Wall Street Journal*, February 8, 2016. https://www.wsj.com/articles/viacom-to-sell-snapchat-ads-in-multi-year-deal-1454988604

Sloane, Garrett. "Snapchat's New Audience-Based Ad Strategy Could Wrest Control from Discover Publishers." DigiDay, February 29, 2016. https://digiday.com/media/snapchats-new-ad-strategy-means-discover-publishers/

———. "Snapchat Is Building an Ad Technology Platform." DigiDay, January 5, 2016. https://digiday.com/media/snapchat-api/

Stone, Brad, and Sarah Frier. "Evan Spiegel Reveals Plan to Turn Snapchat into a Real Business." Bloomberg, May 26, 2015. https://www.bloomberg.com/news/features/2015-05-26/evan-spiegel-reveals-plan-to-turn-snapchat-into-a-real-business

Swisher, Kara, and Walt Mossberg. "Snapchat CEO Evan Spiegel on Diversity, Features for the Olds and More at Code Conference 2015." Recode, June 8, 2015. https://www.recode.net/2015/6/8/11563322/snapchat-ceo-evan-spiegel-on-diversity-features-for-the-olds-and-more

Wagner, Kurt. "Snapchat Is Making Some Pretty Serious Money from Live Stories." Recode, June 17, 2015. https://www.recode.net/2015/6/17/11563634/snapchats-making-some-pretty-serious-money-from-live-stories

Chapter Twenty-Nine: The New TV

Andreeva, Nellie. "Snapchat to Shut Down Snap Channel, Laying Off Team, Changing Content Plans." Deadline, October 12, 2015. http://deadline.com/2015/10/snapchat-snap-channel-shut-down-layoffs-original-content-strategy-1201577855/

Byers, Dylan. "Peter Hamby Leaving CNN for Snapchat." Politico, April 27, 2015. http://www.politico.com/blogs/media/2015/04/peter-hamby-leaving-cnn-for-snapchat-206178

Corasaniti, Nick. "Snapchat Bets Big on Quick-Fire Approach to Campaign Coverage." *New York Times*, February 12, 2016. https://www.nytimes.com/2016/02/13/us/politics/snapchat-bets-big-on-quick-fire-approach-to-campaign-coverage.html

Flynn, Kerry. "President Trump Takes to Snapchat on Inauguration Day." Mashable, January 20, 2017. http://mashable.com/2017/01/20/donald-trump-snapchat/#COriFAOfl5qR

Levine, Sam. "Hillary Clinton Trolls Donald Trump with Custom Snapchat Filter at His Own Rally." *Huffington Post*, May 25, 2016. http://www.huffingtonpost.com/entry/hillary-clinton-donald-trump-snapchat_us_5745f017e4b0dacf7ad3be36

Mahler, Jonathan. "Campaign Coverage via Snapchat Could Shake Up the 2016 Elections." *New York Times*, May 3, 2015. https://www.nytimes.com/2015/05/04/business/media/campaign-coverage-via-snapchat-could-shake-up-the-2016-elections.html

Perlberg, Steven. "Snapchat Debuts Political Campaign Show." *Wall Street Journal*, January 28, 2016. https://www.wsj.com/articles/snapchat-debuts-political-campaign-show-1454015686

Schroeder, Stan. "Snapchat Positions Itself as Breaking News Platform with San Bernardino Coverage." Mashable, December 3, 2015. http://mashable.com/2015/12/03/snapchat-san -bernardino/#COriFAOfl5qR

Shields, Mike. "Bernie Sanders Is Running a 9-Day Snapchat Ad Campaign in Iowa." *Wall Street Journal*, January 26, 2016. https://www.wsj.com/articles/bernie-sanders-is -running-a-9-day-snapchat-ad-campaign-in-iowa-1453806001

Vincent, James. "Ted Cruz Trolled Donald Trump with a Snapchat Filter at Last Night's Debate." *Verge*, January 29, 2016. https://www.theverge.com/2016/1/29/10867830/ted -cruz-donald-trump-snapchat-filter

Wagner, Kurt. "Hillary Clinton Gets a Snapchat Interview, but Donald Trump Doesn't Want One." Recode, October 17, 2016. https://www.recode.net/2016/10/17/13310114/snapchat -hillary-clinton-interview

Chapter Thirty: Discover Falters

Adair, Bill. "What Happens when a 50-Something Journalist Gets a Week's Worth of News from Snapchat Discover?" Nieman Lab, June 6, 2016. http://www.niemanlab.org/2016 /06/what-happens-when-a-50-something-journalist-gets-a-weeks-worth-of-news-from -snapchat-discover/

Carr, Austin. "Inside Snapchat CEO Evan Spiegel's Entertainment Empire." Fast Company, October 19, 2015. https://www.fastcompany.com/3051612/media-tech-and-advertising -to-snapchat-i-aint-afraid-of-no-ghost

Chafkin, Max, and Sarah Frier. "How Snapchat Built a Business by Confusing Olds." Bloomberg, March 3, 2016. https://www.bloomberg.com/features/2016-how-snapchat-built-a -business/

Frier, Sarah. "Snapchat Scores Unique Deal with NBC to Showcase Olympics." Bloomberg, April 29, 2016. https://www.bloomberg.com/amp/news/articles/2016-04-29/snapchat -scores-unprecedented-deal-with-nbc-to-showcase-olympics

Koh, Yoree. "NFL to Get Snapchat Discover Channel This Fall." *Wall Street Journal*, August 2, 2016. https://www.wsj.com/articles/nfl-to-get-snapchat-discover-channel-this-fall -1470150001

Kuchler, Hannah. "Snapchat Strikes Olympic Gold." *Financial Times*, August 15, 2016. https://www.ft.com/content/c463c9fe-6279-11e6-8310-ecf0bddad227

MacMillan, Douglas, and Shalini Ramachandran. "Snapchat Redesign Puts Spotlight on 'Discover' News Portal." *Wall Street Journal*, July 13, 2015. https://blogs.wsj.com/digits /2015/07/13/snapchat-redesign-puts-spotlight-on-discover-news-portal/

Newton, Casey. "Snapchat Redesigns Discover and Lets You Subscribe to Your Favorite Publishers." *Verge*, June 7, 2016. https://www.theverge.com/2016/6/7/11871782/snapchat -discover-redesign-publisher-following

Owen, Laura Hazard. "The *Wall Street Journal* Is the First American Newspaper to Get a Spot on Snapchat Discover." Nieman Lab, January 6, 2016. http://www.niemanlab.org /2016/01/the-wall-street-journal-is-the-first-american-newspaper-to-get-a-spot-on -snapchat-discover/.

Perlberg, Steven. August 12, 2016. "BuzzFeed Has the Keys to NBC's Rio Olympics Snapchat Channel." *Wall Street Journal*, https://www.wsj.com/articles/buzzfeed-has-the-keys -to-nbcs-rio-olympics-snapchat-channel-1470997804

———. "NBCU Signs Deal to Make Snapchat Shows." *Wall Street Journal*, August 8, 2016. https://www.wsj.com/articles/nbcu-signs-deal-to-make-snapchat-shows-1470650401

Peterson, Tim. "Snapchat Is Making Its Own Original Content for Discover Again." Advertising Age, December 28, 2015. http://adage.com/article/digital/snapchat-making -original-content-discover/301942/

Shields, Mike. "Inside Refinery29's Snapchat Discover Operation." *Wall Street Journal*, De-

cember 4, 2015. https://www.wsj.com/articles/inside-refinery29s-snapchat-discover
-operation-1449226800

Slefo, George. "Snapchat Adds Brit & Co to Its Discover Publishers, for Holidays Only."
Advertising Age, March 25, 2016. http://adage.com/article/media/snapchat-partners-brit
-holiday-discover-content/303278/

Sloane, Garrett. "Snapchat's Redesigning Discover to Make It More Like a Newsstand." Digi-
Day, June 1, 2016. https://digiday.com/media/snapchat-publishers-get-redesign-help
-goose-traffic/

———. "Snapchat Finally Enables Publishers to 'Deep Link' to Their Discover Content."
DigiDay, November 30, 2015. https://digiday.com/media/snapchat-publishers-promote
-discover-links-facebook-twitter/

Chapter Thirty-One: Fear and Loathing in Menlo Park

"Bitmoji!" Snapchat, July 19, 2016. https://www.snap.com/en-US/news/post/bitmoji/

Christensen, Clayton M. *The Innovator's Dilemma: When New Technologies Cause Great
Firms to Fail*. Brighton, MA: Harvard Business Review Press, 1997.

Constine, Josh. "Instagram CEO on Stories: Snapchat Deserves All the Credit." *TechCrunch*,
August 2, 2016. https://techcrunch.com/2016/08/02/silicon-copy/

Efrati, Amir, and Cory Weinberg. "Facebook and Twitter Pressure Partners over Snapchat."
The Information, April 14, 2016. https://www.theinformation.com/facebook-and-twitter
-pressure-partners-over-snapchat

Etherington, Darrell. "Snapchat Now Lets You Use Bitmojis in Chat or on Snaps." *Tech-
Crunch*, July 19, 2016. https://techcrunch.com/2016/07/19/snapchat-bitmoji/

Garcia Martinez, Antonio. *Chaos Monkeys: Obscene Fortune and Random Failure in Silicon Valley*. New York: HarperCollins, 2016.

Kafka, Peter. "Facebook Wants Celebrities for Its Live Streaming Service, and It's Willing to
Pay Cash." Recode, March 1, 2016. https://www.recode.net/2016/3/1/11586612/facebook
-wants-celebrities-for-its-live-streaming-service-and-its

Morris, Betsy and Seetharaman, Deepa. "Facebook's Onavo Gives Social-Media Firm Inside Peek at Rivals' Users." *Wall Street Journal*, August 13, 2017. https://www.wsj.com
/articles/facebooks-onavo-gives-social-media-firm-inside-peek-at-rivals-users
-1502622003

Morris, Betsy and Seetharaman, Deepa. "The New Copycats: How Facebook Squashes
Competition From Startups." *Wall Street Journal*, August 9, 2017. https://www.wsj
.com/articles/the-new-copycats-how-facebook-squashes-competition-from-startups
-1502293444

Perlberg, Steven, and Deepa Seetharaman. "Facebook Signs Deals with Media Companies,
Celebrities for Facebook Live." *Wall Street Journal*, June 22, 2016. https://www.wsj.com
/articles/facebook-signs-deals-with-media-companies-celebrities-for-facebook-live
-1466533472

Pierce, David. "Facebook Live Video Is Facebook at Its Most Facebook." *Wired*, December 4,
2015. https://www.wired.com/2015/12/facebook-live-video-is-facebook-at-its-most
-facebook/

Snap Inc. "Snap Inc. Form S-1." US Securities and Exchange Commission, February 2, 2017.
https://www.sec.gov/Archives/edgar/data/1564408/000119312517029199/d270216ds1
.htm

Wagner, Kurt. "Snapchat Hires Exec Who Ran Facebook's Ad Network." Recode, February 29, 2016. https://www.recode.net/2016/2/29/11588316/snapchat-hires-exec-who-ran
-facebooks-ad-network

Chapter Thirty-Two: Snap Inc.

Carman, Ashley. "Snapchat Will Let You Buy Temporary, On-Demand Geofilters for Your Next Party." *Verge*, February 22, 2016. https://www.theverge.com/2016/2/22/11092406/snapchat-rent-custom-geofilter-launch

———. "Snapchat Is Killing Its Lens Store." *Verge*, January 6, 2016. https://www.theverge.com/2016/1/6/10722868/snapchat-lens-store-shutdown

Constine, Josh. "Snapchat Seamlessly Combines Video, Audio, GIFs, Stickers in 'Chat 2.0.'" *TechCrunch*, March 29, 2016. https://techcrunch.com/2016/03/29/snapphone/

Dave, Paresh. "Snapchat Turns Geofilter Digital Stickers into Revenue Source." *Los Angeles Times*, June 15, 2015. http://www.latimes.com/business/la-fi-0613-snapchat-geofilters-20150616-story.html

Del Rey, Jason, and Kurt Wagner. "Shopping Is Coming to Snapchat, Board Member Joanna Coles Says." Recode, February 17, 2016. https://www.recode.net/2016/2/17/11587960/shopping-is-coming-to-snapchat-board-member-joanna-coles-says

Dotan, Tom, and Amir Efrati. "Snapchat Explores New Scannable Ads." The Information, August 2, 2016. https://www.theinformation.com/snapchat-explores-new-scannable-ads

Hamedy, Saba. "You Can Now Buy Your 'X-Men: Apocalypse' Tickets on Snapchat." Mashable, May 23, 2016. http://mashable.com/2016/05/23/x-men-apocalypse-snapchat-takeover/

Heath, Alex. "Snapchat Comes under Fire for 'Digital Blackface' Filter That Turns You into Bob Marley." *Business Insider*, April 20, 2016. http://www.businessinsider.com/snapchat-faces-backlash-for-bob-marley-filter-2016-4

Heath, Alex. "The cult of Evan: What life is like inside Snap right now" *Business Insider*, August 1, 2017. http://www.businessinsider.com/snapchat-employees-prepare-sell-stock-lock-up-ipo-2017-7

Isaac, Mike. "AMC Unveils 'Preacher' Clip on Snapchat." *New York Times*, May 16, 2016. https://www.nytimes.com/2016/05/17/business/media/amc-unveils-preacher-clip-on-snapchat.html

Johnson, Lauren. "Taco Bell's Cinco de Mayo Snapchat Lens Was Viewed 224 Million Times." Ad Week, May 11, 2016. http://www.adweek.com/digital/taco-bells-cinco-de-mayo-snapchat-lens-was-viewed-224-million-times-171390/

Kokalitcheva, Kia. "Cosmopolitan's Editor-In-Chief Joins Snapchat's Board." *Fortune*, January 26, 2016. http://fortune.com/2016/01/26/snapchat-joanna-coles/

Primack, Dan. "Exclusive: Snapchat Buys Bitmoji Maker." *Fortune*, March 24, 2016. http://fortune.com/2016/03/24/exclusive-snapchat-buys-bitmoji-maker/

Shields, Mike. "Publishers Flock to New Instagram Stories." *Wall Street Journal*, August 12, 2016. https://www.wsj.com/articles/publishers-flock-to-new-instagram-stories-1470999602

Snap Inc. "Snap Inc. Form S-1." US Securities and Exchange Commission, February 2, 2017. https://www.sec.gov/Archives/edgar/data/1564408/000119312517029199/d270216ds1.htm

Stevenson, Seth. "Snapchat Releases First Hardware Product, Spectacles." *Wall Street Journal*, September 24, 2016. https://www.wsj.com/articles/snapchat-releases-first-hardware-product-spectacles-1474682719

Swisher, Kara, and Walt Mossberg. "Snapchat CEO Evan Spiegel on Diversity, Features for the Olds and More at Code Conference 2015." Recode, June 8, 2015. https://www.recode.net/2015/6/8/11563322/snapchat-ceo-evan-spiegel-on-diversity-features-for-the-olds-and-more

Thompson, Ben. "Snapchat's Ladder." Stratechery, March 30, 2016. https://stratechery.com/2016/snapchats-ladder/

Wagner, Kurt. "Inside Evan Spiegel's Very Private Snapchat Story." Recode, May 9, 2016. https://www.recode.net/2016/5/9/11594144/evan-spiegel-snapchat

———. "Snapchat Hires Longtime Pandora Executive Tom Conrad as VP of Product." Re-code, March 15, 2016. https://www.recode.net/2016/3/15/11587006/snapchat-hires-longtime-pandora-exec-tom-conrad-as-vp-of-product

———. "Snapchat's New Money-Maker: Discover Channels for Advertisers." Recode, Oc-tober 26, 2015. https://www.recode.net/2015/10/26/11620050/snapchats-new-money-maker-discover-channels-for-advertisers

Chapter Thirty-Three: Spectacles

Connolly, Kevin. "Snapshot Affair: The Enduring Power of the Polaroid." BBC, June 22, 2010. http://www.bbc.com/news/10355526

Dave, Paresh. "Snapchat Has Changed through Acquisitions, and It's Hunting for More People and Tech to Buy." *Los Angeles Times*, May 10, 2017. http://www.latimes.com/business/technology/la-fi-tn-snapchat-acquisitions-20170510-htmlstory.html

———. "Exclusive Interview: How Snapchat Founder Evan Spiegel Feels after the Historic IPO." *Los Angeles Times*, March 2, 2017. http://www.latimes.com/business/technology/la-fi-tn-evan-spiegel-bobby-murphy-20170302-story.html

Evans, Benedict. "Imaging, Snapchat and Mobile." Benedict Evans, August 15, 2016. http://ben-evans.com/benedictevans/2016/8/15/imaging-snapchat-and-mobile

Farrell, Maureen, and Corrie Driebusch. "Snap's IPO Roadshow Message: We're the Next Facebook, Not the Next Twitter." *Wall Street Journal*, December 29, 2016. https://www.wsj.com/articles/snaps-ipo-roadshow-message-were-the-next-facebook-not-the-next-twitter-1483007406

Flynn, Kerry. "Snapchat Spectacles Latest Vending Machine Drops in Los Angeles." Mash-able, December 1, 2016. http://mashable.com/2016/12/01/snapbot-spectacles-/#hKfNS8KrXSq9

Frier, Sarah. "Snapchat Passes Twitter in Daily Usage." Bloomberg, June 2, 2016. https://www.bloombergquint.com/business/2016/06/02/snapchat-passes-twitter-in-daily-usage

Singer, Daniel. "A Real Teen's Take on Snapchat's Hot New Spectacles." *TechCrunch*, No-vember 14, 2016. https://techcrunch.com/2016/11/14/a-real-teens-take-on-snapchats-hot-new-spectacles/

Swisher, Kara, and Walt Mossberg. "Snapchat CEO Evan Spiegel on Diversity, Features for the Olds and More at Code Conference 2015." Recode, June 8, 2015. https://www.recode.net/2015/6/8/11563322/snapchat-ceo-evan-spiegel-on-diversity-features-for-the-olds-and-more

Additional Sources

While researching and writing this book, I also found the following books helpful:

Bilton, Nick. *Hatching Twitter: A True Story of Money, Power, Friendship, and Betrayal.* New York: Portfolio, 2013.

boyd, danah. *It's Complicated: The Social Lives of Networked Teens.* New Haven, CT: Yale University Press, 2014.

Burrough, Bryan, and John Helyar. *Barbarians at the Gate: The Fall of RJR Nabisco.* New York: Harper and Row, 1990.

Carlson, Nicholas. *Marissa Mayer and the Fight to Save Yahoo!* New York: Twelve, 2015.

Christensen, Clayton M. *The Innovator's Dilemma: When New Technologies Cause Great Firms to Fail.* Brighton, MA: Harvard Business Review Press, 1997.

Fagan, Kate. *What Made Maddy Run: The Secret Struggles and Tragic Death of an All-American Teen.* New York: Little, Brown and Company, 2017.

Gottschall, Jonathan. *The Storytelling Animal: How Stories Make Us Human.* New York: Houghton Mifflin Harcourt, 2012.

Grove, Andrew S. *Only the Paranoid Survive: How to Exploit the Crisis Points That Challenge Every Company.* New York: Doubleday, 1996.

Harris, Blake J. *Console Wars: Sega, Nintendo, and the Battle that Defined a Generation.* New York: It Books, 2014.

Isaacson, Walter. *Steve Jobs.* New York: Simon and Schuster, 2011.

Knight, Phil. *Shoe Dog: A Memoir by the Creator of Nike.* New York: Scribner, 2016.

Lamott, Anne. *Bird by Bird: Some Instructions on Writing and Life.* New York: Anchor, 1995.

Lowenstein, Roger. *When Genius Failed: The Rise and Fall of Long-Term Capital Management.* New York: Random House, 2000.

Martinez, Antonio Garcia. *Chaos Monkeys: Obscene Fortune and Random Failure in Silicon Valley.* New York: HarperCollins, 2016.

Mezrich, Ben. *The Accidental Billionaires: The Founding of Facebook; A Tale of Sex, Money, Genius and Betrayal.* New York: Anchor Books, 2010.

Miller, James Andrew. *Powerhouse: The Untold Story of Hollywood's Creative Artists Agency.* New York: Custom House, 2016.

Miller, James Andrew, and Tom Shales. *Those Guys Have All the Fun: Inside the World of ESPN.* New York: Little, Brown and Company, 2011.

———. *Live From New York: The Complete, Uncensored History of Saturday Night Live as Told by Its Stars, Writers, and Guests.* New York: Little, Brown and Company, 2016.

Moritz. Michael. *Return to the Little Kingdom: How Apple and Steve Jobs Changed the World.* New York: Overlook Press, 2009.

Reis, Eric. *The Lean Startup: How Today's Entrepreneurs Use Continuous Innovation to Create Radically Successful Businesses.* New York: Crown Business, 2011.

Roose, Kevin. *Young Money: Inside the Hidden World of Wall Street's Post-Crash Recruits.* New York: Grand Central Publishing, 2014.

Rose, Todd. *The End of Average: How We Succeed in a World That Values Sameness.* New York: HarperOne, 2016.

Schlender, Brent, and Rick Tetzeli. *Becoming Steve Jobs.* New York: Crown Business, 2015.

Sorkin, Andrew Ross. *Too Big to Fail: The Inside Story of How Wall Street and Washington Fought to Save the Financial System—and Themselves.* New York: Viking, 2009.

Stone, Brad. *The Everything Store: Jeff Bezos and the Age of Amazon.* New York: Little, Brown and Company, 2013.

———. *The Upstarts: How Uber, Airbnb, and the Killer Companies of the New Silicon Valley Are Changing the World.* New York: Little, Brown and Company, 2017.

Taleb, Nassim Nicholas. *The Black Swan: The Impact of the Highly Improbable.* New York: Random House, 2007.

Thompson, Derek. *Hit Makers: The Science of Popularity in an Age of Distraction.* New York: Penguin, 2017.

Tzu, Sun. *The Art of War.* date unknown; https://www.amazon.com/Art-War-Sun-Tzu/dp/1599869772/ref=sr_1_1?s=books&ie=UTF8&qid=1501497433&sr=1-1&keywords=the+art+of+war

Vance, Ashlee. *Elon Musk: Tesla, SpaceX, and the Quest for a Fantastic Future.* New York: HarperCollins, 2015.

Walsh, Bill, Steve Jamison, and Craig Walsh. *The Score Takes Care of Itself: My Philosophy of Leadership.* New York: Portfolio, 2009.

Walton, Sam. *Sam Walton: Made in America.* New York: Doubleday, 1992.

Wu, Tim. *The Attention Merchants: The Epic Scramble to Get inside Our Heads.* New York: Knopf, 2016.

INDEX